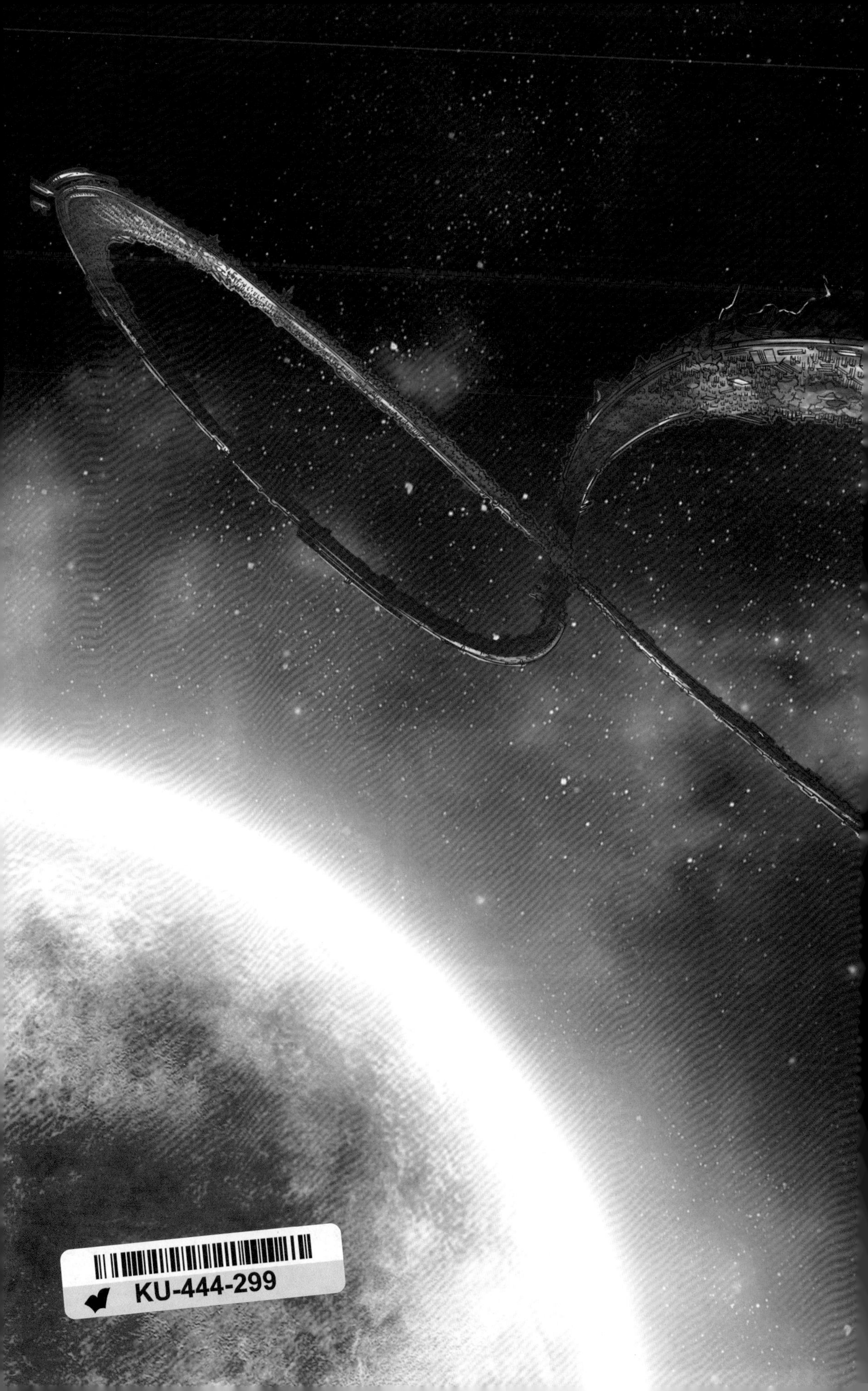

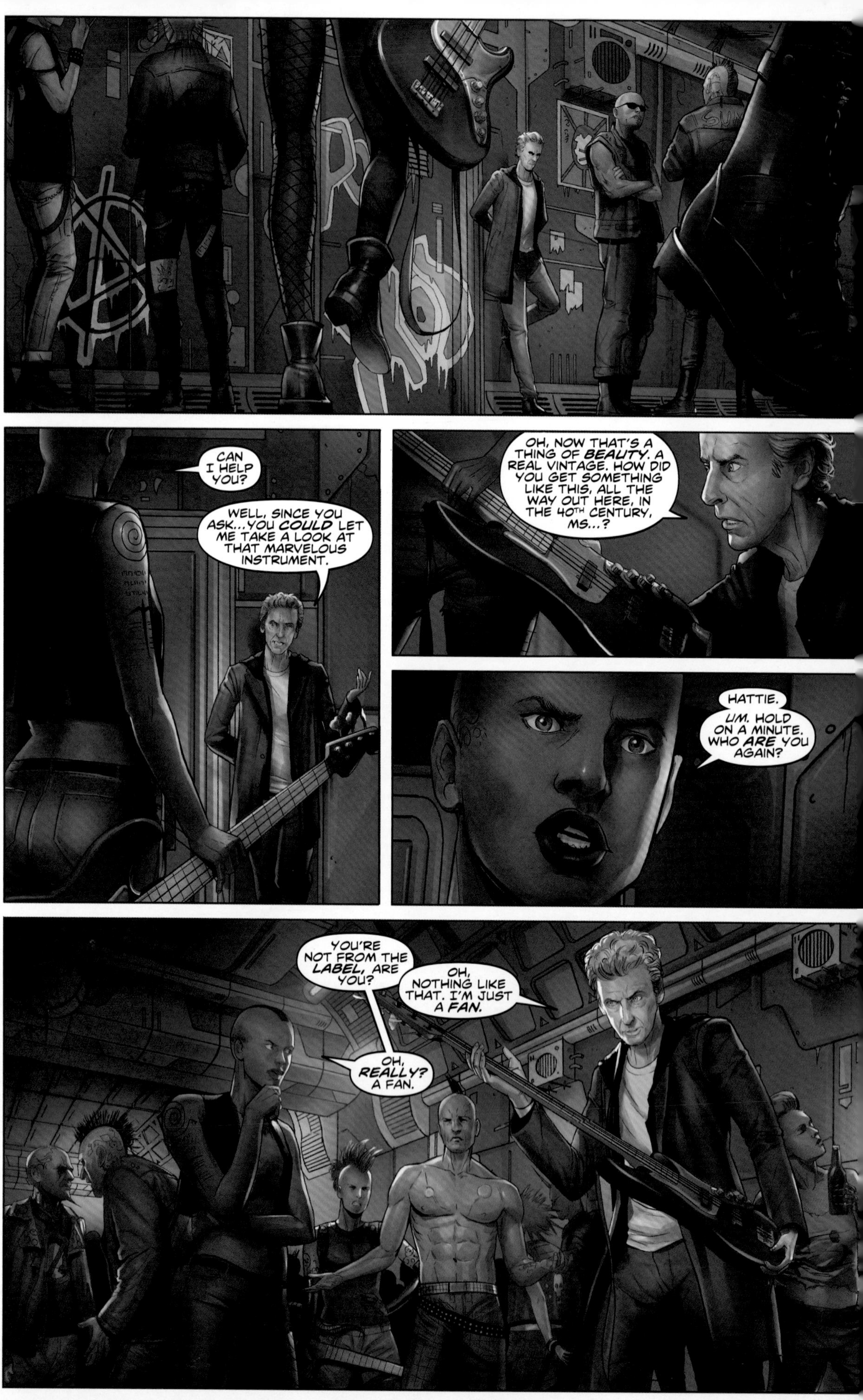
CAN I HELP YOU?
WELL, SINCE YOU ASK...YOU COULD LET ME TAKE A LOOK AT THAT MARVELOUS INSTRUMENT.
OH, NOW THAT'S A THING OF BEAUTY. A REAL VINTAGE. HOW DID YOU GET SOMETHING LIKE THIS, ALL THE WAY OUT HERE, IN THE 40TH CENTURY, MS...?
HATTIE.
UM. HOLD ON A MINUTE. WHO ARE YOU AGAIN?
YOU'RE NOT FROM THE LABEL, ARE YOU?
OH, NOTHING LIKE THAT. I'M JUST A FAN.
OH, REALLY? A FAN.

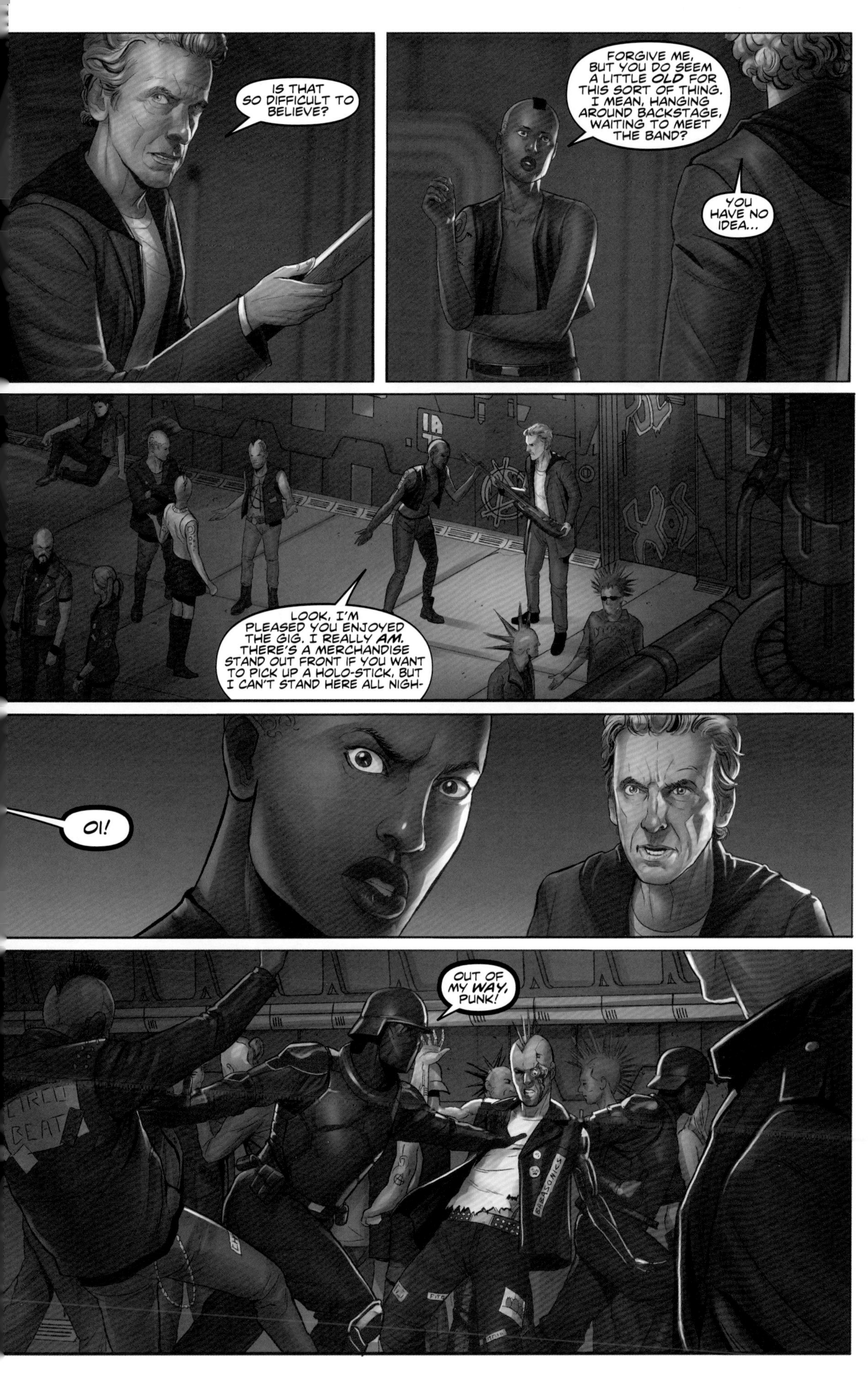
IS THAT SO DIFFICULT TO BELIEVE?
FORGIVE ME, BUT YOU DO SEEM A LITTLE OLD FOR THIS SORT OF THING. I MEAN, HANGING AROUND BACKSTAGE, WAITING TO MEET THE BAND?
YOU HAVE NO IDEA...
LOOK, I'M PLEASED YOU ENJOYED THE GIG. I REALLY AM. THERE'S A MERCHANDISE STAND OUT FRONT IF YOU WANT TO PICK UP A HOLO-STICK, BUT I CAN'T STAND HERE ALL NIGH-
OI!
OUT OF MY WAY, PUNK!

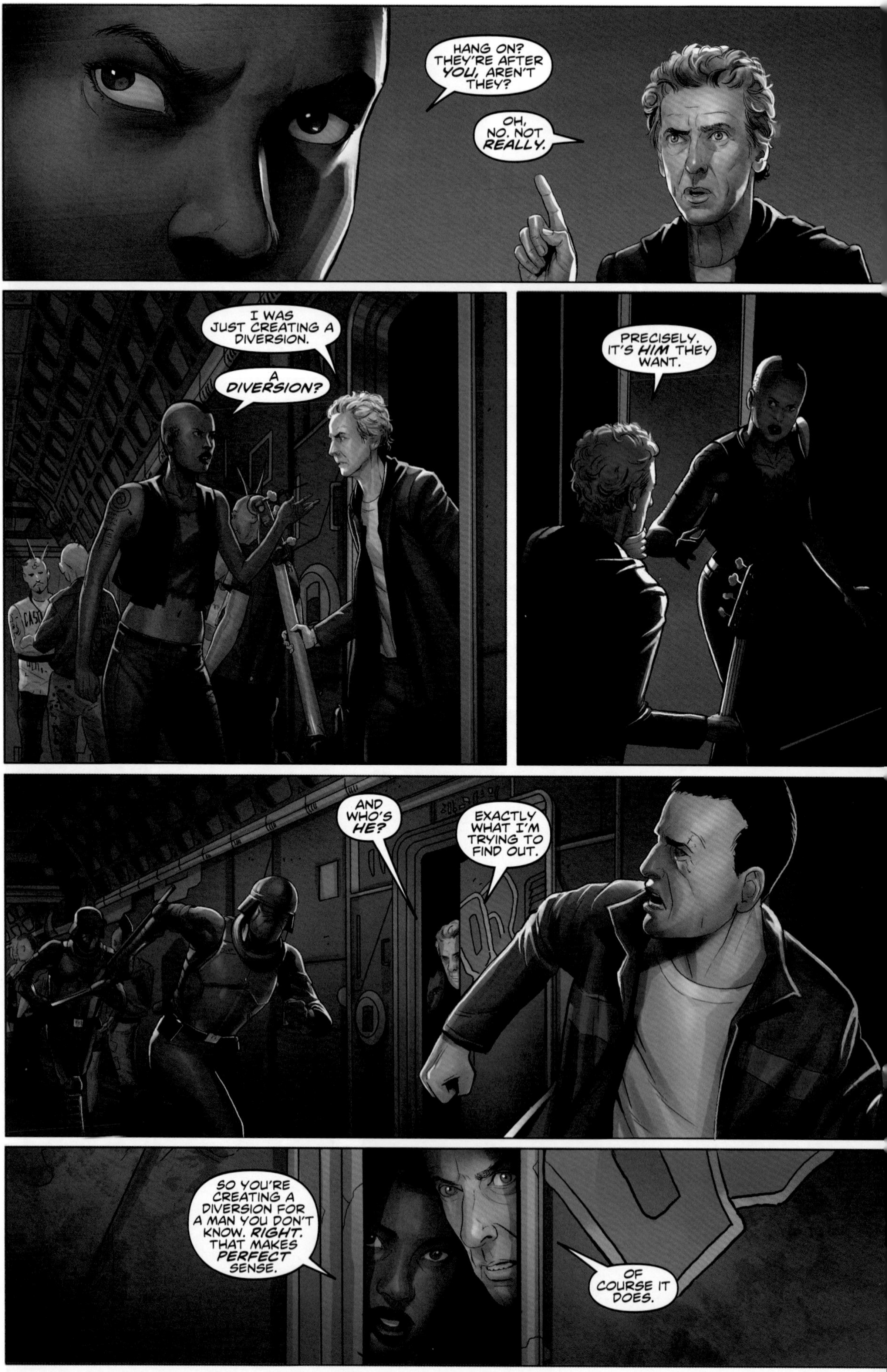
HANG ON? THEY'RE AFTER YOU, AREN'T THEY?
OH, NO. NOT REALLY.
I WAS JUST CREATING A DIVERSION.
A DIVERSION?
PRECISELY. IT'S HIM THEY WANT.
AND WHO'S HE?
EXACTLY WHAT I'M TRYING TO FIND OUT.
SO YOU'RE CREATING A DIVERSION FOR A MAN YOU DON'T KNOW. RIGHT. THAT MAKES PERFECT SENSE.
OF COURSE IT DOES.

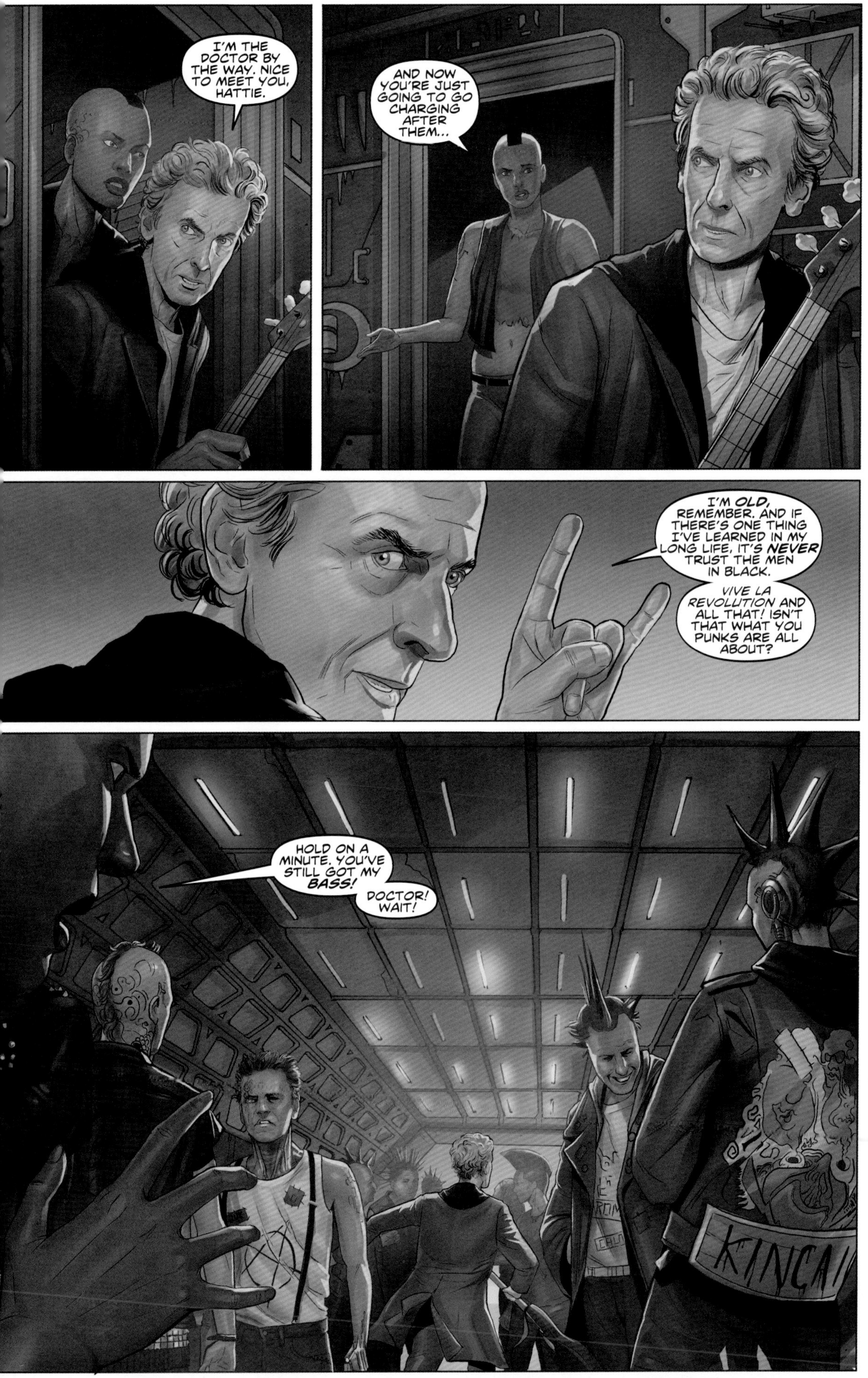
I'M THE DOCTOR BY THE WAY. NICE TO MEET YOU, HATTIE.
AND NOW YOU'RE JUST GOING TO GO CHARGING AFTER THEM...
I'M *OLD*, REMEMBER. AND IF THERE'S ONE THING I'VE LEARNED IN MY LONG LIFE, IT'S *NEVER* TRUST THE MEN IN BLACK.
VIVE LA REVOLUTION AND ALL THAT! ISN'T THAT WHAT YOU PUNKS ARE ALL ABOUT?
HOLD ON A MINUTE. YOU'VE STILL GOT MY *BASS!*
DOCTOR! WAIT!
KINCAI

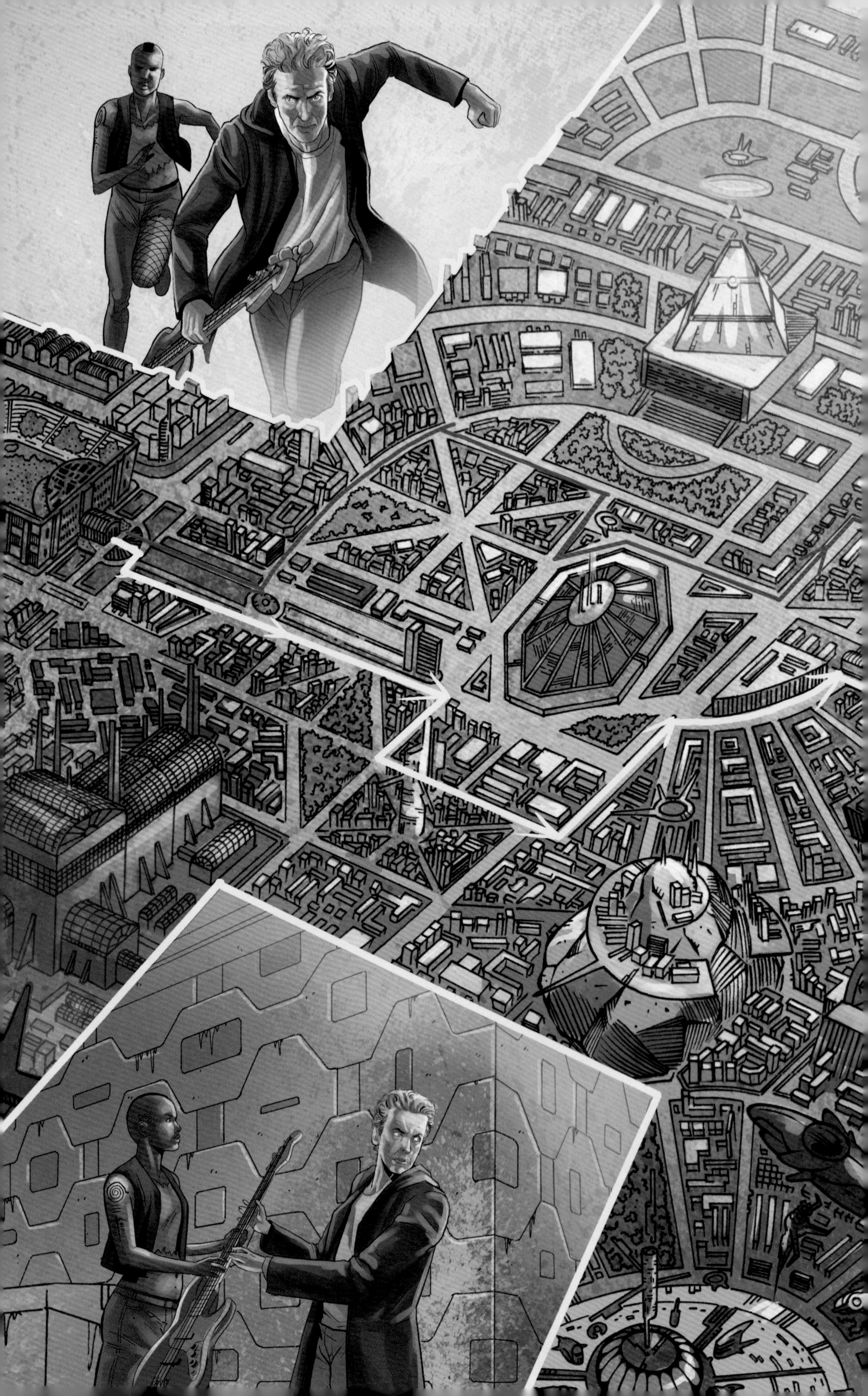

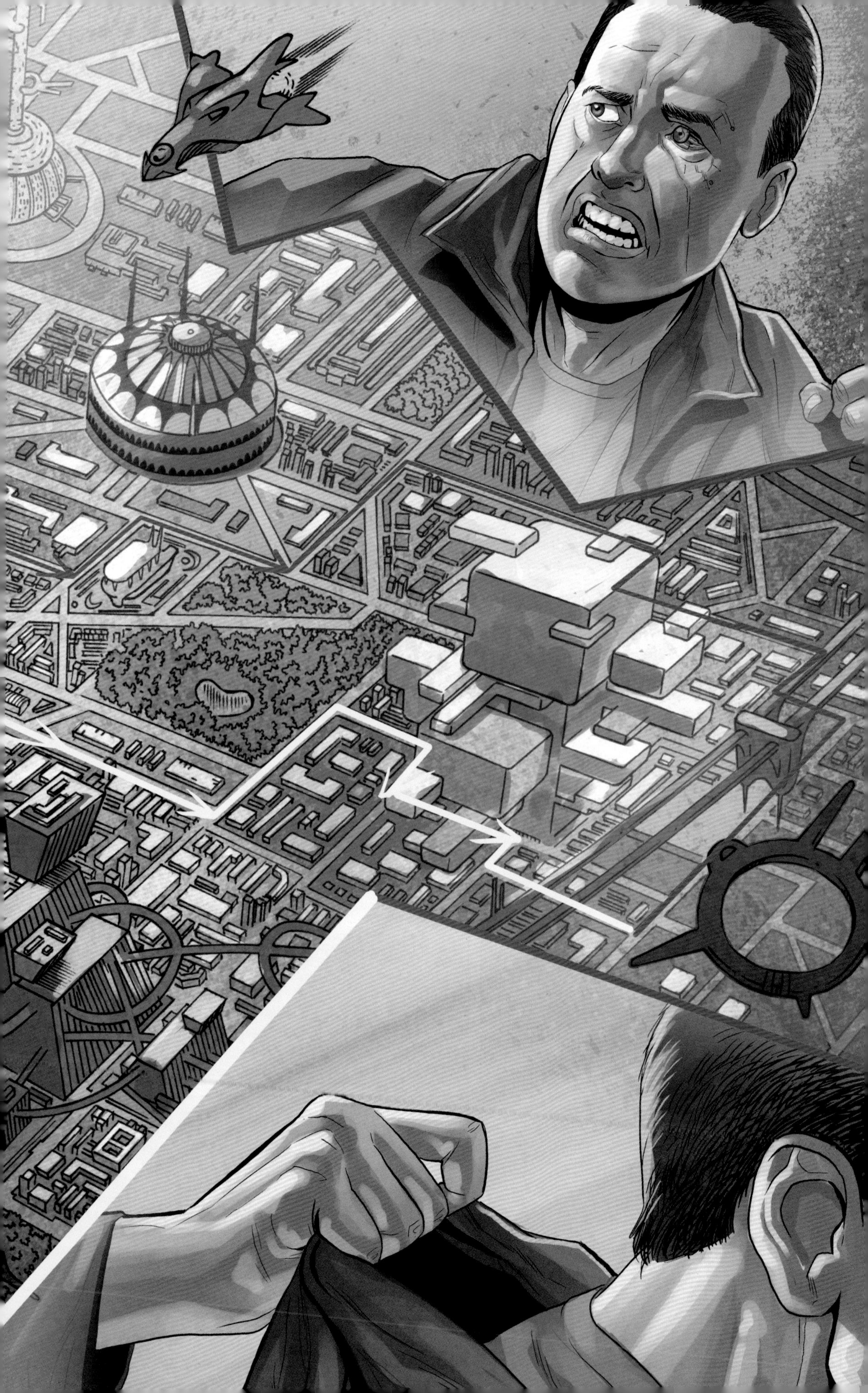

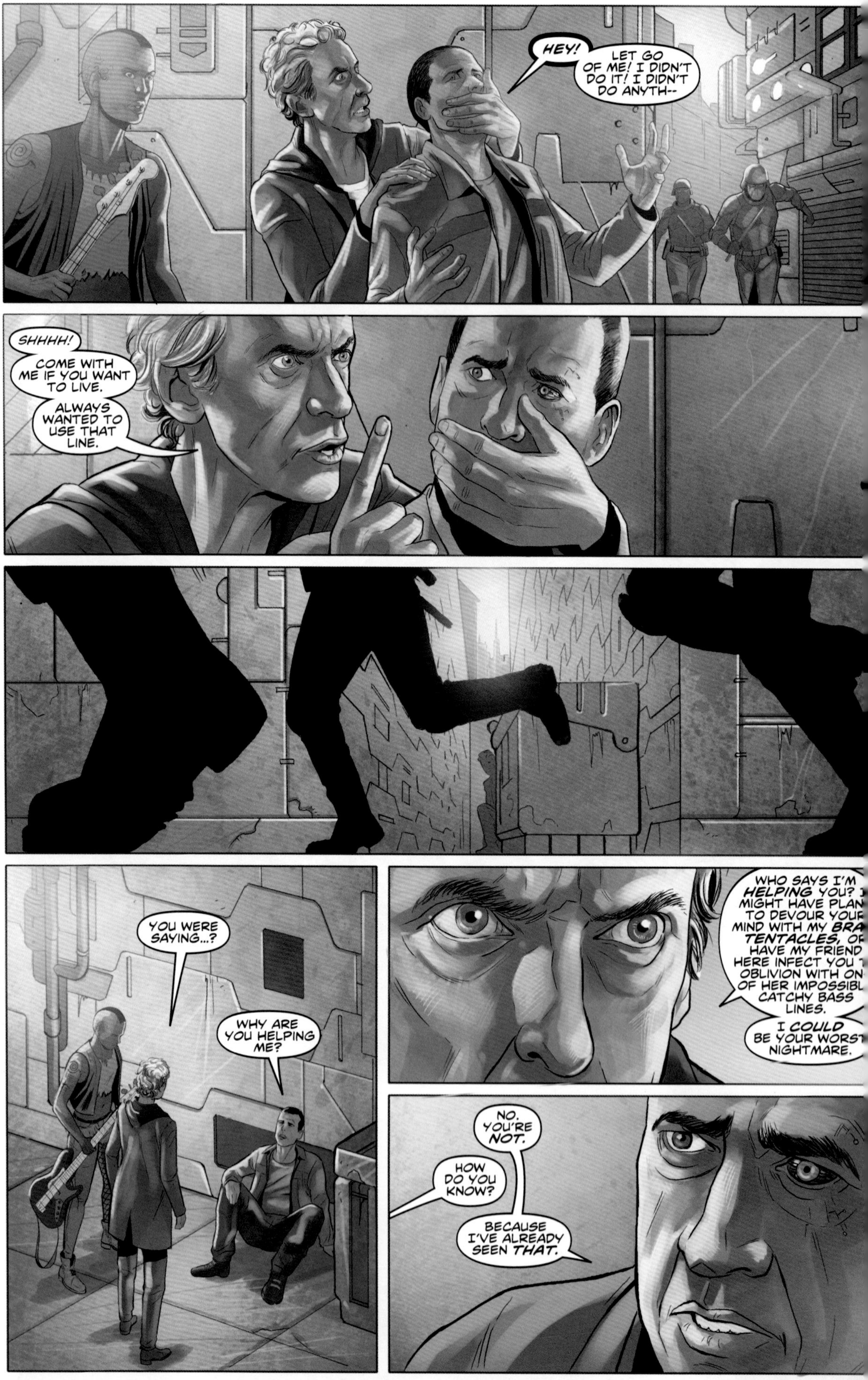

HEY!
LET GO OF ME! I DIDN'T DO IT! I DIDN'T DO ANYTH--
SHHHH!
COME WITH ME IF YOU WANT TO LIVE.
ALWAYS WANTED TO USE THAT LINE.
YOU WERE SAYING...?
WHY ARE YOU HELPING ME?
WHO SAYS I'M HELPING YOU? I MIGHT HAVE PLAN TO DEVOUR YOUR MIND WITH MY BRA TENTACLES, OR HAVE MY FRIEND HERE INFECT YOU T OBLIVION WITH ON OF HER IMPOSSIBL CATCHY BASS LINES.
I COULD BE YOUR WORST NIGHTMARE.
NO. YOU'RE NOT.
HOW DO YOU KNOW?
BECAUSE I'VE ALREADY SEEN THAT.

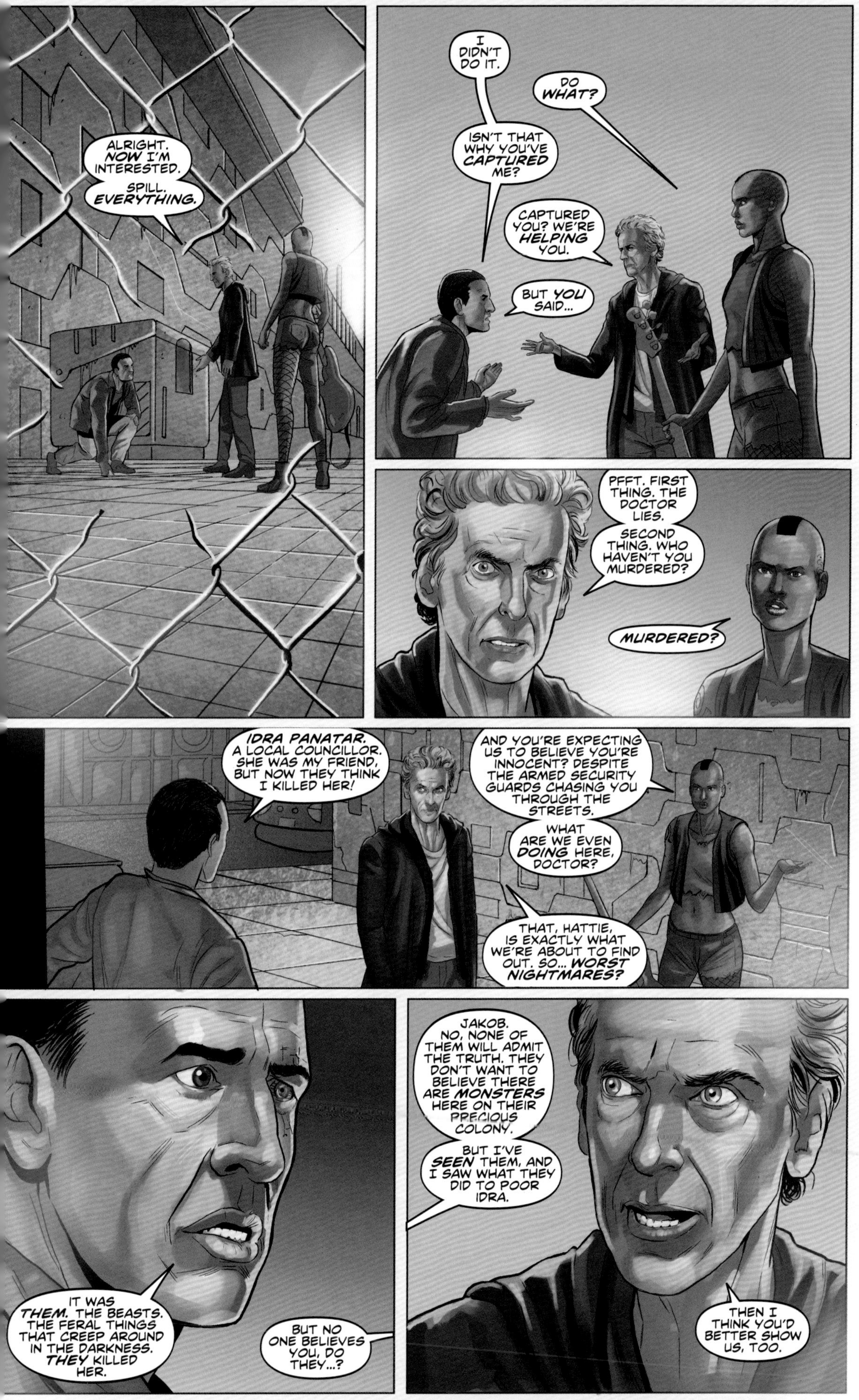
ALRIGHT. NOW I'M INTERESTED.
SPILL. EVERYTHING.
I DIDN'T DO IT.
DO WHAT?
ISN'T THAT WHY YOU'VE CAPTURED ME?
CAPTURED YOU? WE'RE HELPING YOU.
BUT YOU SAID...
PFFT. FIRST THING. THE DOCTOR LIES.
SECOND THING. WHO HAVEN'T YOU MURDERED?
MURDERED?
IDRA PANATAR. A LOCAL COUNCILLOR. SHE WAS MY FRIEND, BUT NOW THEY THINK I KILLED HER!
AND YOU'RE EXPECTING US TO BELIEVE YOU'RE INNOCENT? DESPITE THE ARMED SECURITY GUARDS CHASING YOU THROUGH THE STREETS.
WHAT ARE WE EVEN DOING HERE, DOCTOR?
THAT, HATTIE, IS EXACTLY WHAT WE'RE ABOUT TO FIND OUT. SO... WORST NIGHTMARES?
IT WAS THEM. THE BEASTS. THE FERAL THINGS THAT CREEP AROUND IN THE DARKNESS. THEY KILLED HER.
BUT NO ONE BELIEVES YOU, DO THEY...?
JAKOB. NO, NONE OF THEM WILL ADMIT THE TRUTH. THEY DON'T WANT TO BELIEVE THERE ARE MONSTERS HERE ON THEIR PRECIOUS COLONY.
BUT I'VE SEEN THEM, AND I SAW WHAT THEY DID TO POOR IDRA.
THEN I THINK YOU'D BETTER SHOW US, TOO.

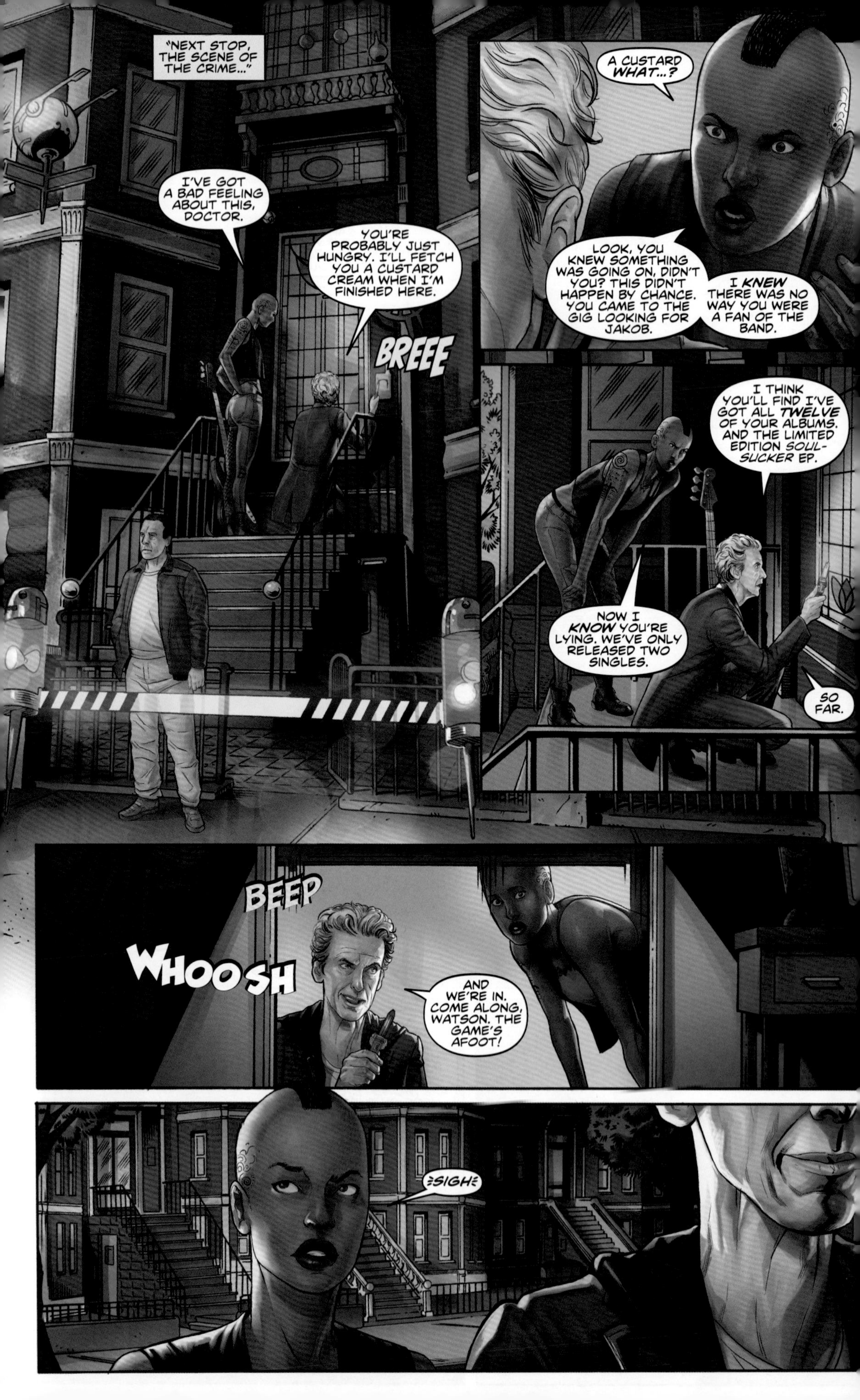
"NEXT STOP, THE SCENE OF THE CRIME..."
I'VE GOT A BAD FEELING ABOUT THIS, DOCTOR.
YOU'RE PROBABLY JUST HUNGRY. I'LL FETCH YOU A CUSTARD CREAM WHEN I'M FINISHED HERE.
BREEE
A CUSTARD WHAT...?
LOOK, YOU KNEW SOMETHING WAS GOING ON, DIDN'T YOU? THIS DIDN'T HAPPEN BY CHANCE. YOU CAME TO THE GIG LOOKING FOR JAKOB.
I KNEW THERE WAS NO WAY YOU WERE A FAN OF THE BAND.
I THINK YOU'LL FIND I'VE GOT ALL TWELVE OF YOUR ALBUMS. AND THE LIMITED EDITION SOUL-SUCKER EP.
NOW I KNOW YOU'RE LYING. WE'VE ONLY RELEASED TWO SINGLES.
SO FAR.
BEEP
WHOOSH
AND WE'RE IN. COME ALONG, WATSON. THE GAME'S AFOOT!
SIGH

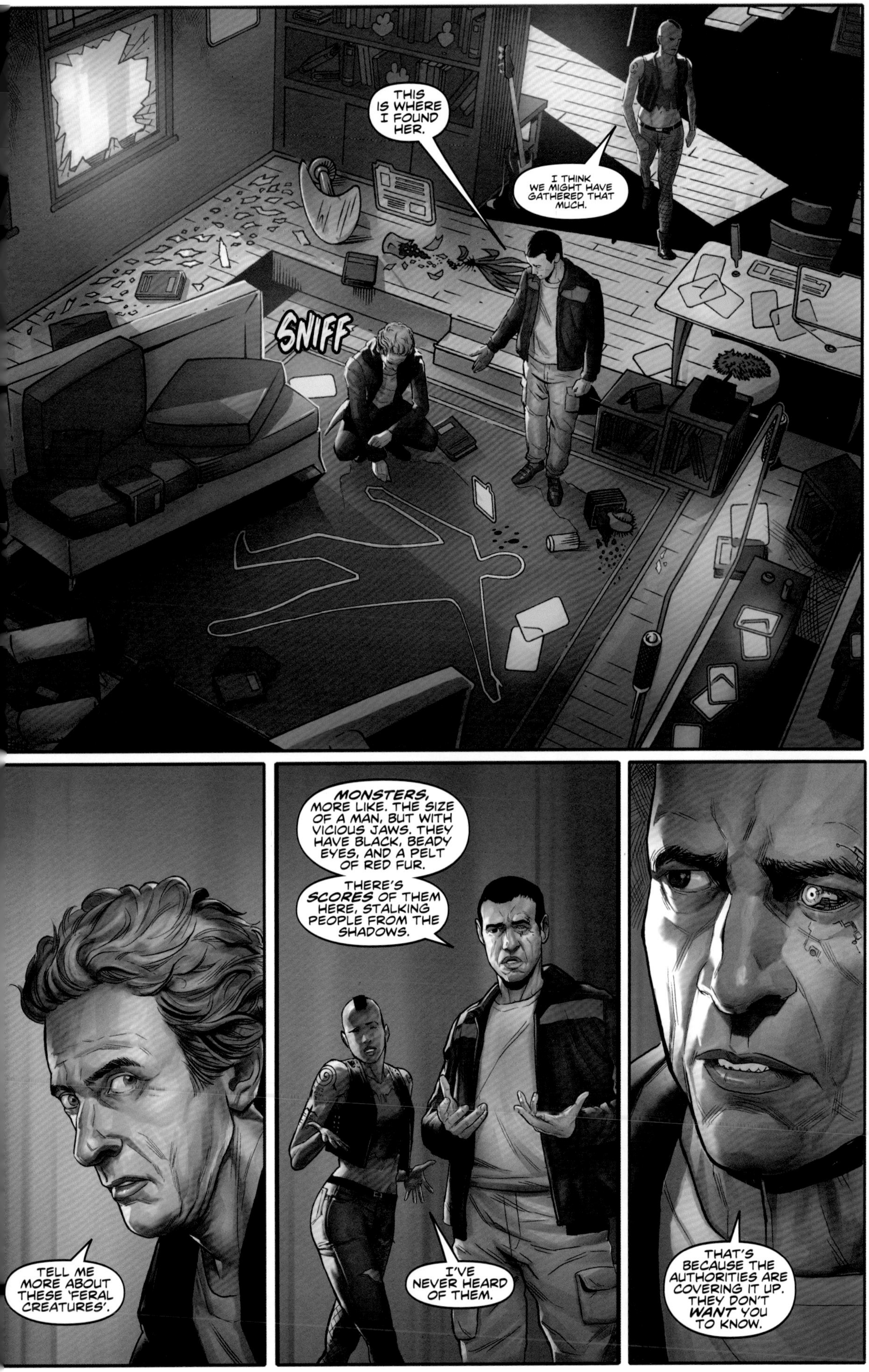
THIS IS WHERE I FOUND HER.
I THINK WE MIGHT HAVE GATHERED THAT MUCH.
SNIFF
TELL ME MORE ABOUT THESE 'FERAL CREATURES'.
MONSTERS, MORE LIKE. THE SIZE OF A MAN, BUT WITH VICIOUS JAWS. THEY HAVE BLACK, BEADY EYES, AND A PELT OF RED FUR.
THERE'S SCORES OF THEM HERE, STALKING PEOPLE FROM THE SHADOWS.
I'VE NEVER HEARD OF THEM.
THAT'S BECAUSE THE AUTHORITIES ARE COVERING IT UP. THEY DON'T WANT YOU TO KNOW.

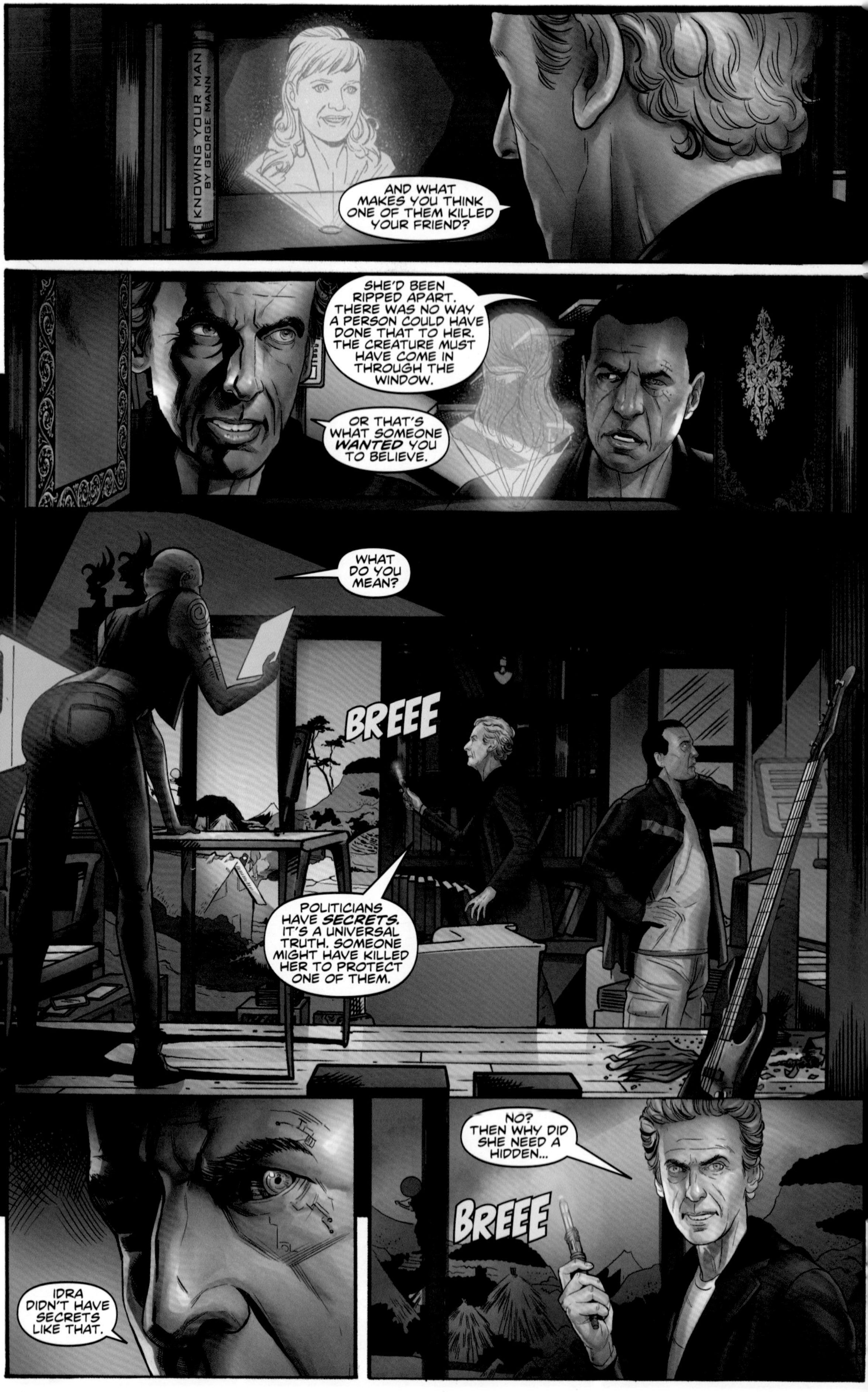
KNOWING YOUR MAN BY GEORGE MANN
AND WHAT MAKES YOU THINK ONE OF THEM KILLED YOUR FRIEND?
SHE'D BEEN RIPPED APART. THERE WAS NO WAY A PERSON COULD HAVE DONE THAT TO HER. THE CREATURE MUST HAVE COME IN THROUGH THE WINDOW.
OR THAT'S WHAT SOMEONE *WANTED* YOU TO BELIEVE.
WHAT DO YOU MEAN?
BREEE
POLITICIANS HAVE *SECRETS.* IT'S A UNIVERSAL TRUTH. SOMEONE MIGHT HAVE KILLED HER TO PROTECT ONE OF THEM.
IDRA DIDN'T HAVE SECRETS LIKE THAT.
NO? THEN WHY DID SHE NEED A HIDDEN...
BREEE

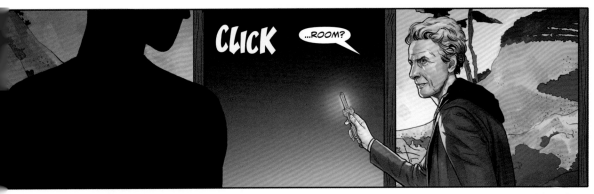

CLICK

...ROOM?

SECRETS, SECRETS, SECRETS...

THESE PICTURES... THEY'RE FROM ALL OVER THE TWIST.

AND THEY'RE ALL SHOTS OF THE CREATURES. THIS IS THE PROOF I'VE BEEN LOOKING FOR.

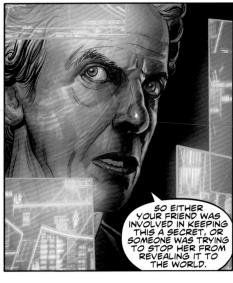

SO EITHER YOUR FRIEND WAS INVOLVED IN KEEPING THIS A SECRET, OR SOMEONE WAS TRYING TO STOP HER FROM REVEALING IT TO THE WORLD.

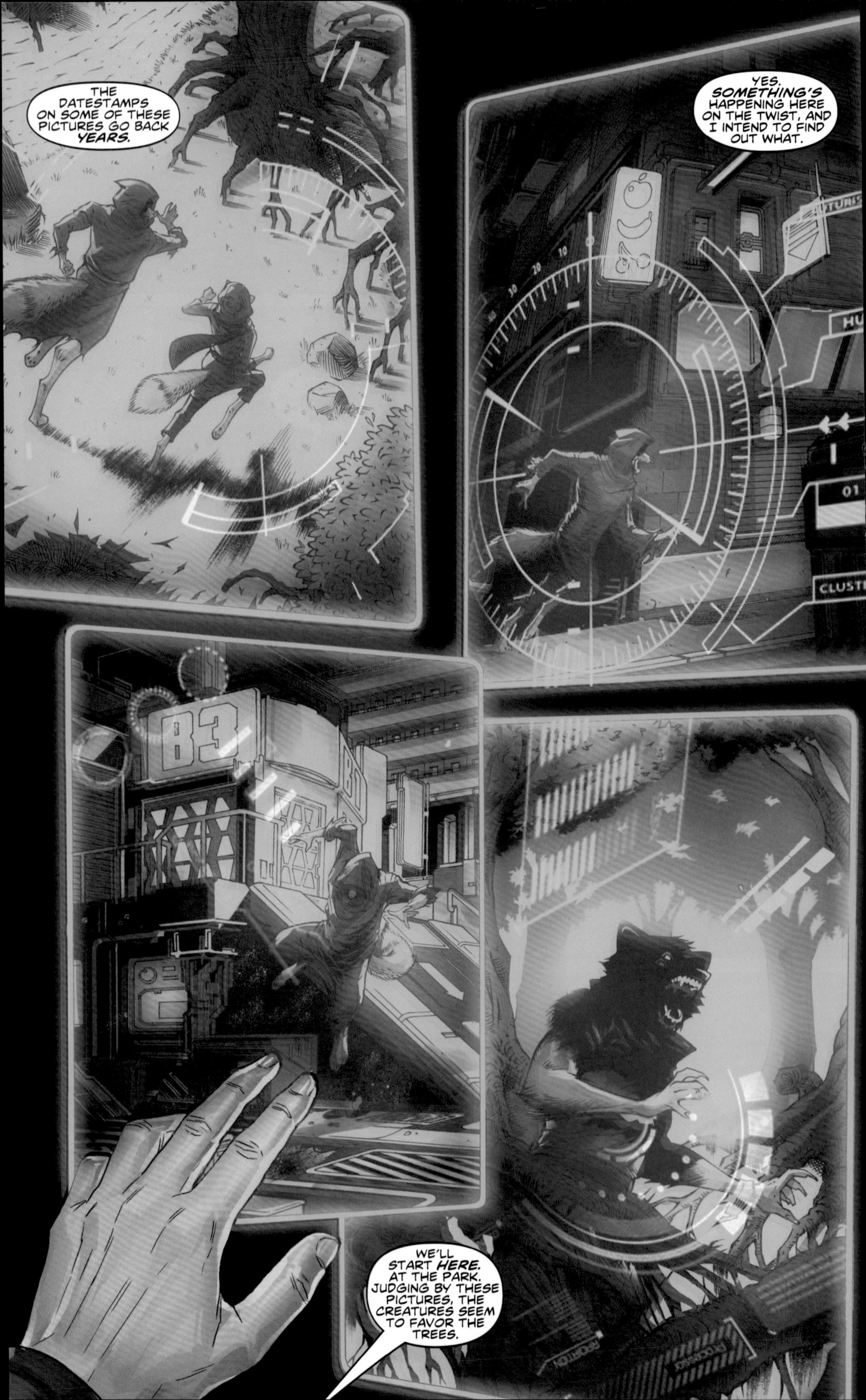
THE DATESTAMPS ON SOME OF THESE PICTURES GO BACK YEARS.
YES. SOMETHING'S HAPPENING HERE ON THE TWIST, AND I INTEND TO FIND OUT WHAT.
B3
WE'LL START HERE. AT THE PARK. JUDGING BY THESE PICTURES, THE CREATURES SEEM TO FAVOR THE TREES.

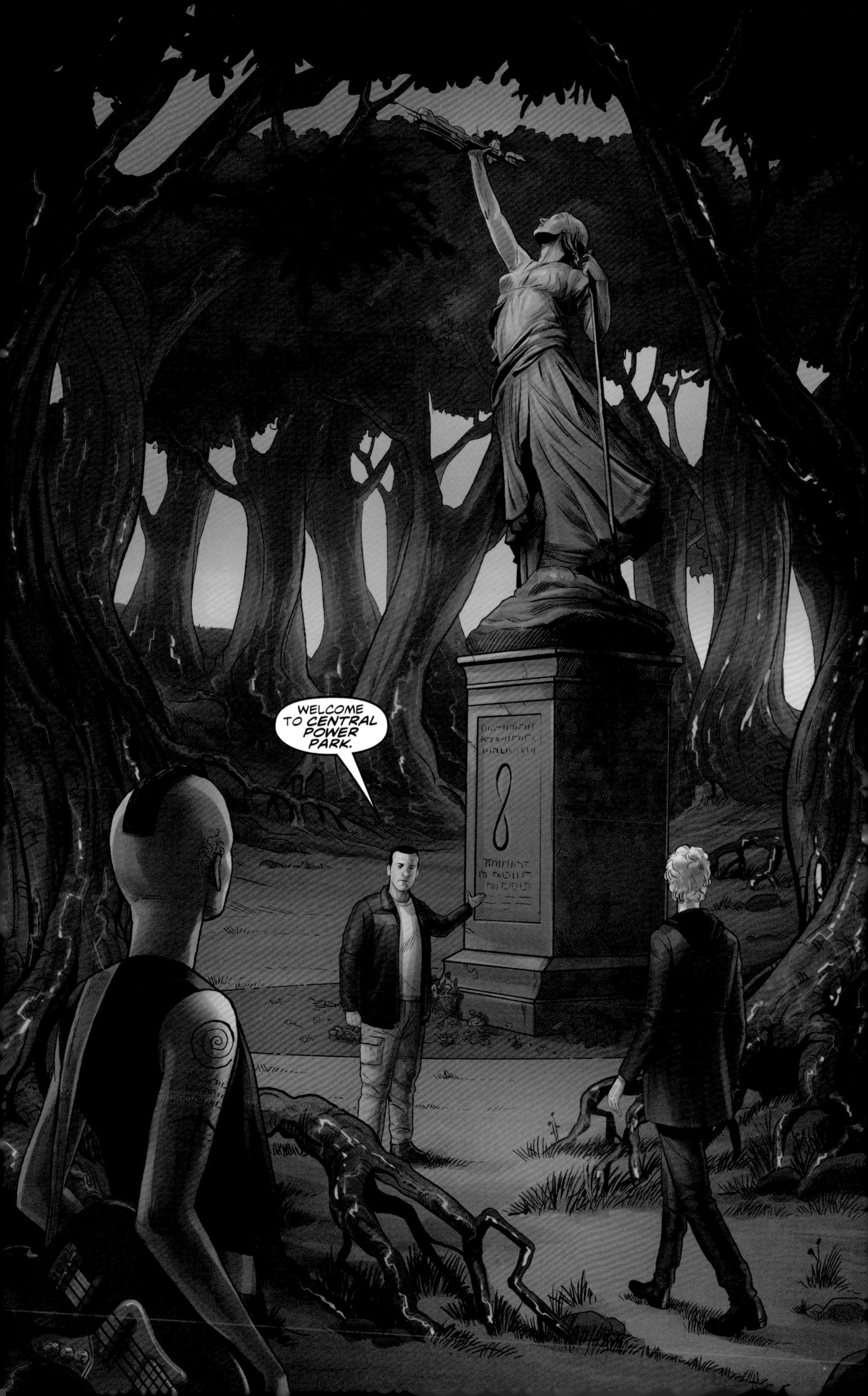
WELCOME TO CENTRAL POWER PARK.

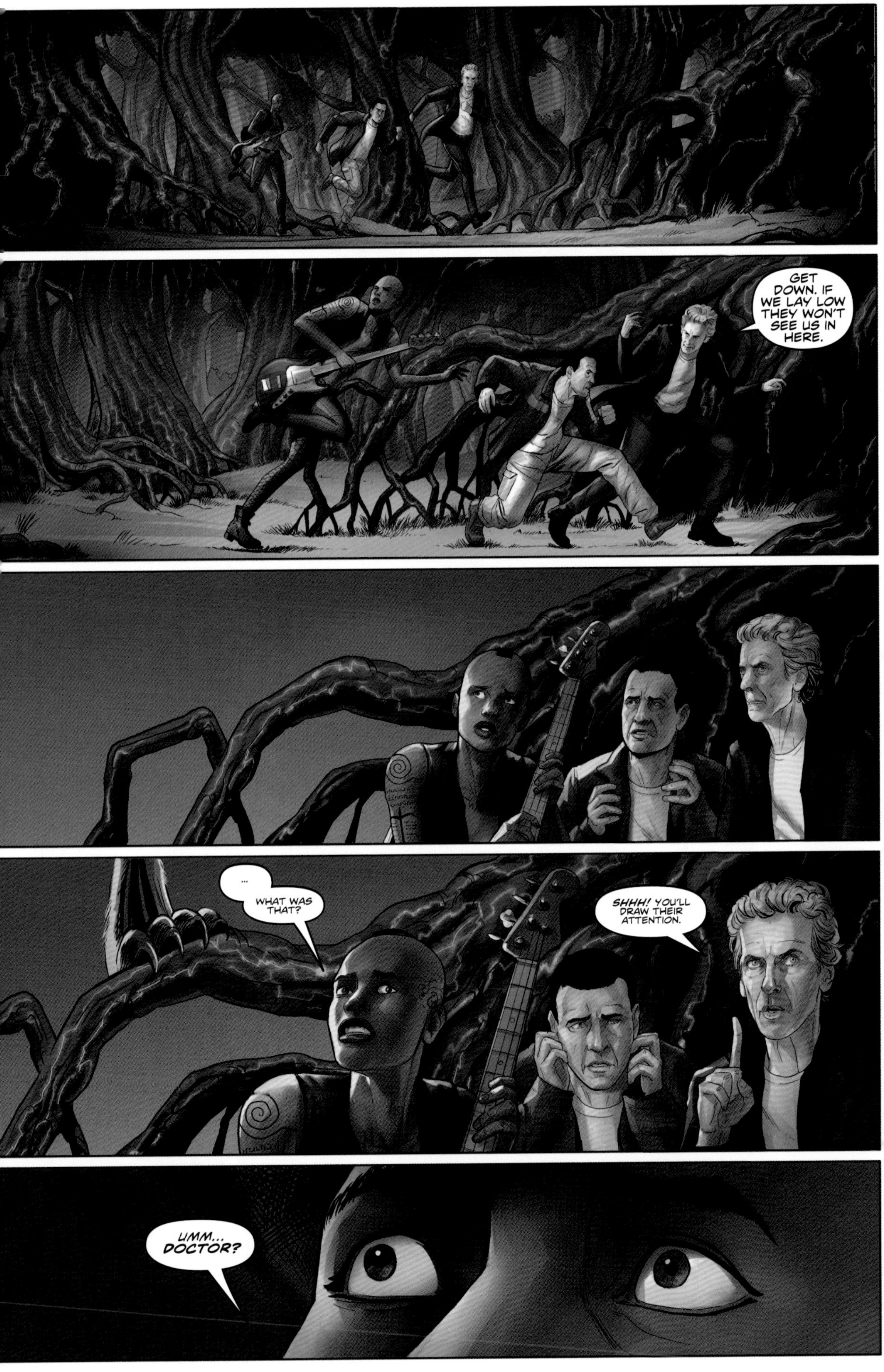
GET DOWN. IF WE LAY LOW THEY WON'T SEE US IN HERE.
...
WHAT WAS THAT?
SHHH! YOU'LL DRAW THEIR ATTENTION.
UMM... DOCTOR?

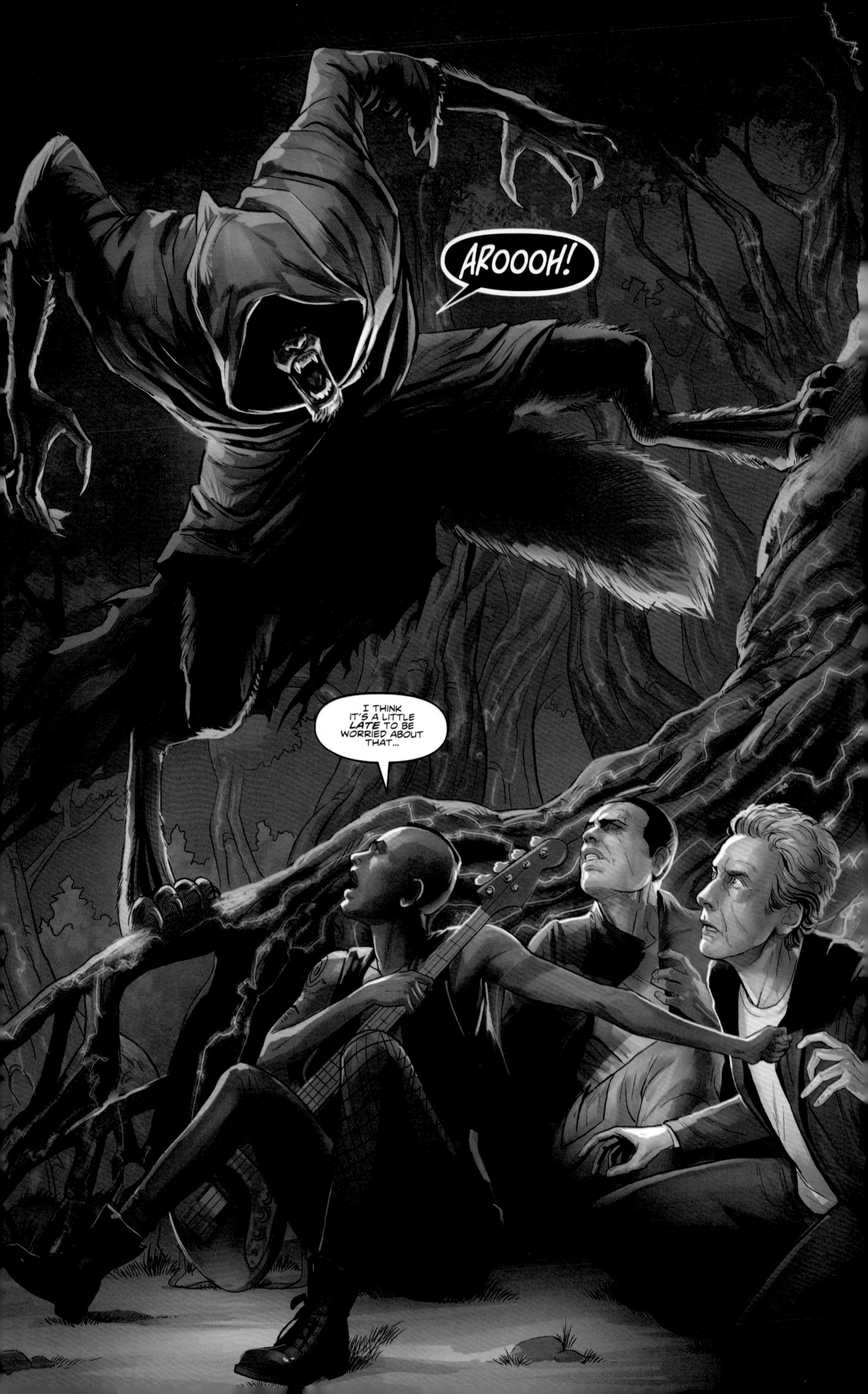
AROOOH!
I THINK IT'S A LITTLE LATE TO BE WORRIED ABOUT THAT...

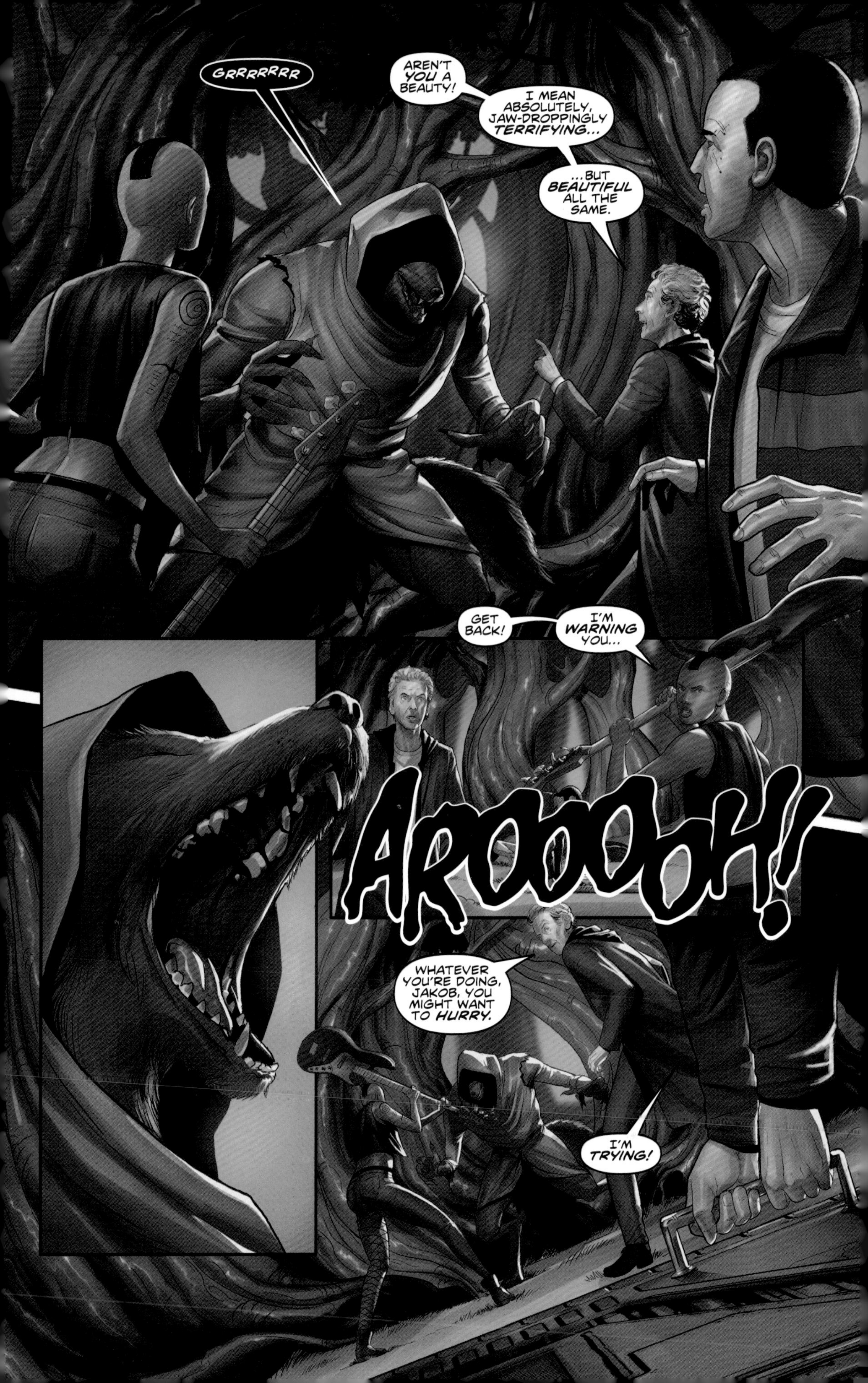
GRRRRRRR
AREN'T YOU A BEAUTY!
I MEAN ABSOLUTELY, JAW-DROPPINGLY TERRIFYING...
...BUT BEAUTIFUL ALL THE SAME.
GET BACK!
I'M WARNING YOU...
AROOOOH!
WHATEVER YOU'RE DOING, JAKOB, YOU MIGHT WANT TO HURRY.
I'M TRYING!

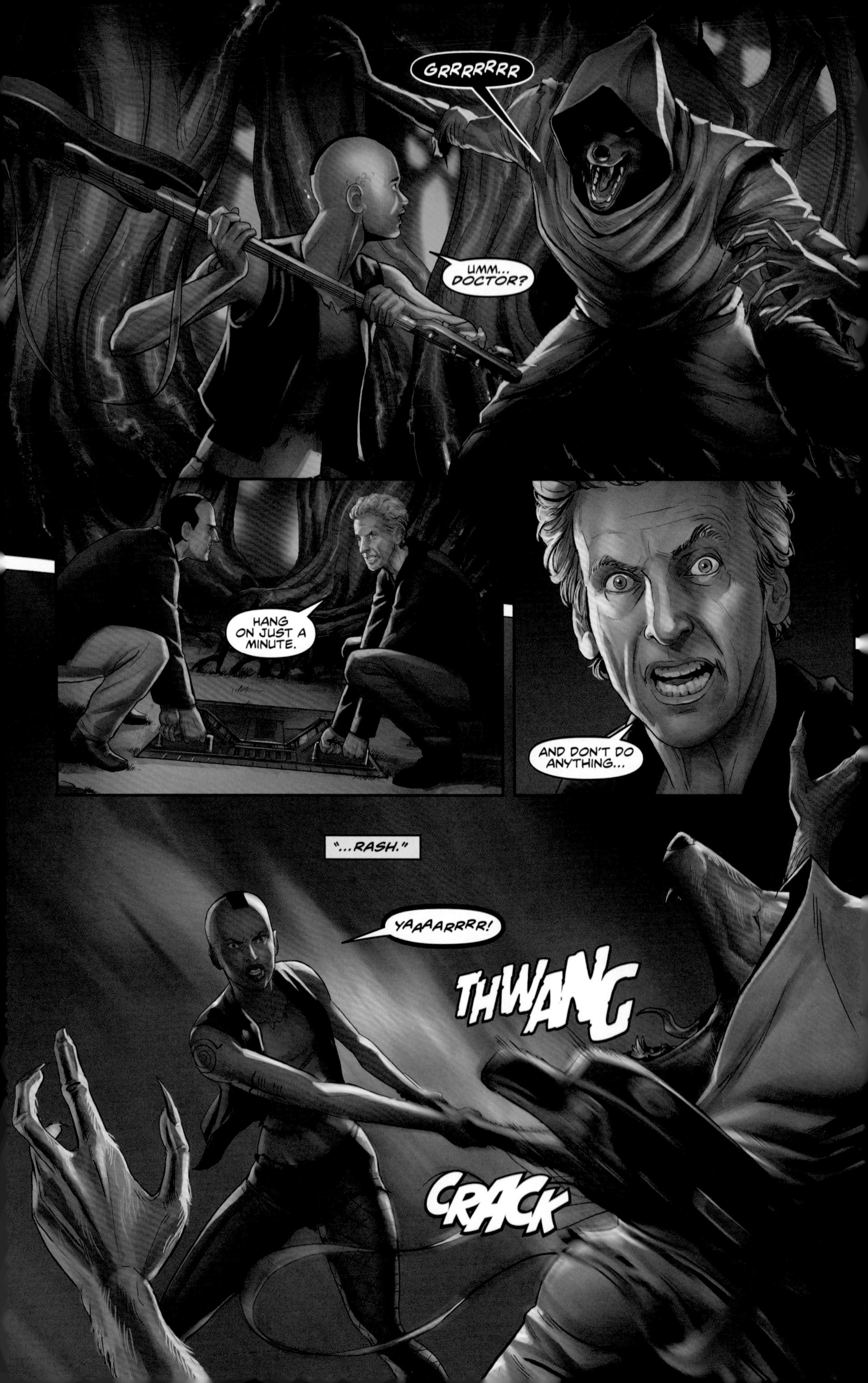
GRRRRRRR
UMM... DOCTOR?
HANG ON JUST A MINUTE.
AND DON'T DO ANYTHING...
"...RASH."
YAAAARRRR!
THWANG
CRACK

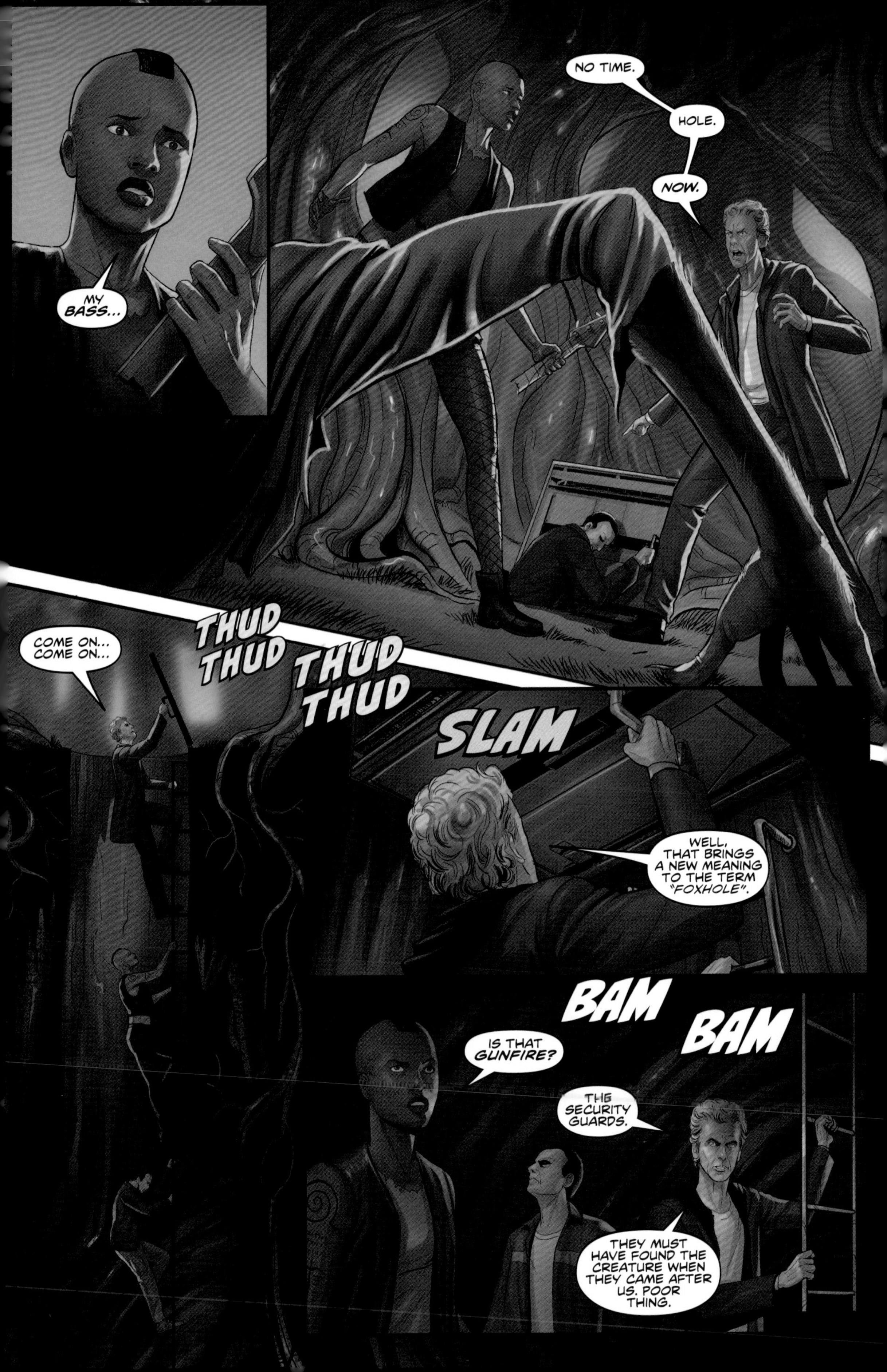
MY BASS...
NO TIME.
HOLE.
NOW.
THUD THUD
THUD THUD
COME ON... COME ON...
SLAM
WELL, THAT BRINGS A NEW MEANING TO THE TERM "FOXHOLE".
BAM
BAM
IS THAT GUNFIRE?
THE SECURITY GUARDS.
THEY MUST HAVE FOUND THE CREATURE WHEN THEY CAME AFTER US. POOR THING.

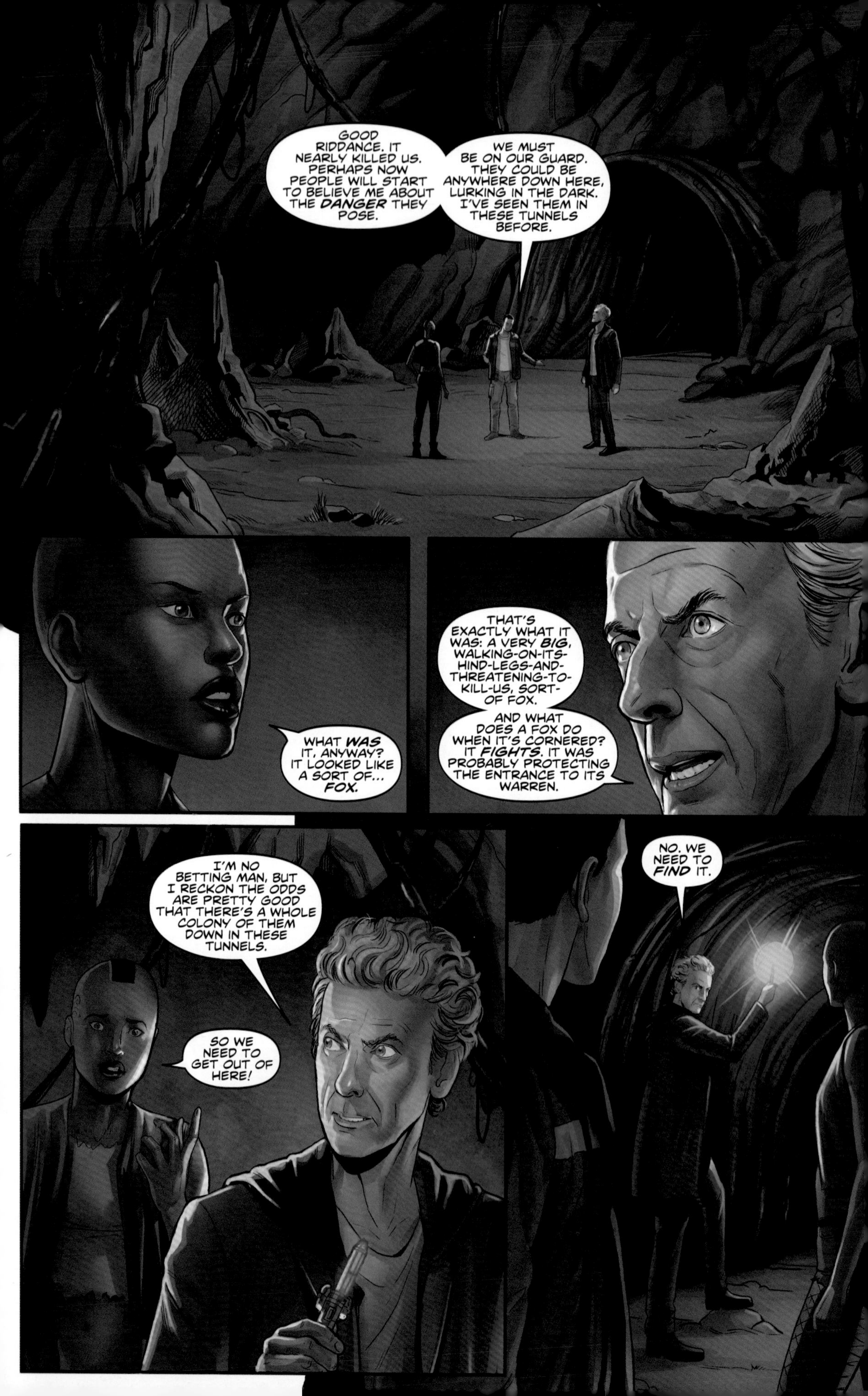
GOOD RIDDANCE. IT NEARLY KILLED US. PERHAPS NOW PEOPLE WILL START TO BELIEVE ME ABOUT THE *DANGER* THEY POSE.
WE MUST BE ON OUR GUARD. THEY COULD BE ANYWHERE DOWN HERE, LURKING IN THE DARK. I'VE SEEN THEM IN THESE TUNNELS BEFORE.
WHAT *WAS* IT, ANYWAY? IT LOOKED LIKE A SORT OF... *FOX.*
THAT'S EXACTLY WHAT IT WAS: A VERY *BIG*, WALKING-ON-ITS-HIND-LEGS-AND-THREATENING-TO-KILL-US, SORT-OF FOX.
AND WHAT DOES A FOX DO WHEN IT'S CORNERED? IT *FIGHTS*. IT WAS PROBABLY PROTECTING THE ENTRANCE TO ITS WARREN.
I'M NO BETTING MAN, BUT I RECKON THE ODDS ARE PRETTY GOOD THAT THERE'S A WHOLE COLONY OF THEM DOWN IN THESE TUNNELS.
SO WE NEED TO GET OUT OF HERE!
NO. WE NEED TO *FIND* IT.

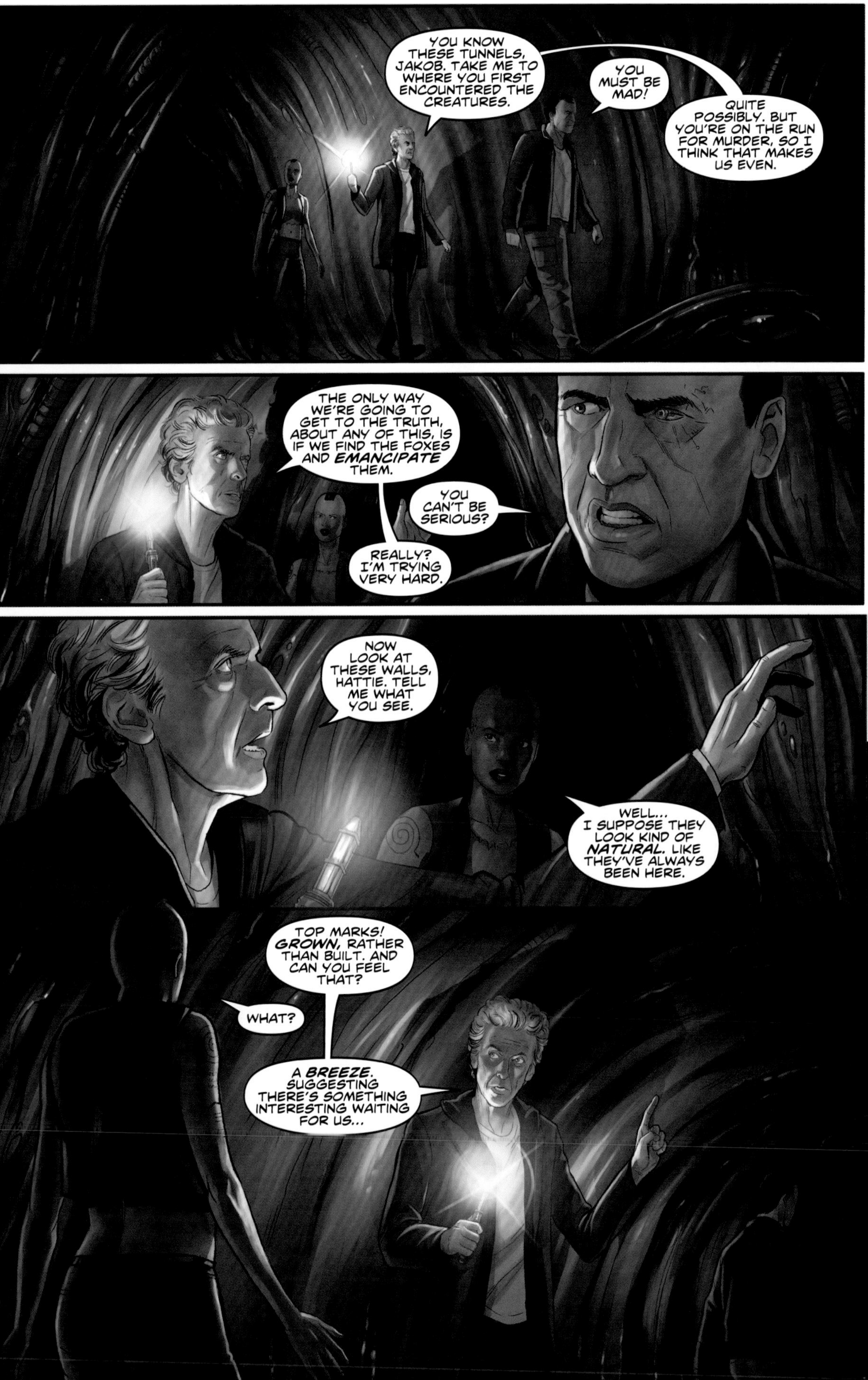
YOU KNOW THESE TUNNELS, JAKOB. TAKE ME TO WHERE YOU FIRST ENCOUNTERED THE CREATURES.
YOU MUST BE MAD!
QUITE POSSIBLY. BUT YOU'RE ON THE RUN FOR MURDER, SO I THINK THAT MAKES US EVEN.
THE ONLY WAY WE'RE GOING TO GET TO THE TRUTH, ABOUT ANY OF THIS, IS IF WE FIND THE FOXES AND *EMANCIPATE* THEM.
YOU CAN'T BE SERIOUS?
REALLY? I'M TRYING VERY HARD.
NOW LOOK AT THESE WALLS, HATTIE. TELL ME WHAT YOU SEE.
WELL... I SUPPOSE THEY LOOK KIND OF *NATURAL.* LIKE THEY'VE ALWAYS BEEN HERE.
TOP MARKS! *GROWN,* RATHER THAN BUILT. AND CAN YOU FEEL THAT?
WHAT?
A *BREEZE.* SUGGESTING THERE'S SOMETHING INTERESTING WAITING FOR US...

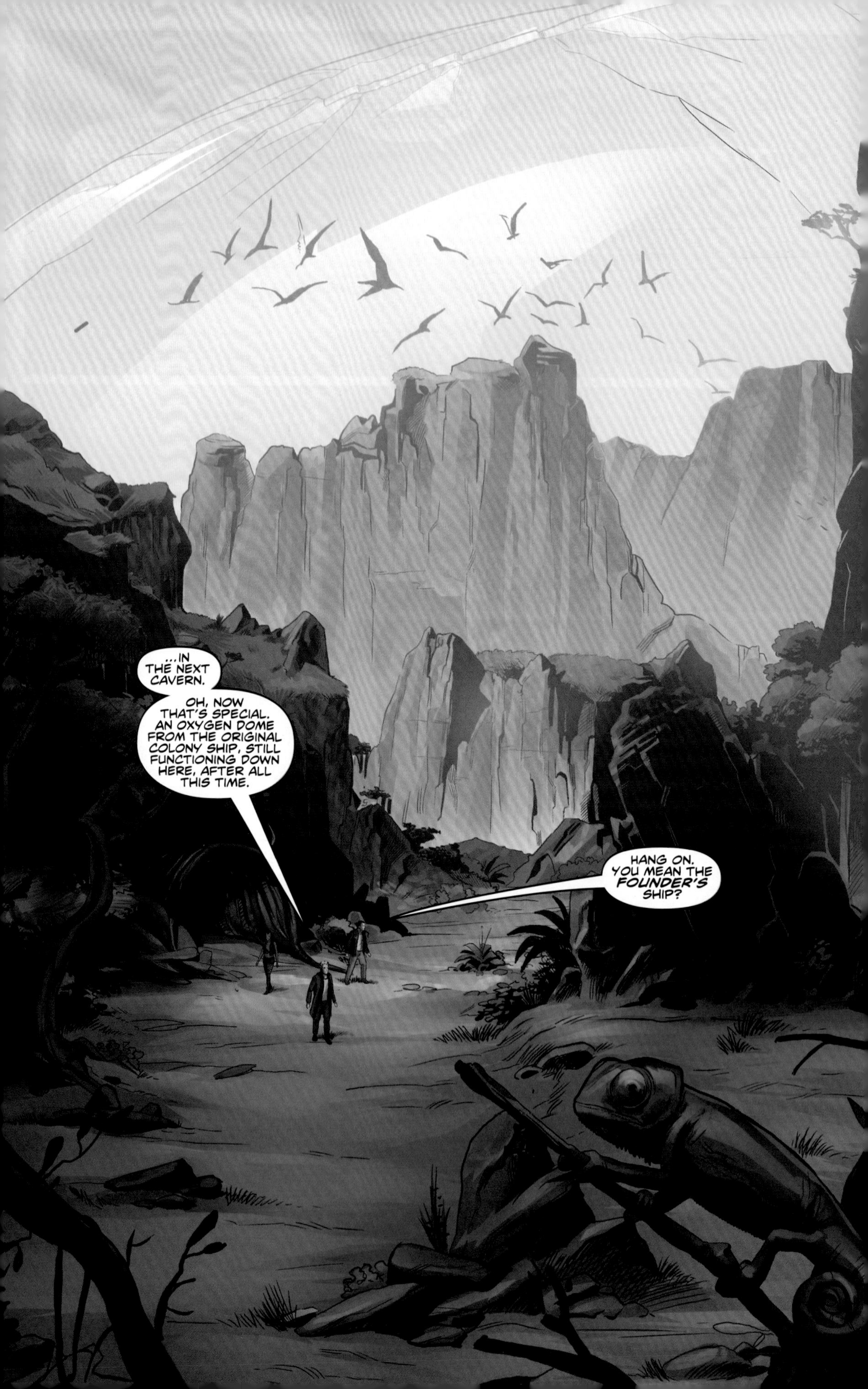
...IN THE NEXT CAVERN.
OH, NOW THAT'S SPECIAL. AN OXYGEN DOME FROM THE ORIGINAL COLONY SHIP, STILL FUNCTIONING DOWN HERE, AFTER ALL THIS TIME.
HANG ON. YOU MEAN THE FOUNDER'S SHIP?

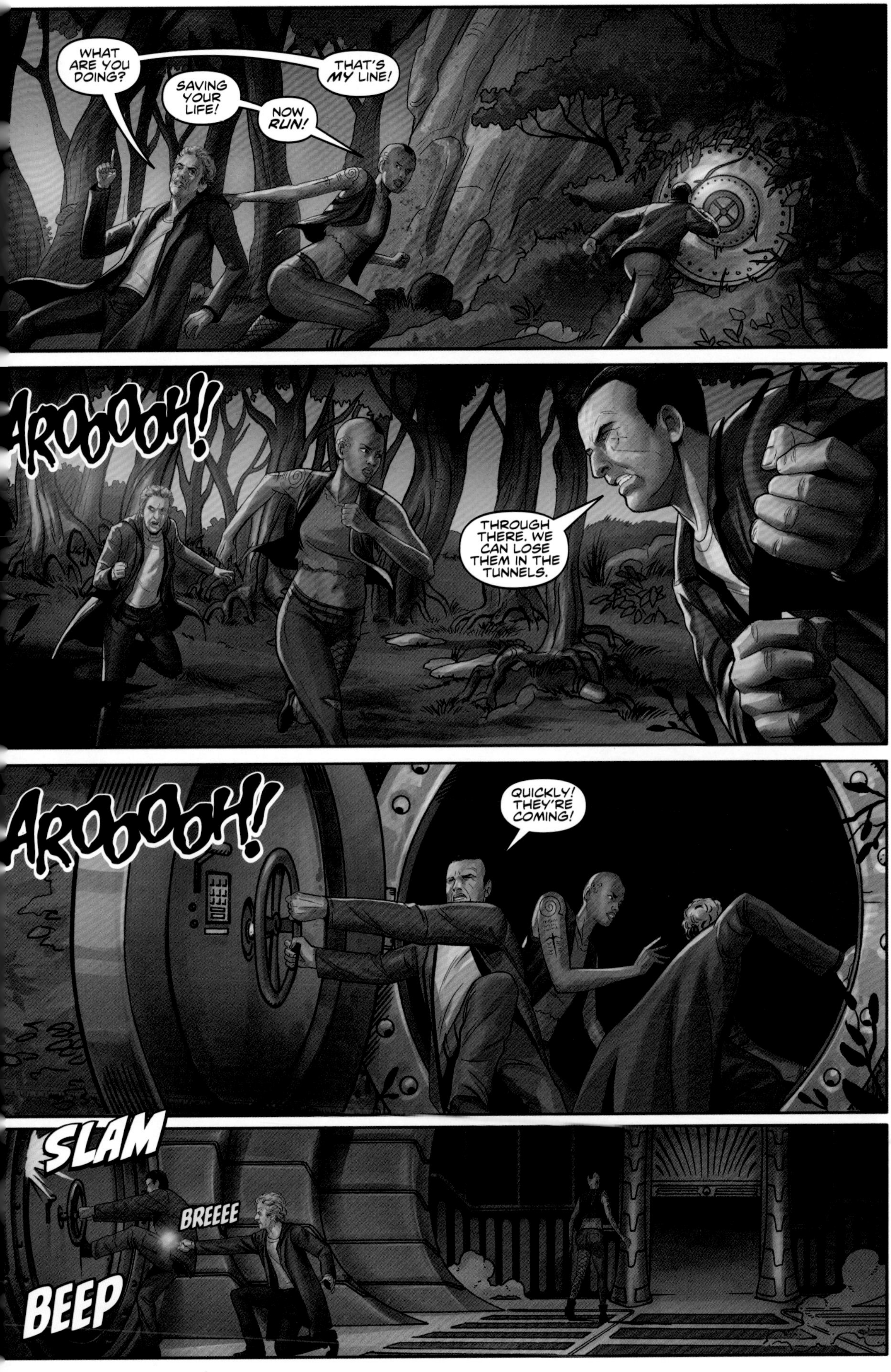
WHAT ARE YOU DOING?
SAVING YOUR LIFE!
THAT'S MY LINE!
NOW RUN!
AROOOOH!
THROUGH THERE. WE CAN LOSE THEM IN THE TUNNELS.
AROOOOH!
QUICKLY! THEY'RE COMING!
SLAM
BREEEE
BEEP

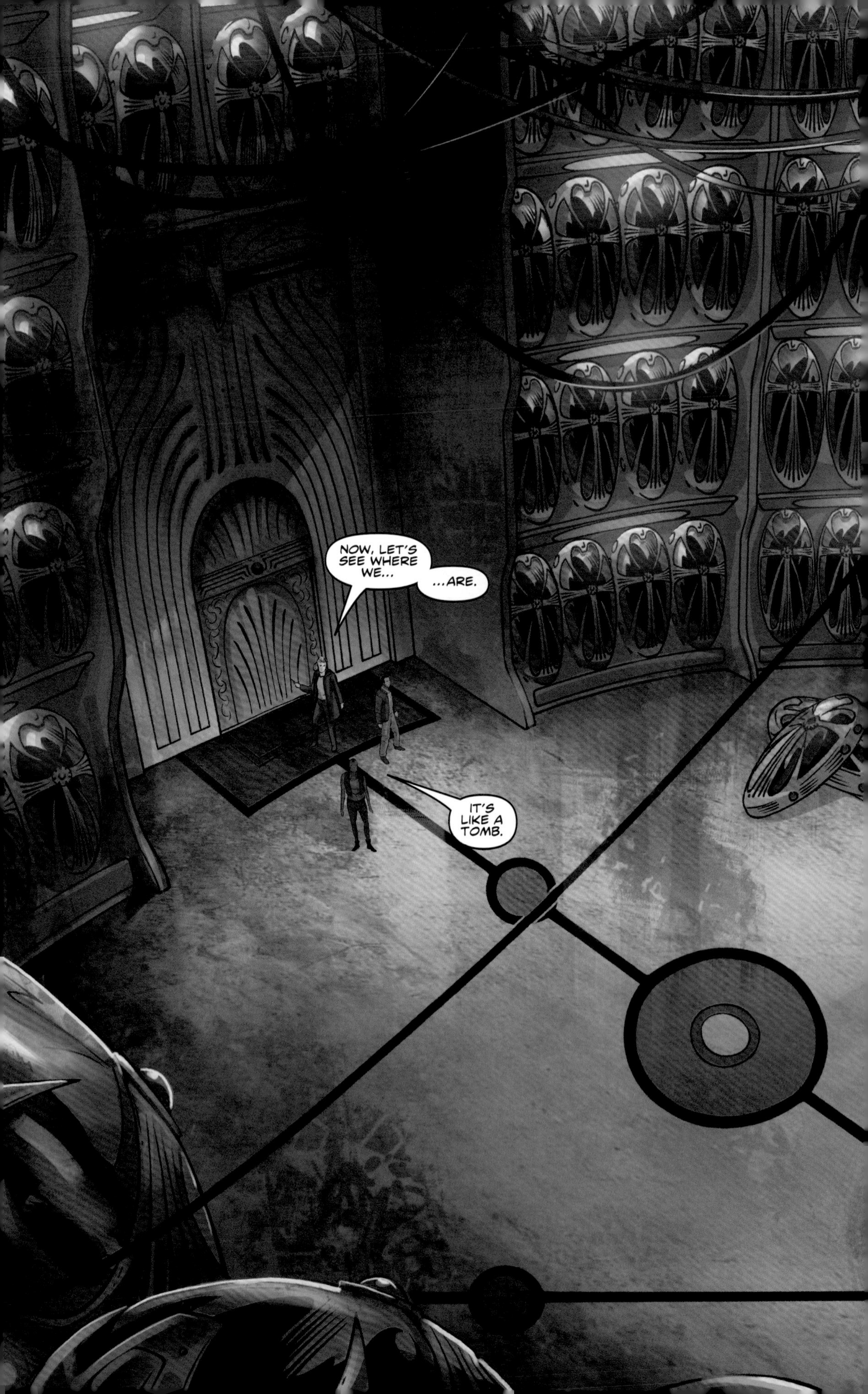
NOW, LET'S SEE WHERE WE...
...ARE.
IT'S LIKE A TOMB.

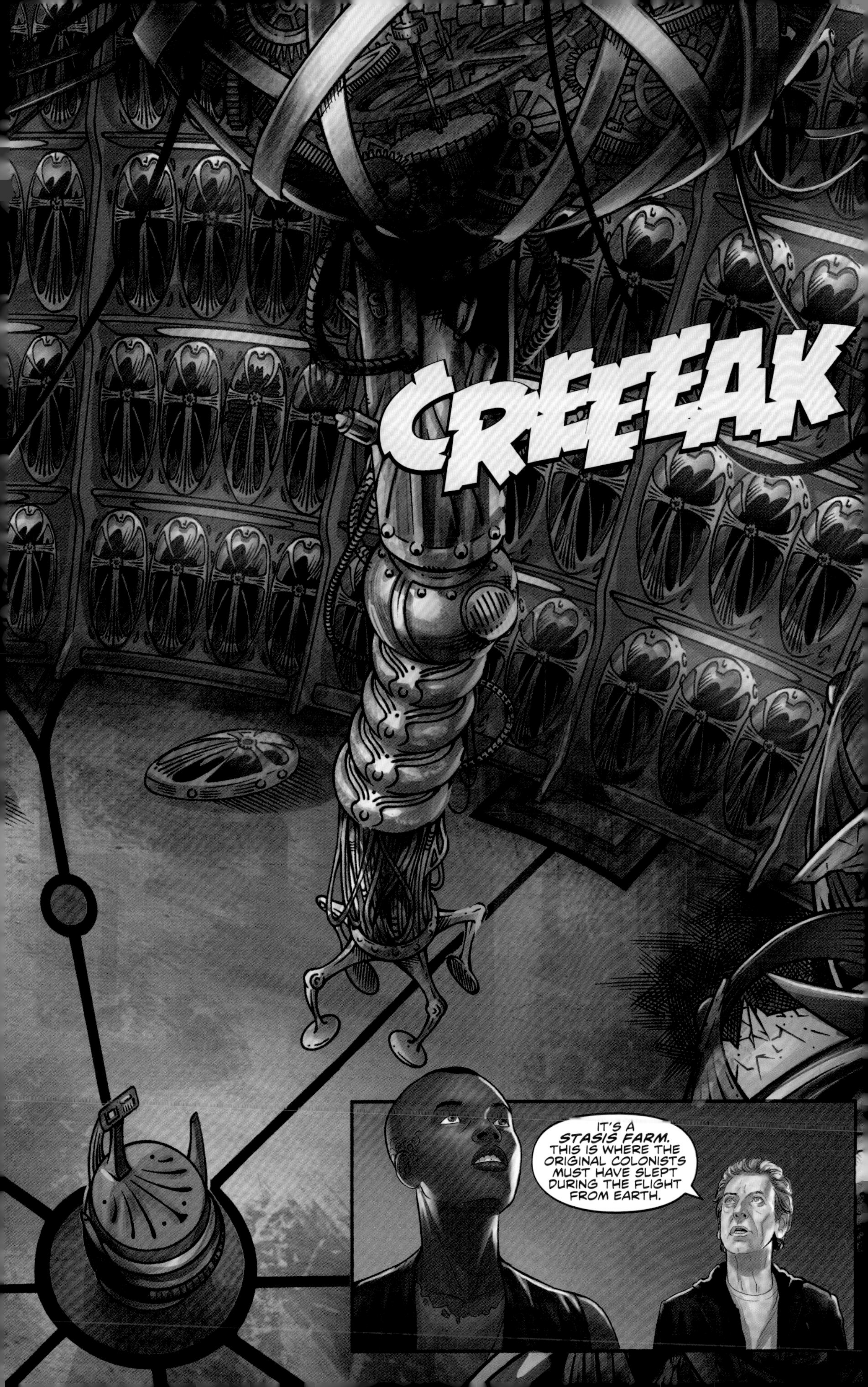
CREEEAK
IT'S A *STASIS FARM.* THIS IS WHERE THE ORIGINAL COLONISTS MUST HAVE SLEPT DURING THE FLIGHT FROM EARTH.

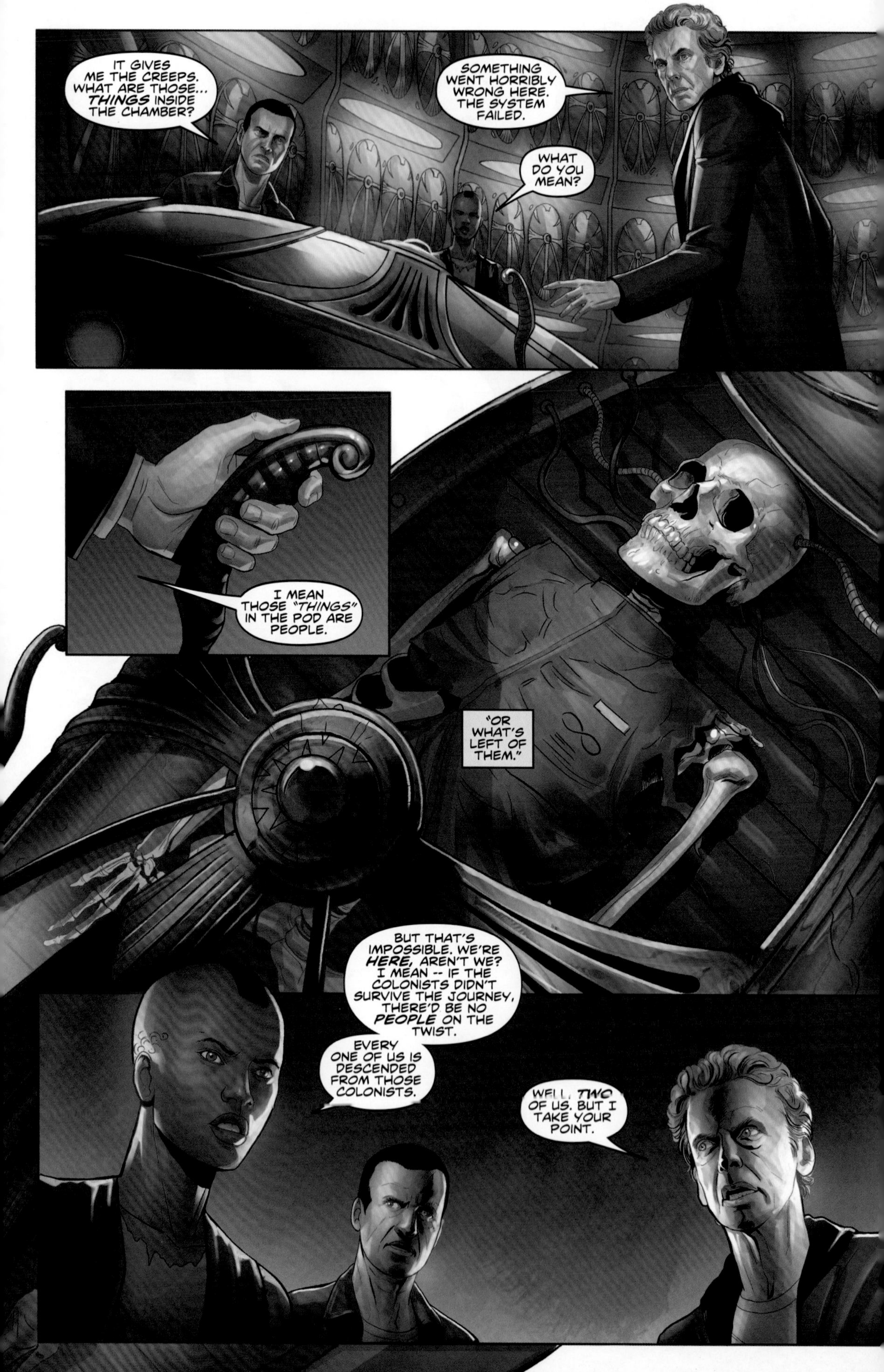

IT GIVES ME THE CREEPS. WHAT ARE THOSE... THINGS INSIDE THE CHAMBER?
SOMETHING WENT HORRIBLY WRONG HERE. THE SYSTEM FAILED.
WHAT DO YOU MEAN?
I MEAN THOSE "THINGS" IN THE POD ARE PEOPLE.
"OR WHAT'S LEFT OF THEM."
BUT THAT'S IMPOSSIBLE. WE'RE HERE, AREN'T WE? I MEAN -- IF THE COLONISTS DIDN'T SURVIVE THE JOURNEY, THERE'D BE NO PEOPLE ON THE TWIST.
EVERY ONE OF US IS DESCENDED FROM THOSE COLONISTS.
WELL, TWO OF US. BUT I TAKE YOUR POINT.

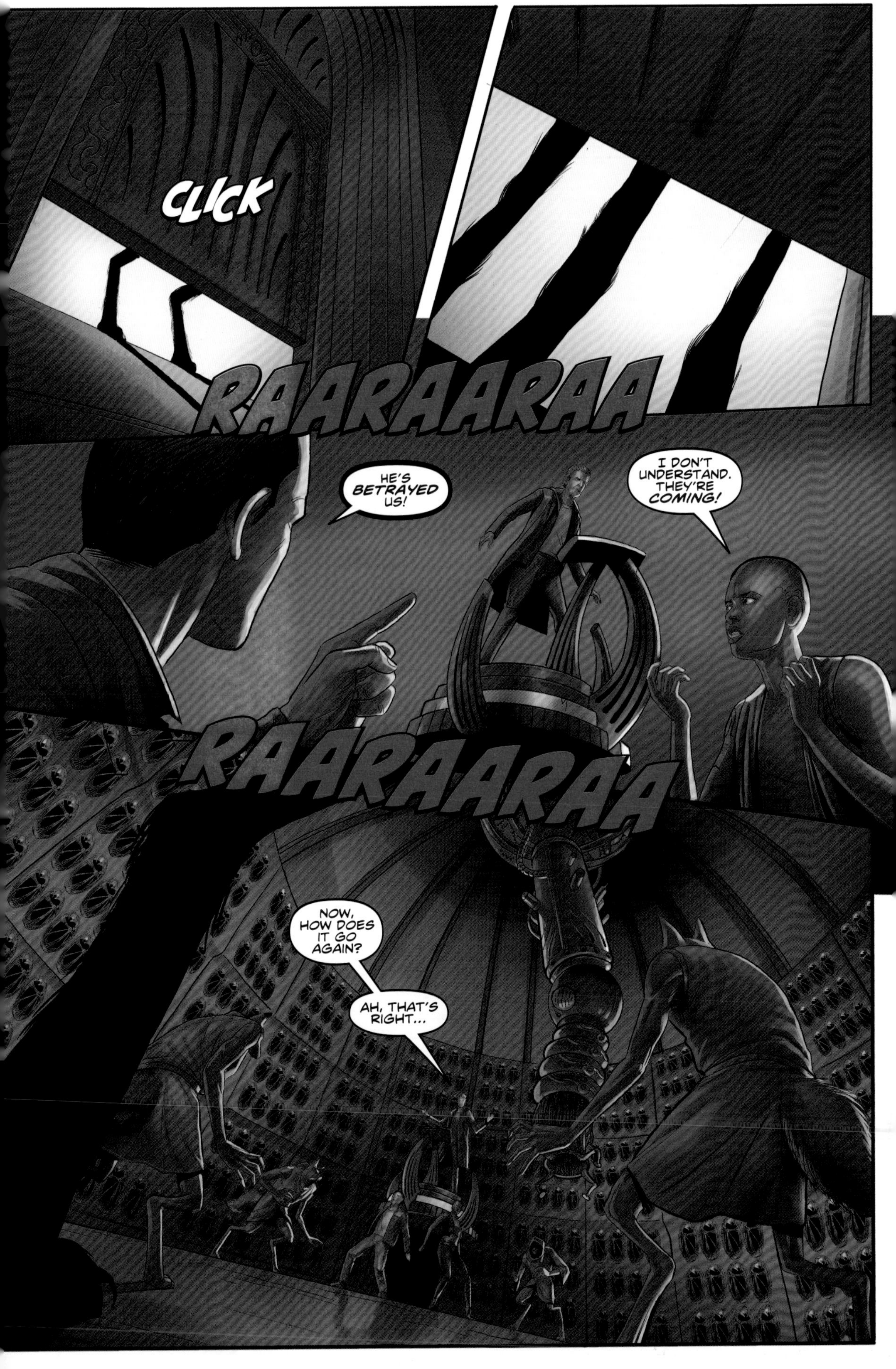
CLICK
RAARAARAA
HE'S BETRAYED US!
I DON'T UNDERSTAND. THEY'RE COMING!
RAARAARAA
NOW, HOW DOES IT GO AGAIN?
AH, THAT'S RIGHT...

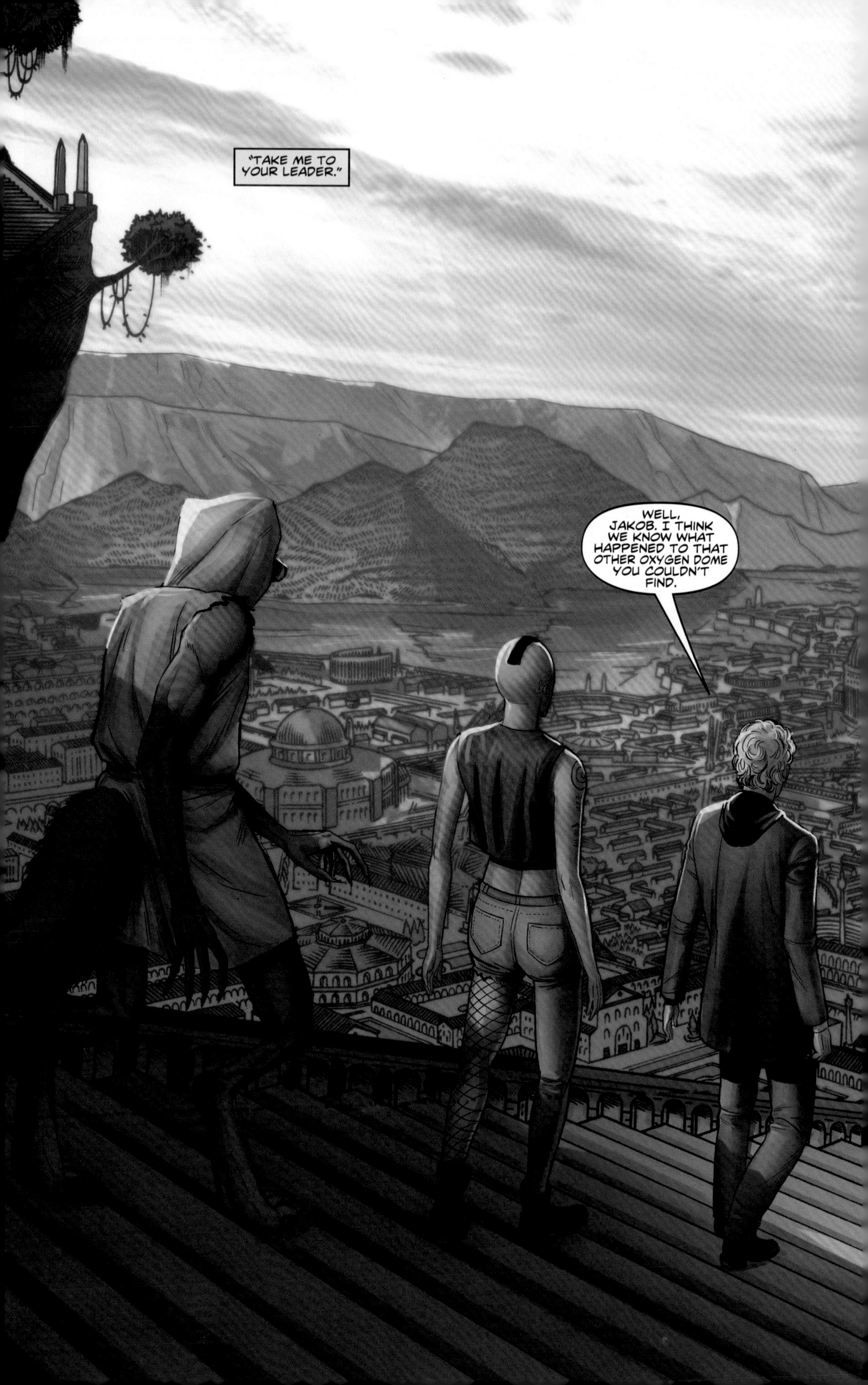
"TAKE ME TO YOUR LEADER."
WELL, JAKOB. I THINK WE KNOW WHAT HAPPENED TO THAT OTHER OXYGEN DOME YOU COULDN'T FIND.

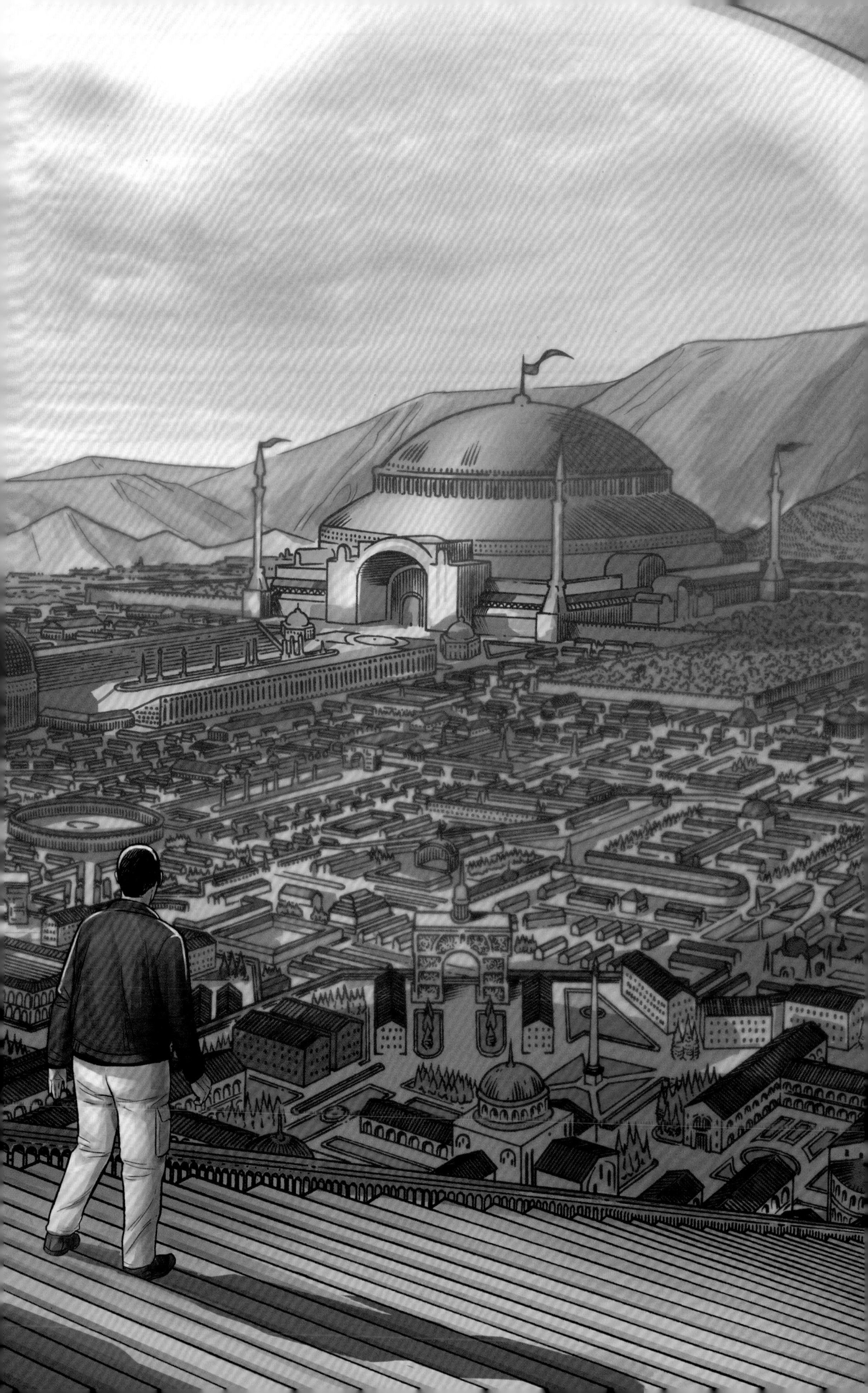

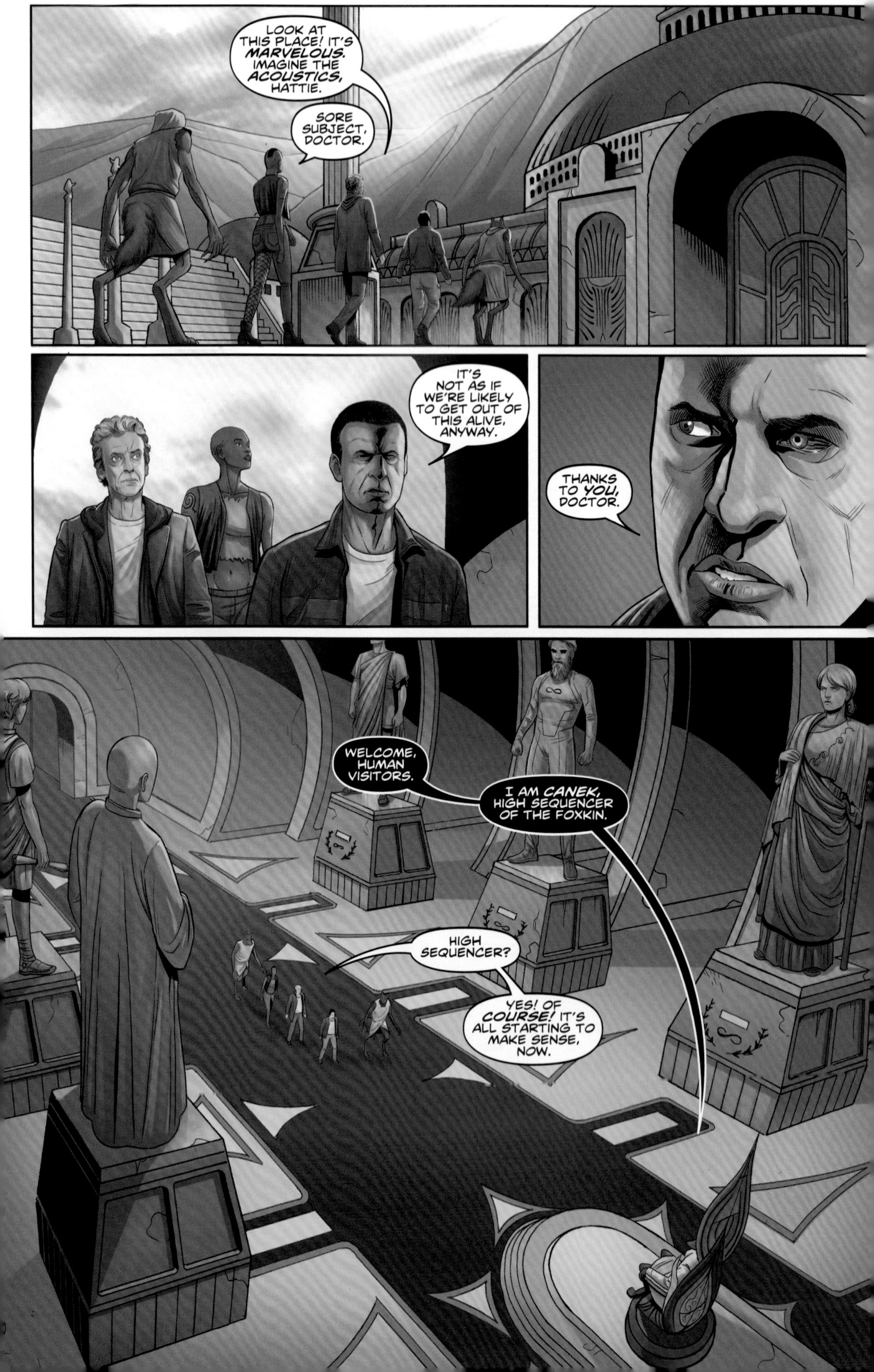
LOOK AT THIS PLACE! IT'S MARVELOUS. IMAGINE THE ACOUSTICS, HATTIE.
SORE SUBJECT, DOCTOR.
IT'S NOT AS IF WE'RE LIKELY TO GET OUT OF THIS ALIVE, ANYWAY.
THANKS TO YOU, DOCTOR.
WELCOME, HUMAN VISITORS.
I AM CANEK, HIGH SEQUENCER OF THE FOXKIN.
HIGH SEQUENCER?
YES! OF COURSE! IT'S ALL STARTING TO MAKE SENSE, NOW.

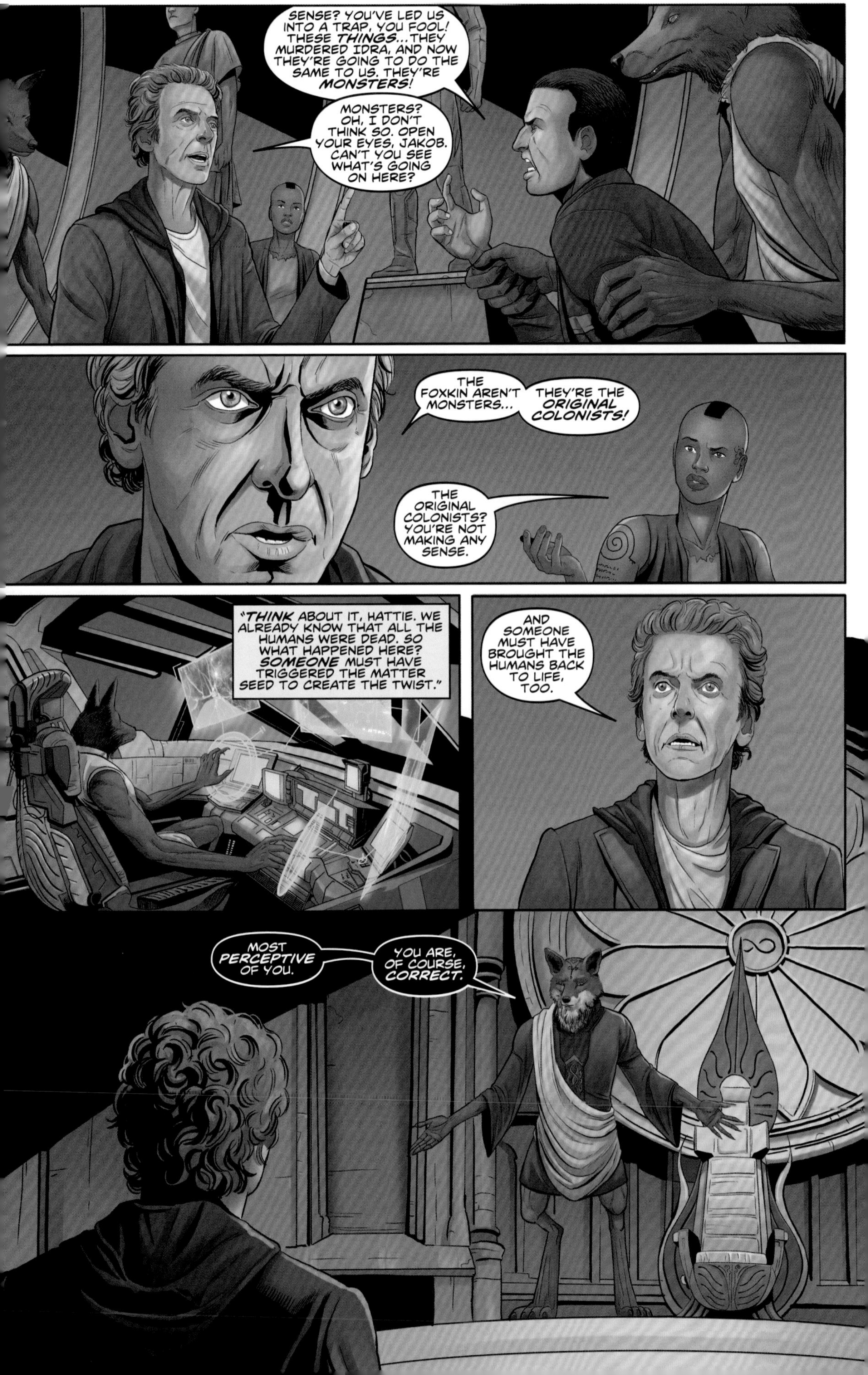
SENSE? YOU'VE LED US INTO A TRAP, YOU FOOL! THESE *THINGS*... THEY MURDERED IDRA, AND NOW THEY'RE GOING TO DO THE SAME TO US. THEY'RE ***MONSTERS***!
MONSTERS? OH, I DON'T THINK SO. OPEN YOUR EYES, JAKOB. CAN'T YOU SEE WHAT'S GOING ON HERE?
THE FOXKIN AREN'T MONSTERS...
THEY'RE THE *ORIGINAL* ***COLONISTS!***
THE ORIGINAL COLONISTS? YOU'RE NOT MAKING ANY SENSE.
"***THINK*** ABOUT IT, HATTIE. WE ALREADY KNOW THAT ALL THE HUMANS WERE DEAD. SO WHAT HAPPENED HERE? ***SOMEONE*** MUST HAVE TRIGGERED THE MATTER SEED TO CREATE THE TWIST."
AND SOMEONE MUST HAVE BROUGHT THE HUMANS BACK TO LIFE, TOO.
MOST ***PERCEPTIVE*** OF YOU.
YOU ARE, OF COURSE, ***CORRECT.***

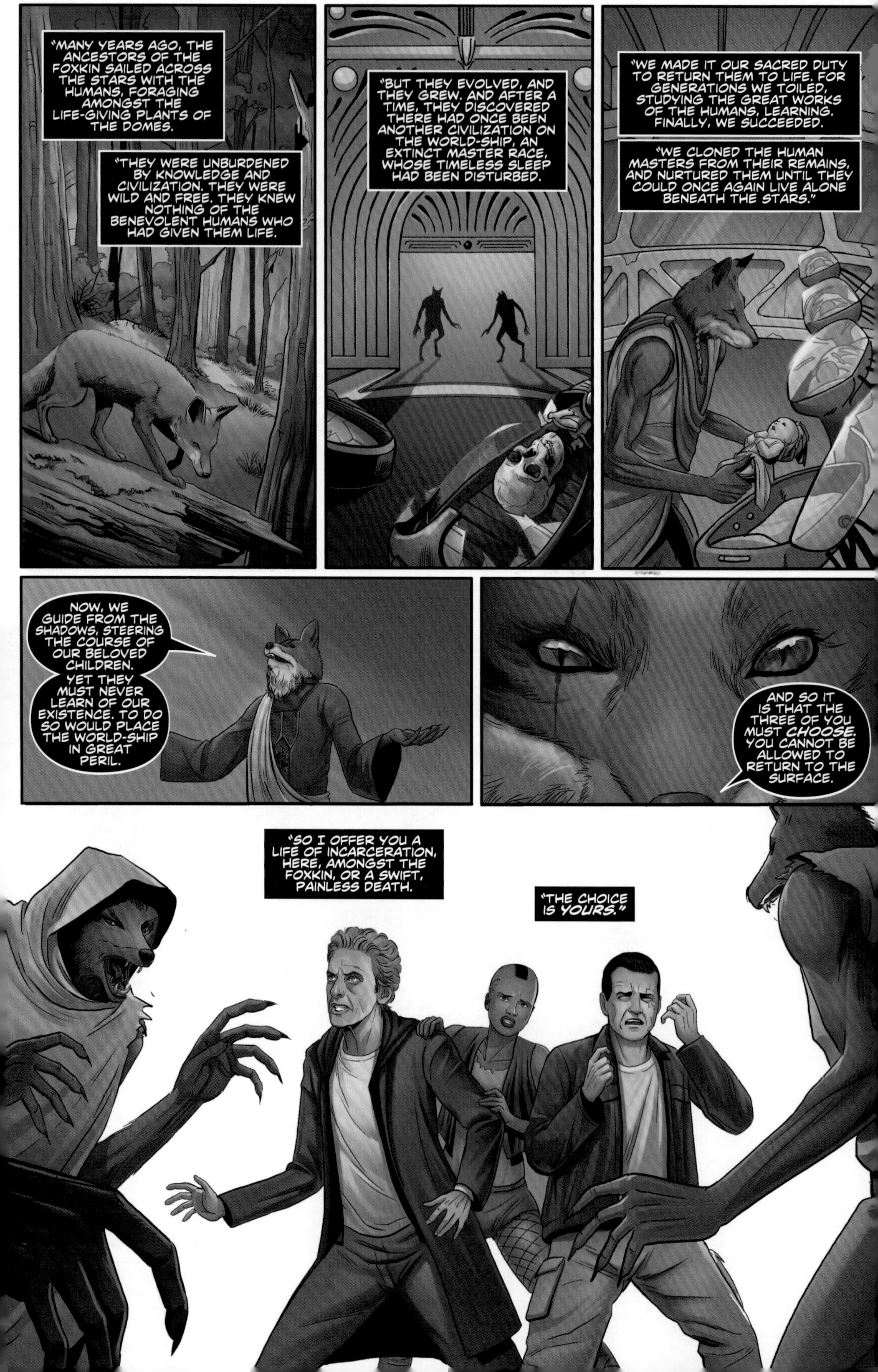
"MANY YEARS AGO, THE ANCESTORS OF THE FOXKIN SAILED ACROSS THE STARS WITH THE HUMANS, FORAGING AMONGST THE LIFE-GIVING PLANTS OF THE DOMES.
"THEY WERE UNBURDENED BY KNOWLEDGE AND CIVILIZATION. THEY WERE WILD AND FREE. THEY KNEW NOTHING OF THE BENEVOLENT HUMANS WHO HAD GIVEN THEM LIFE.
"BUT THEY EVOLVED, AND THEY GREW. AND AFTER A TIME, THEY DISCOVERED THERE HAD ONCE BEEN ANOTHER CIVILIZATION ON THE WORLD-SHIP, AN EXTINCT MASTER RACE, WHOSE TIMELESS SLEEP HAD BEEN DISTURBED.
"WE MADE IT OUR SACRED DUTY TO RETURN THEM TO LIFE. FOR GENERATIONS WE TOILED, STUDYING THE GREAT WORKS OF THE HUMANS, LEARNING. FINALLY, WE SUCCEEDED.
"WE CLONED THE HUMAN MASTERS FROM THEIR REMAINS, AND NURTURED THEM UNTIL THEY COULD ONCE AGAIN LIVE ALONE BENEATH THE STARS."
NOW, WE GUIDE FROM THE SHADOWS, STEERING THE COURSE OF OUR BELOVED CHILDREN.
YET THEY MUST NEVER LEARN OF OUR EXISTENCE. TO DO SO WOULD PLACE THE WORLD-SHIP IN GREAT PERIL.
AND SO IT IS THAT THE THREE OF YOU MUST *CHOOSE*. YOU CANNOT BE ALLOWED TO RETURN TO THE SURFACE.
"SO I OFFER YOU A LIFE OF INCARCERATION, HERE, AMONGST THE FOXKIN, OR A SWIFT, PAINLESS DEATH.
"THE CHOICE IS *YOURS*."

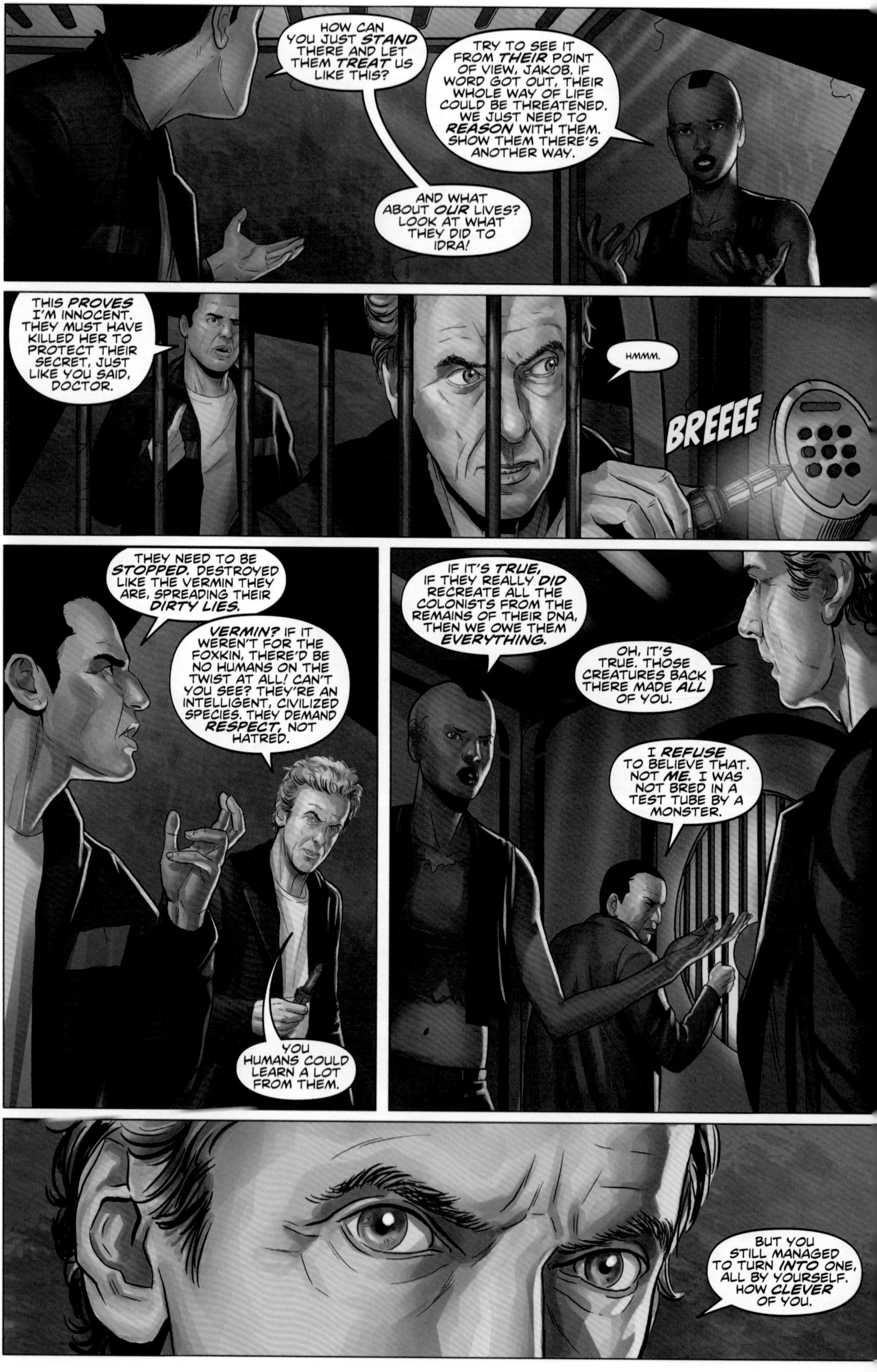
HOW CAN YOU JUST STAND THERE AND LET THEM TREAT US LIKE THIS?
TRY TO SEE IT FROM THEIR POINT OF VIEW, JAKOB. IF WORD GOT OUT, THEIR WHOLE WAY OF LIFE COULD BE THREATENED. WE JUST NEED TO REASON WITH THEM. SHOW THEM THERE'S ANOTHER WAY.
AND WHAT ABOUT OUR LIVES? LOOK AT WHAT THEY DID TO IDRA!
THIS PROVES I'M INNOCENT. THEY MUST HAVE KILLED HER TO PROTECT THEIR SECRET, JUST LIKE YOU SAID, DOCTOR.
HMMM.
BREEEE
THEY NEED TO BE STOPPED. DESTROYED LIKE THE VERMIN THEY ARE, SPREADING THEIR DIRTY LIES.
VERMIN? IF IT WEREN'T FOR THE FOXKIN, THERE'D BE NO HUMANS ON THE TWIST AT ALL! CAN'T YOU SEE? THEY'RE AN INTELLIGENT, CIVILIZED SPECIES. THEY DEMAND RESPECT, NOT HATRED.
YOU HUMANS COULD LEARN A LOT FROM THEM.
IF IT'S TRUE, IF THEY REALLY DID RECREATE ALL THE COLONISTS FROM THE REMAINS OF THEIR DNA, THEN WE OWE THEM EVERYTHING.
OH, IT'S TRUE. THOSE CREATURES BACK THERE MADE ALL OF YOU.
I REFUSE TO BELIEVE THAT. NOT ME. I WAS NOT BRED IN A TEST TUBE BY A MONSTER.
BUT YOU STILL MANAGED TO TURN INTO ONE, ALL BY YOURSELF. HOW CLEVER OF YOU.

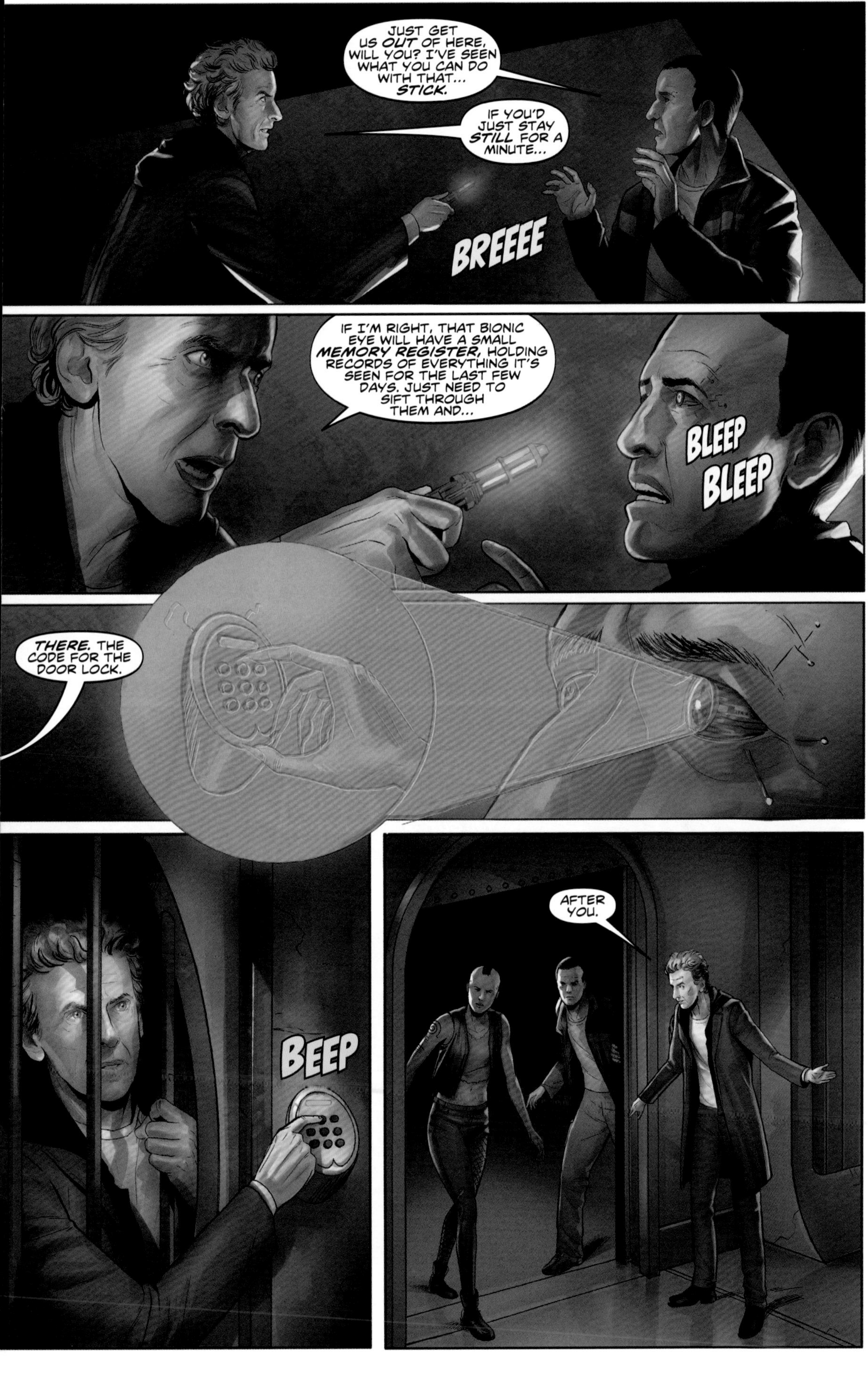
JUST GET US OUT OF HERE, WILL YOU? I'VE SEEN WHAT YOU CAN DO WITH THAT... STICK.
IF YOU'D JUST STAY STILL FOR A MINUTE...
BREEEE
IF I'M RIGHT, THAT BIONIC EYE WILL HAVE A SMALL MEMORY REGISTER, HOLDING RECORDS OF EVERYTHING IT'S SEEN FOR THE LAST FEW DAYS. JUST NEED TO SIFT THROUGH THEM AND...
BLEEP
BLEEP
THERE. THE CODE FOR THE DOOR LOCK.
BEEP
AFTER YOU.

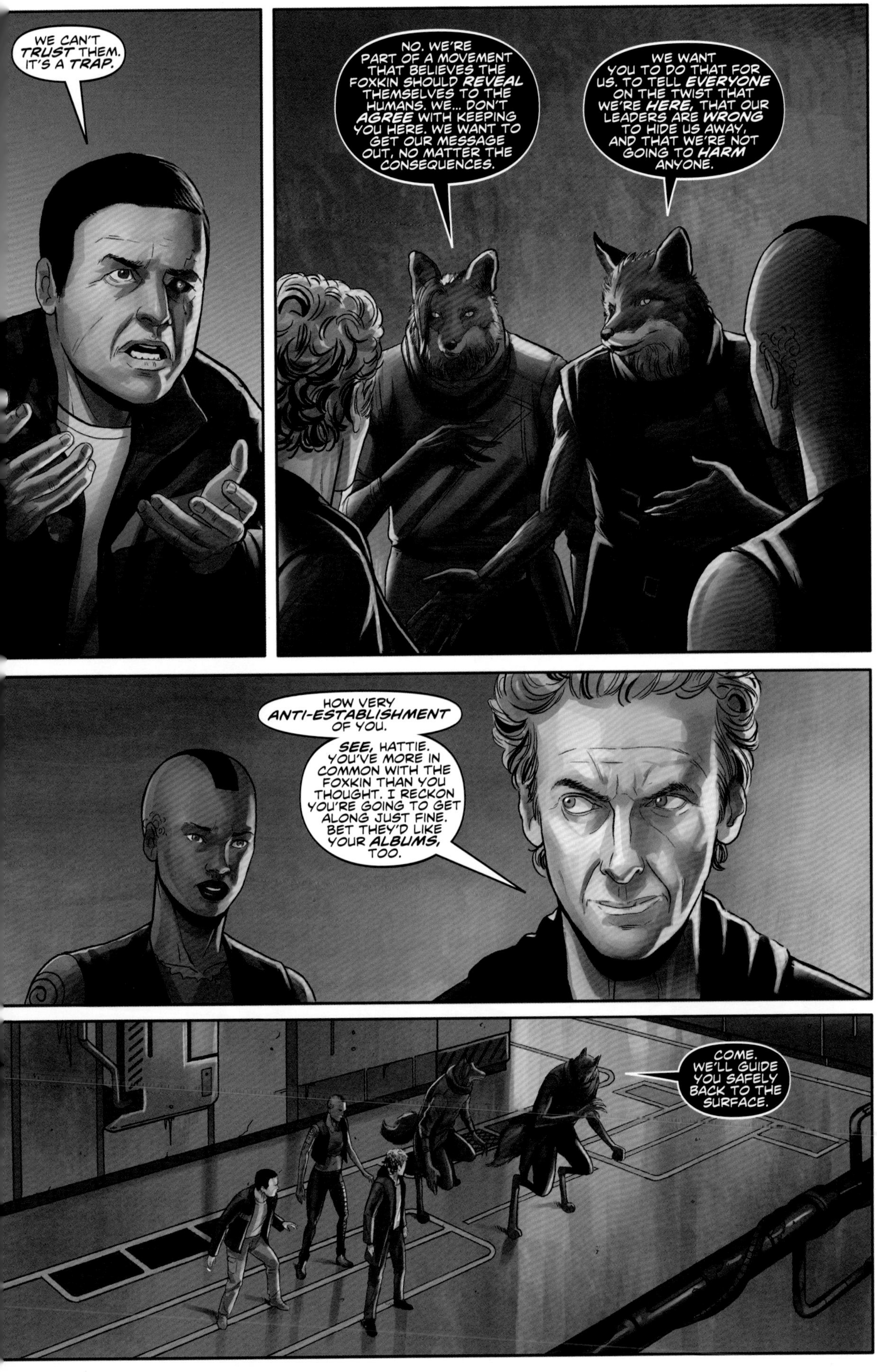
WE CAN'T *TRUST* THEM. IT'S A *TRAP.*
NO. WE'RE PART OF A MOVEMENT THAT BELIEVES THE FOXKIN SHOULD *REVEAL* THEMSELVES TO THE HUMANS. WE... DON'T *AGREE* WITH KEEPING YOU HERE. WE WANT TO GET OUR MESSAGE OUT, NO MATTER THE CONSEQUENCES.
WE WANT YOU TO DO THAT FOR US. TO TELL *EVERYONE* ON THE TWIST THAT WE'RE *HERE,* THAT OUR LEADERS ARE *WRONG* TO HIDE US AWAY, AND THAT WE'RE NOT GOING TO *HARM* ANYONE.
HOW VERY *ANTI-ESTABLISHMENT* OF YOU.
SEE, HATTIE. YOU'VE MORE IN COMMON WITH THE FOXKIN THAN YOU THOUGHT. I RECKON YOU'RE GOING TO GET ALONG JUST FINE. BET THEY'D LIKE YOUR *ALBUMS,* TOO.
COME. WE'LL GUIDE YOU SAFELY BACK TO THE SURFACE.

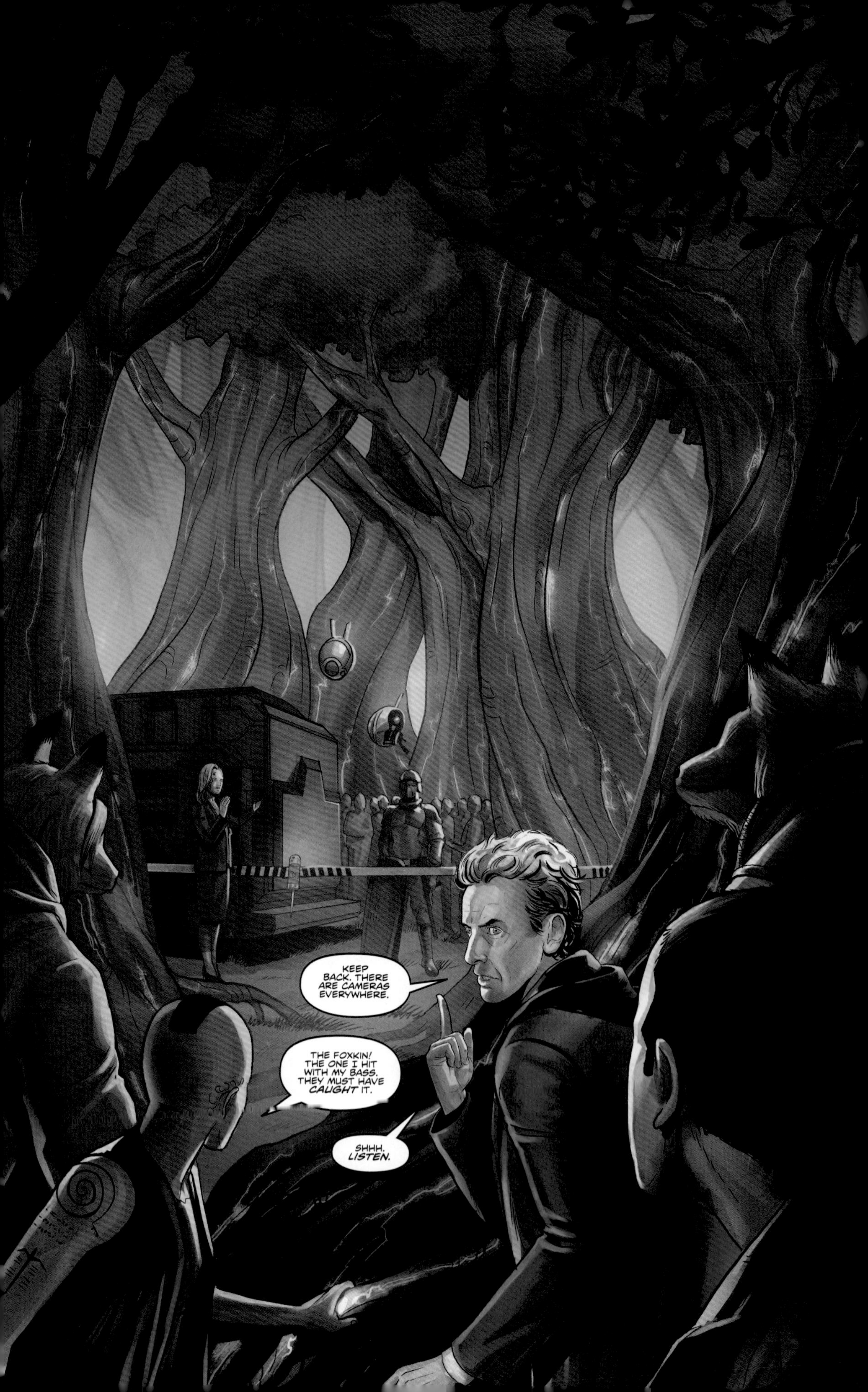
KEEP BACK. THERE ARE CAMERAS EVERYWHERE.
THE FOXKIN! THE ONE I HIT WITH MY BASS. THEY MUST HAVE *CAUGHT* IT.
SHHH. *LISTEN.*

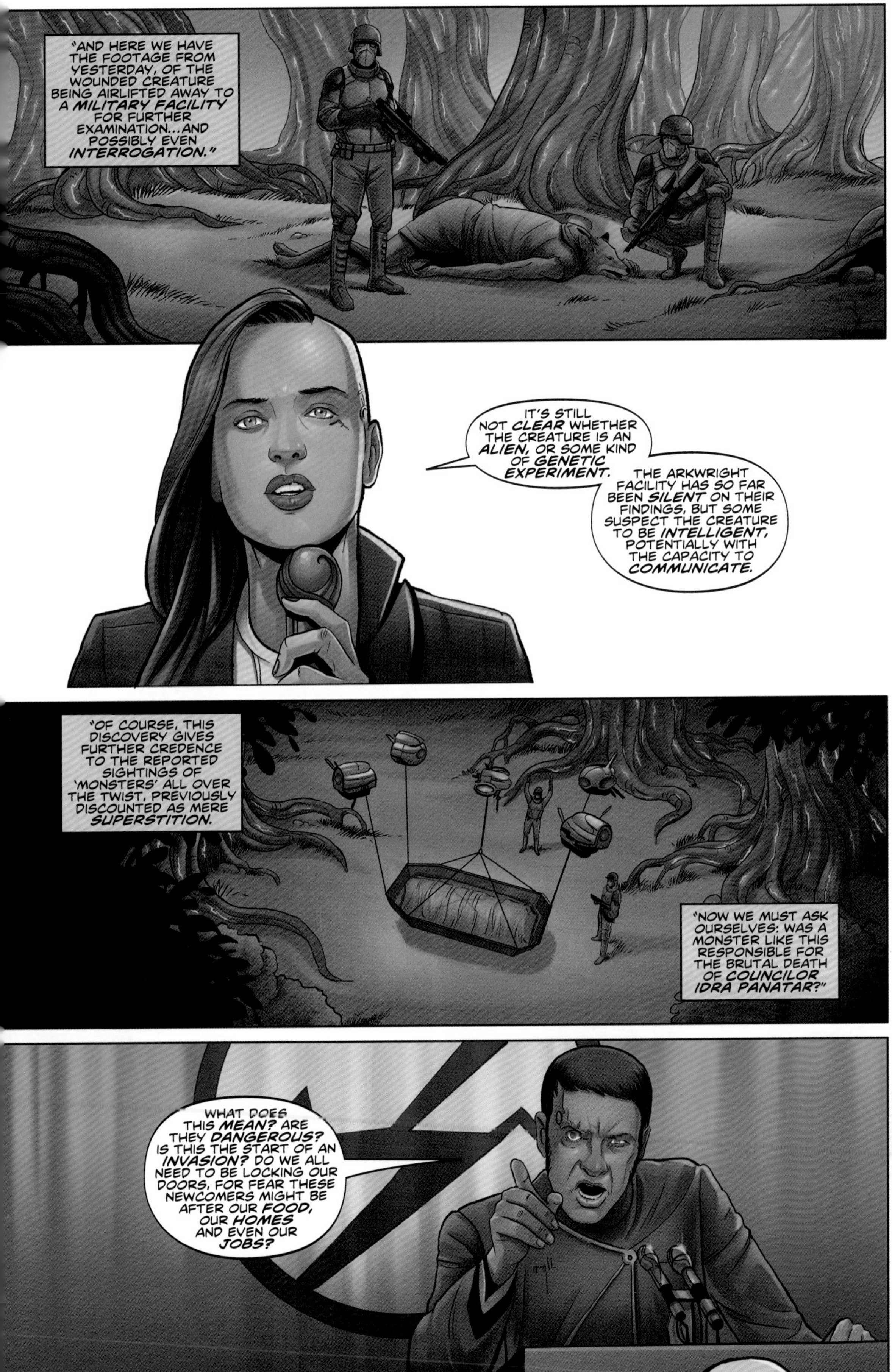
"AND HERE WE HAVE THE FOOTAGE FROM YESTERDAY, OF THE WOUNDED CREATURE BEING AIRLIFTED AWAY TO A MILITARY FACILITY FOR FURTHER EXAMINATION... AND POSSIBLY EVEN INTERROGATION."
IT'S STILL NOT CLEAR WHETHER THE CREATURE IS AN ALIEN, OR SOME KIND OF GENETIC EXPERIMENT.
THE ARKWRIGHT FACILITY HAS SO FAR BEEN SILENT ON THEIR FINDINGS, BUT SOME SUSPECT THE CREATURE TO BE INTELLIGENT, POTENTIALLY WITH THE CAPACITY TO COMMUNICATE.
"OF COURSE, THIS DISCOVERY GIVES FURTHER CREDENCE TO THE REPORTED SIGHTINGS OF 'MONSTERS' ALL OVER THE TWIST, PREVIOUSLY DISCOUNTED AS MERE SUPERSTITION.
"NOW WE MUST ASK OURSELVES: WAS A MONSTER LIKE THIS RESPONSIBLE FOR THE BRUTAL DEATH OF COUNCILOR IDRA PANATAR?"
WHAT DOES THIS MEAN? ARE THEY DANGEROUS? IS THIS THE START OF AN INVASION? DO WE ALL NEED TO BE LOCKING OUR DOORS, FOR FEAR THESE NEWCOMERS MIGHT BE AFTER OUR FOOD, OUR HOMES AND EVEN OUR JOBS?

WE'RE TOO LATE. THE FOX IS ALREADY OUT OF THE BAG.

NO GOING BACK NOW.

GOING *BACK* WAS NEVER AN OPTION.

FINALLY! THIS IS THE CHANCE I'VE BEEN WAITING FOR. NOW SOMETHING CAN BE *DONE.* *NOW* PEOPLE WILL LISTEN.

I CAN SHOW EVERYONE WHAT A DANGER THEY ARE, WHAT THEY DID TO IDRA. I CAN LEAD THEM TO THE CREATURE'S NEST. *DESTROY* THEM.

THAT'S *ENOUGH.*

OH *NO,* DOCTOR. THIS IS JUST THE *START.*

NO, JAKOB. IT'S TIME YOU FACED UP TO WHAT YOU'VE DONE.

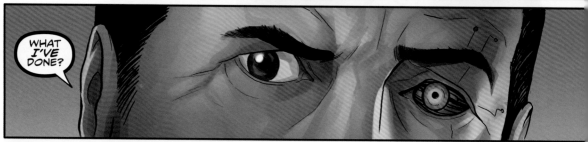

WHAT *I'VE* DONE?

IT'S TIME TO STOP THE *LIES.* YOU WERE *WRONG,* JAKOB. ABOUT THE FOXKIN, ABOUT IDRA...

YOU CROSSED A LINE YOU CAN NEVER COME BACK FROM.

DOCTOR?

IT WAS OBVIOUS FROM THE START. I JUST WANTED TO KNOW *WHY.* AND NOW I SEE IT. IDRA WAS GOING TO *TELL* EVERYONE, WASN'T SHE? SHE WAS GOING TO TELL THEM THE *TRUTH.*

WHAT...? I DON'T KNOW WHAT YOU'RE TALKING ABOUT...

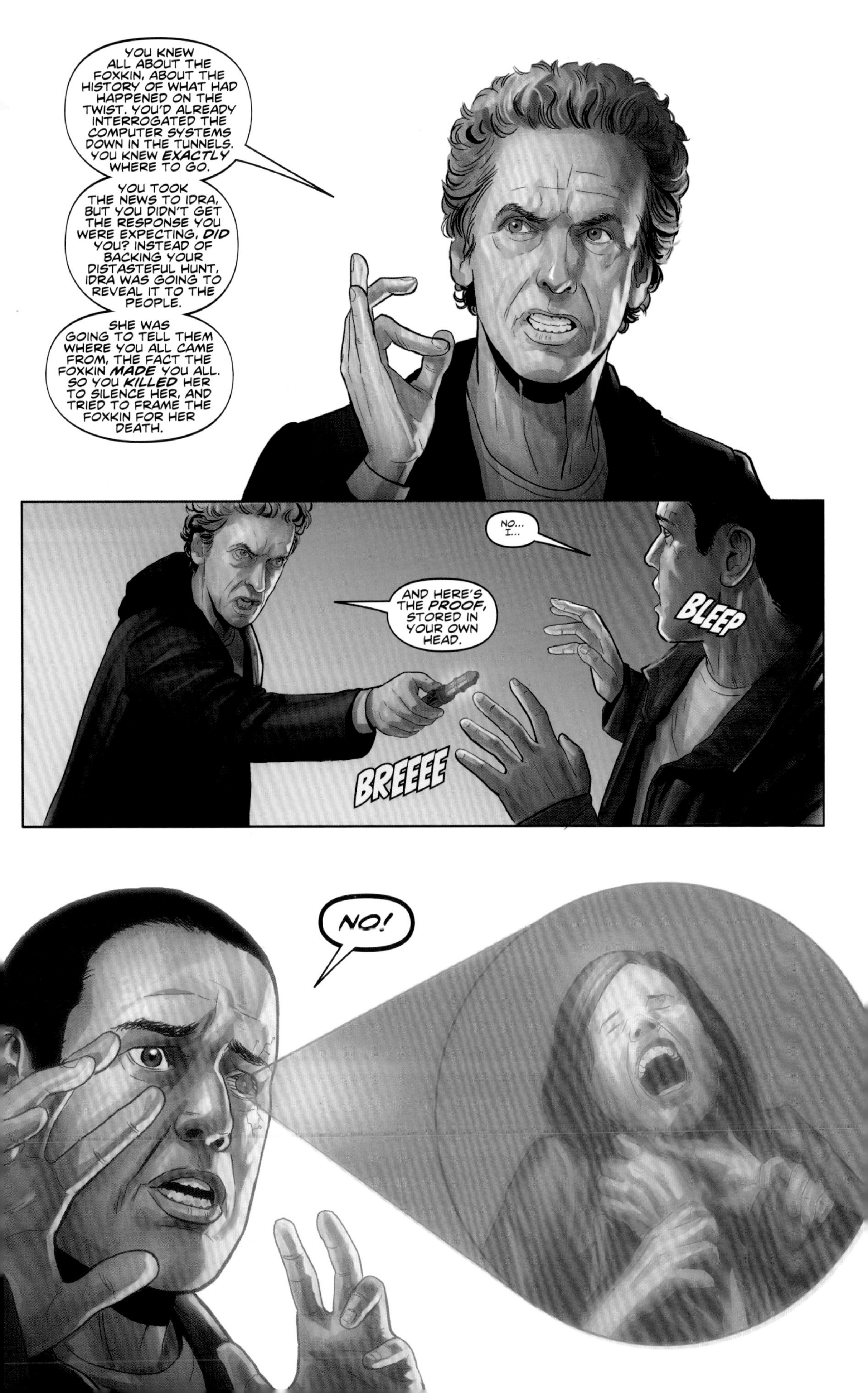
YOU KNEW ALL ABOUT THE FOXKIN, ABOUT THE HISTORY OF WHAT HAD HAPPENED ON THE TWIST. YOU'D ALREADY INTERROGATED THE COMPUTER SYSTEMS DOWN IN THE TUNNELS. YOU KNEW EXACTLY WHERE TO GO.
YOU TOOK THE NEWS TO IDRA, BUT YOU DIDN'T GET THE RESPONSE YOU WERE EXPECTING, DID YOU? INSTEAD OF BACKING YOUR DISTASTEFUL HUNT, IDRA WAS GOING TO REVEAL IT TO THE PEOPLE.
SHE WAS GOING TO TELL THEM WHERE YOU ALL CAME FROM, THE FACT THE FOXKIN MADE YOU ALL. SO YOU KILLED HER TO SILENCE HER, AND TRIED TO FRAME THE FOXKIN FOR HER DEATH.
NO... I...
AND HERE'S THE PROOF, STORED IN YOUR OWN HEAD.
BLEEP
BREEEE
NO!

IT WAS *HIM?* *HE* KILLED IDRA?

I DID IT FOR THE *GREATER GOOD.* WHY CAN'T ANY OF YOU *SEE* THAT?

WE'RE LIVING ON TOP OF A NEST OF MONSTERS. THEY CONTROL OUR VERY *DNA.* THEY *HAVE* TO BE STOPPED!

THIS WAY, *EVERYONE* COULD SEE WHAT SORT OF MONSTERS THEY REALLY ARE.

HATTIE!

GRRRRRR

GRRRR.

LET HIM *GO,* THERE'S BEEN *ENOUGH* BLOODSHED. DON'T GIVE HIM THE SATISFACTION OF LAYING ANOTHER DEATH AT YOUR DOOR.

WE CAN'T *JUST* LET HIM GET *AWAY* WITH IT!

WE'RE *NOT.* HE WON'T GET FAR. THERE ARE CAMERAS SWARMING ALL OVER THE PLACE. LET THE MEN IN BLACK DO THEIR JOB.

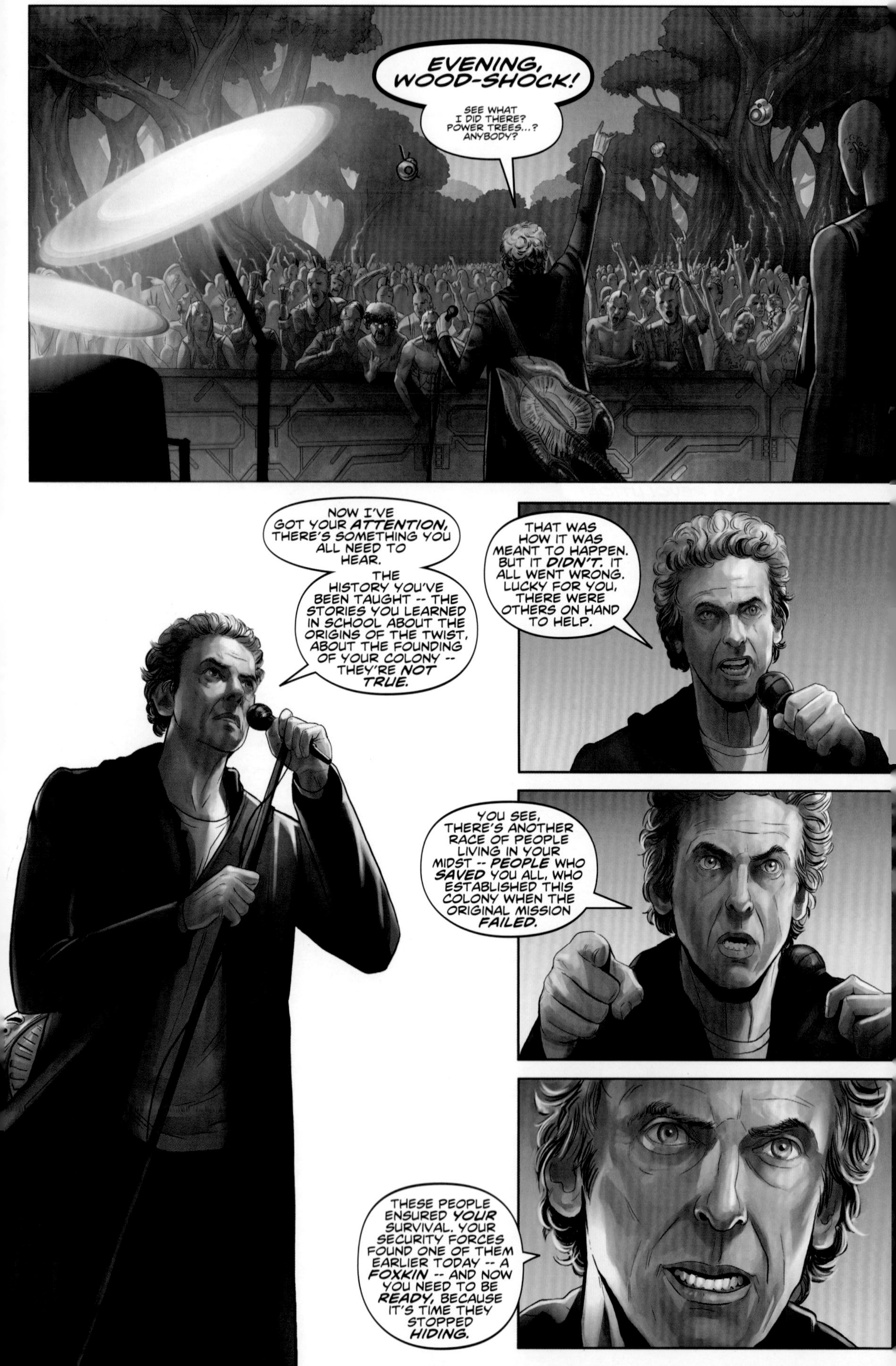
EVENING, WOOD-SHOCK!
SEE WHAT I DID THERE? POWER TREES...? ANYBODY?
NOW I'VE GOT YOUR ATTENTION, THERE'S SOMETHING YOU ALL NEED TO HEAR.
THE HISTORY YOU'VE BEEN TAUGHT -- THE STORIES YOU LEARNED IN SCHOOL ABOUT THE ORIGINS OF THE TWIST, ABOUT THE FOUNDING OF YOUR COLONY -- THEY'RE NOT TRUE.
THAT WAS HOW IT WAS MEANT TO HAPPEN. BUT IT DIDN'T. IT ALL WENT WRONG. LUCKY FOR YOU, THERE WERE OTHERS ON HAND TO HELP.
YOU SEE, THERE'S ANOTHER RACE OF PEOPLE LIVING IN YOUR MIDST -- PEOPLE WHO SAVED YOU ALL, WHO ESTABLISHED THIS COLONY WHEN THE ORIGINAL MISSION FAILED.
THESE PEOPLE ENSURED YOUR SURVIVAL. YOUR SECURITY FORCES FOUND ONE OF THEM EARLIER TODAY -- A FOXKIN -- AND NOW YOU NEED TO BE READY, BECAUSE IT'S TIME THEY STOPPED HIDING.

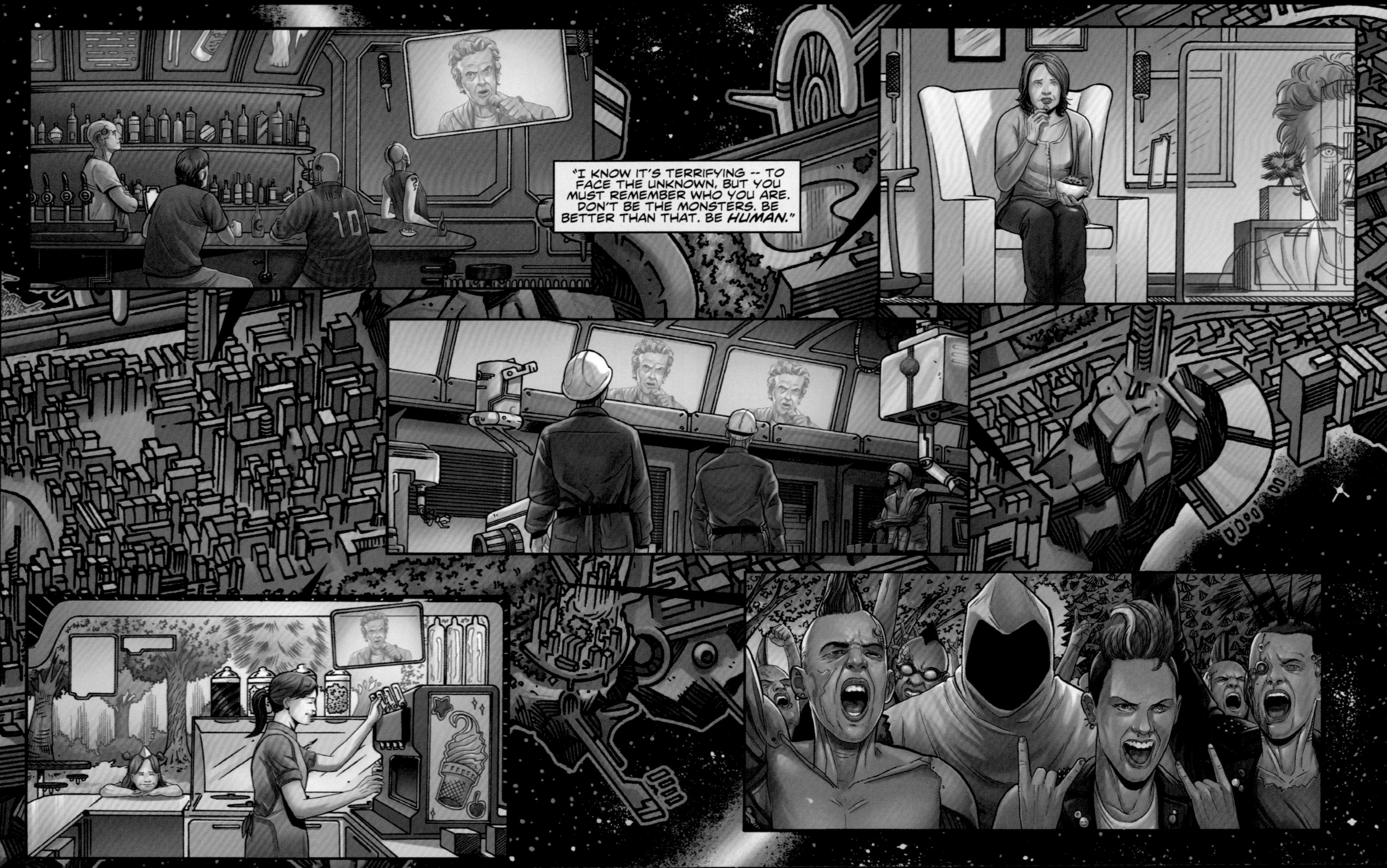
"I KNOW IT'S TERRIFYING -- TO FACE THE UNKNOWN, BUT YOU MUST REMEMBER WHO YOU ARE. DON'T BE THE MONSTERS. BE BETTER THAN THAT. BE *HUMAN.*"

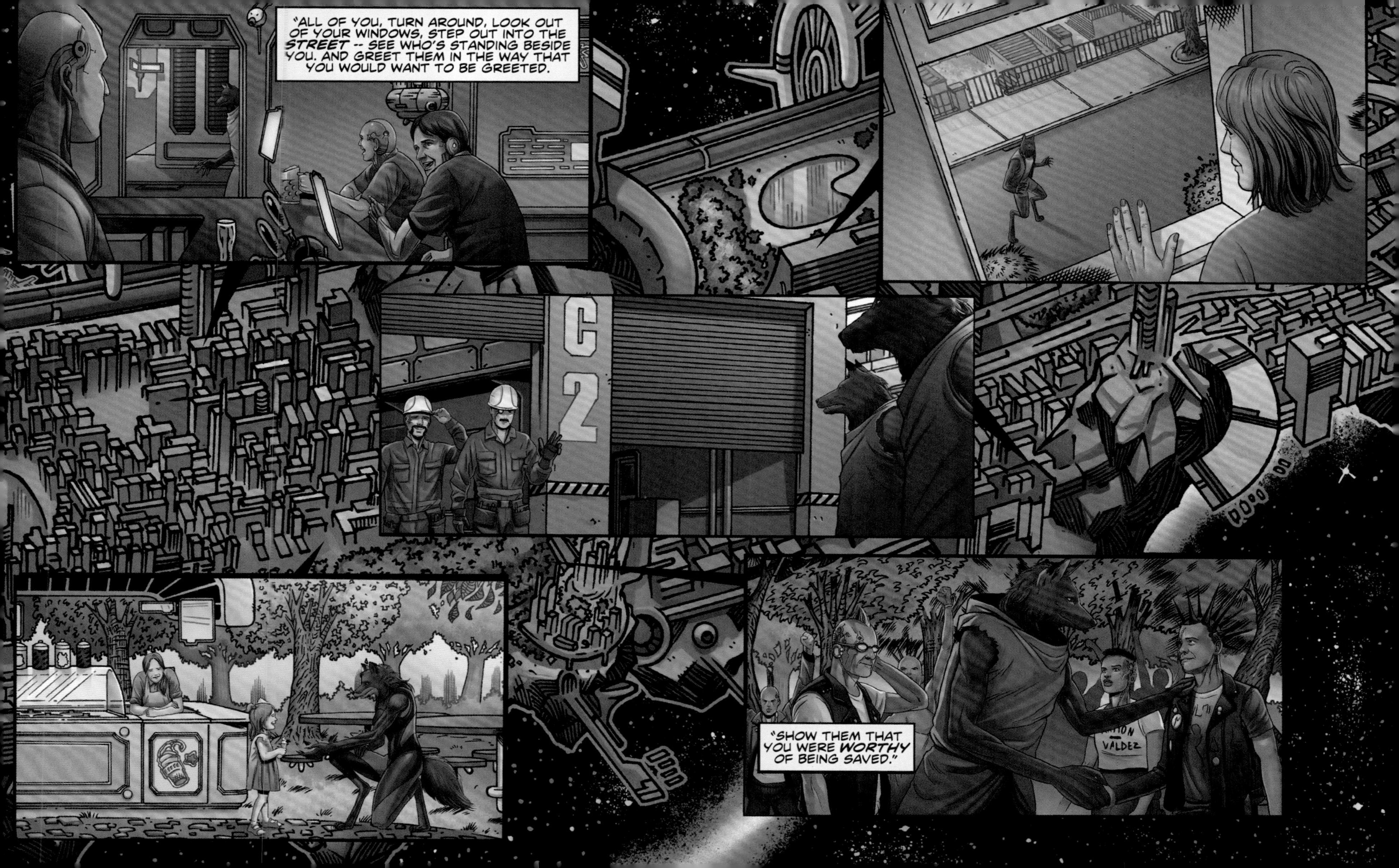
"ALL OF YOU, TURN AROUND, LOOK OUT OF YOUR WINDOWS, STEP OUT INTO THE *STREET* -- SEE WHO'S STANDING BESIDE YOU. AND GREET THEM IN THE WAY THAT YOU WOULD WANT TO BE GREETED.
C2
VALDEZ
"SHOW THEM THAT YOU WERE *WORTHY* OF BEING SAVED."

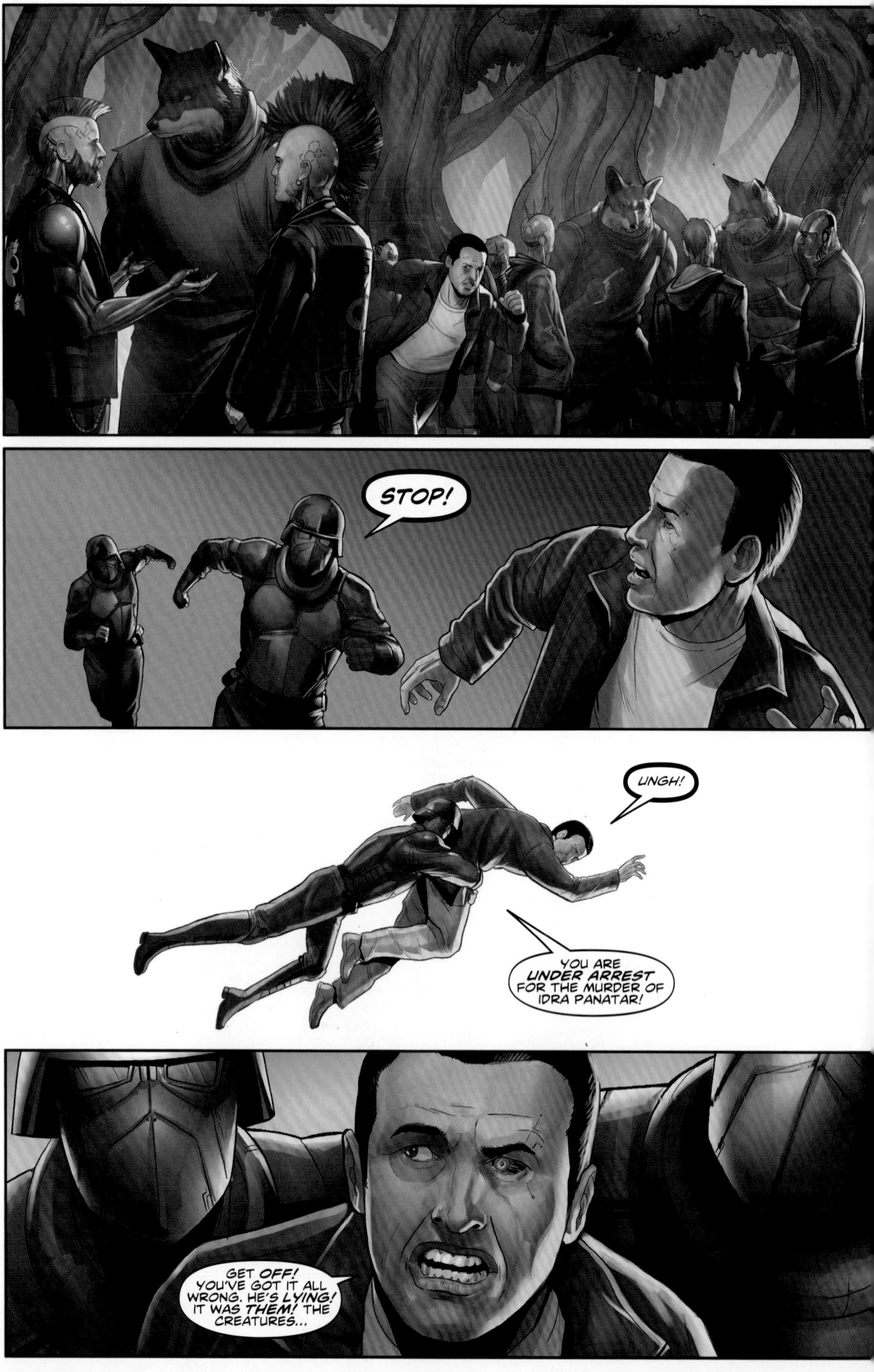
STOP!
UNGH!
YOU ARE UNDER ARREST FOR THE MURDER OF IDRA PANATAR!
GET OFF! YOU'VE GOT IT ALL WRONG. HE'S LYING! IT WAS THEM! THE CREATURES...

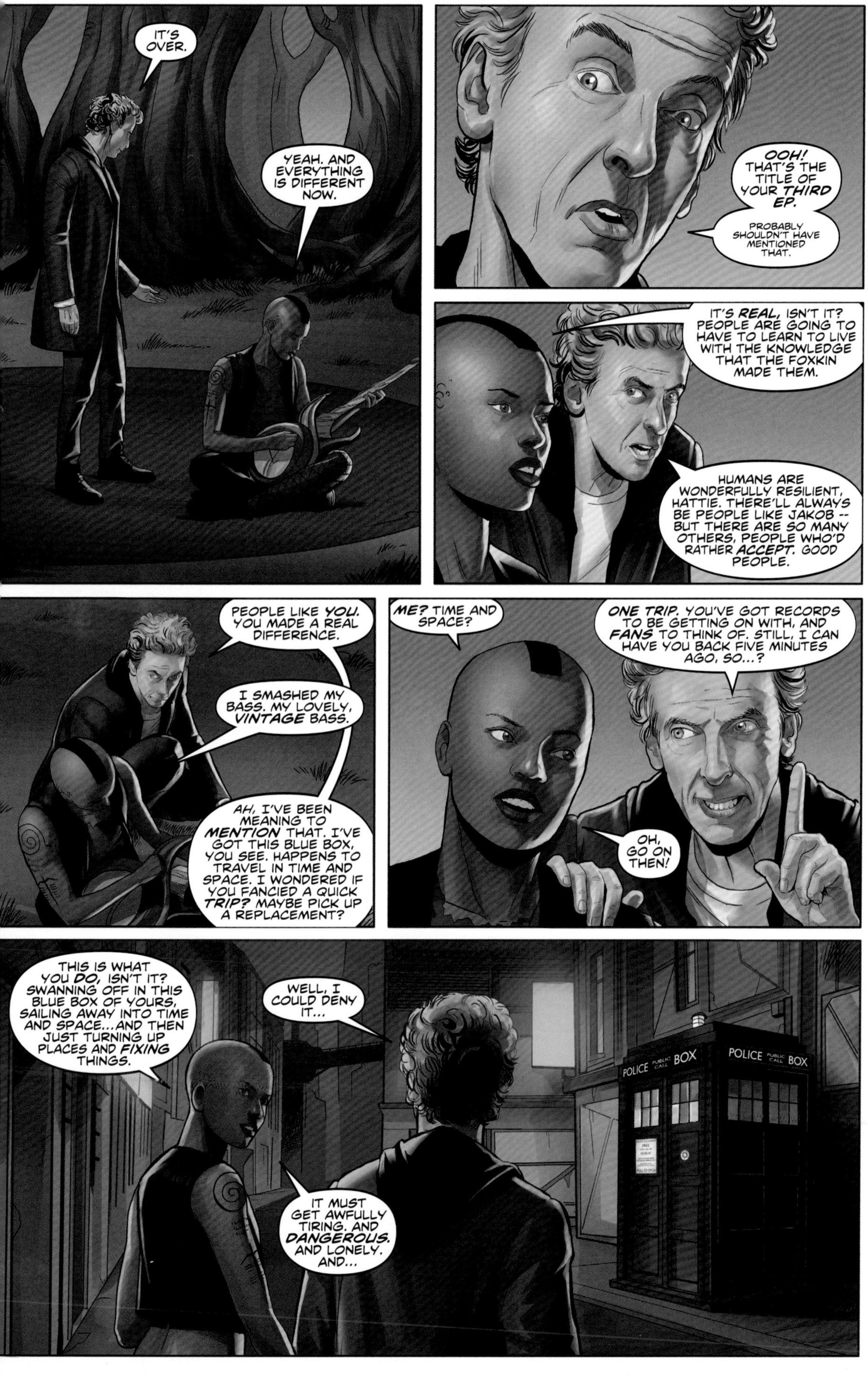
IT'S OVER.
YEAH. AND EVERYTHING IS DIFFERENT NOW.
OOH! THAT'S THE TITLE OF YOUR THIRD EP.
PROBABLY SHOULDN'T HAVE MENTIONED THAT.
IT'S REAL, ISN'T IT? PEOPLE ARE GOING TO HAVE TO LEARN TO LIVE WITH THE KNOWLEDGE THAT THE FOXKIN MADE THEM.
HUMANS ARE WONDERFULLY RESILIENT, HATTIE. THERE'LL ALWAYS BE PEOPLE LIKE JAKOB -- BUT THERE ARE SO MANY OTHERS, PEOPLE WHO'D RATHER ACCEPT. GOOD PEOPLE.
PEOPLE LIKE YOU. YOU MADE A REAL DIFFERENCE.
I SMASHED MY BASS. MY LOVELY, VINTAGE BASS.
AH, I'VE BEEN MEANING TO MENTION THAT. I'VE GOT THIS BLUE BOX, YOU SEE. HAPPENS TO TRAVEL IN TIME AND SPACE. I WONDERED IF YOU FANCIED A QUICK TRIP? MAYBE PICK UP A REPLACEMENT?
ME? TIME AND SPACE?
ONE TRIP. YOU'VE GOT RECORDS TO BE GETTING ON WITH, AND FANS TO THINK OF. STILL, I CAN HAVE YOU BACK FIVE MINUTES AGO, SO...?
OH, GO ON THEN!
THIS IS WHAT YOU DO, ISN'T IT? SWANNING OFF IN THIS BLUE BOX OF YOURS, SAILING AWAY INTO TIME AND SPACE...AND THEN JUST TURNING UP PLACES AND FIXING THINGS.
WELL, I COULD DENY IT...
IT MUST GET AWFULLY TIRING. AND DANGEROUS. AND LONELY. AND...
POLICE PUBLIC CALL BOX
POLICE PUBLIC CALL BOX

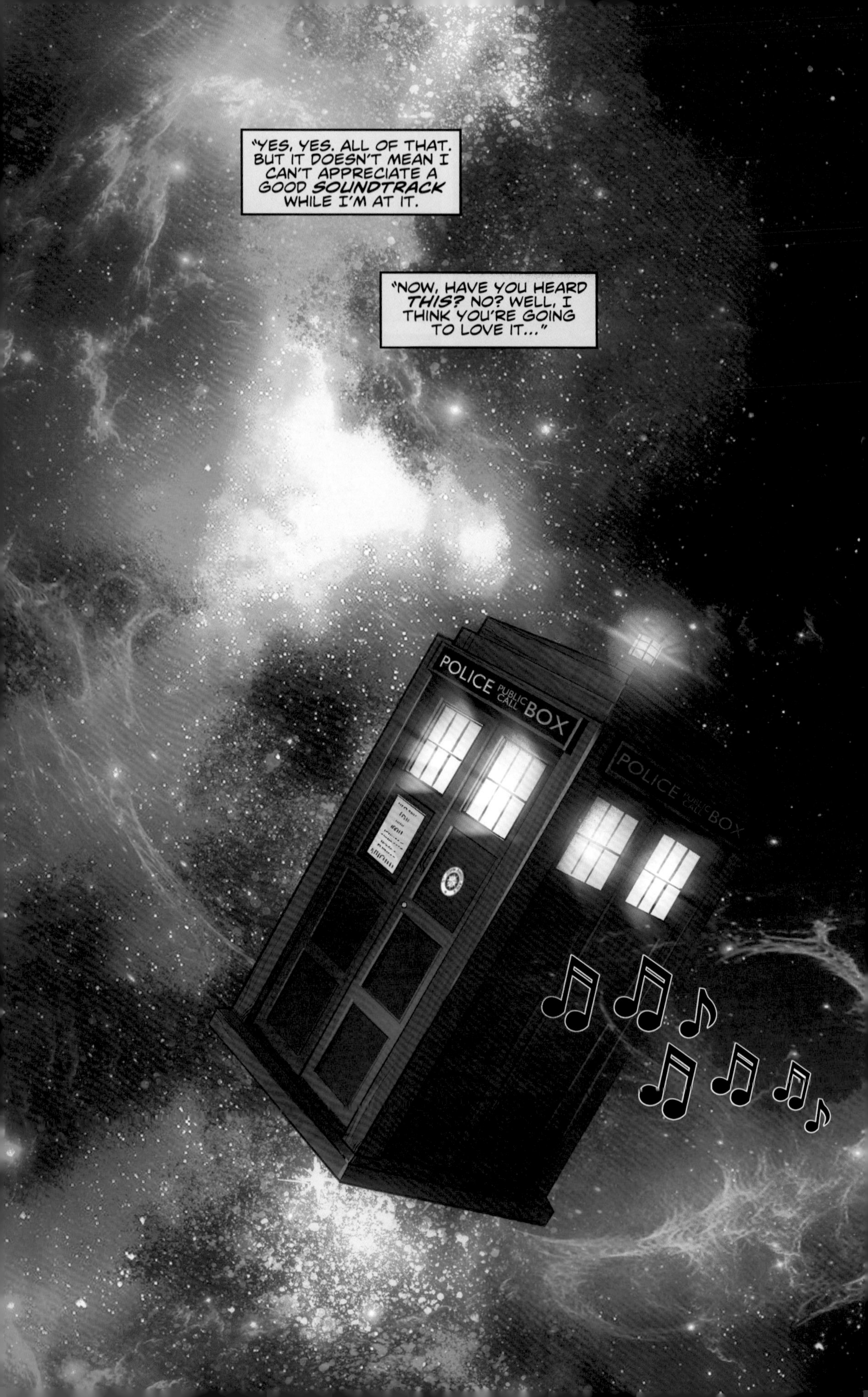
"YES, YES. ALL OF THAT. BUT IT DOESN'T MEAN I CAN'T APPRECIATE A GOOD SOUNDTRACK WHILE I'M AT IT.
"NOW, HAVE YOU HEARD THIS? NO? WELL, I THINK YOU'RE GOING TO LOVE IT..."
POLICE PUBLIC CALL BOX
POLICE PUBLIC CALL BOX

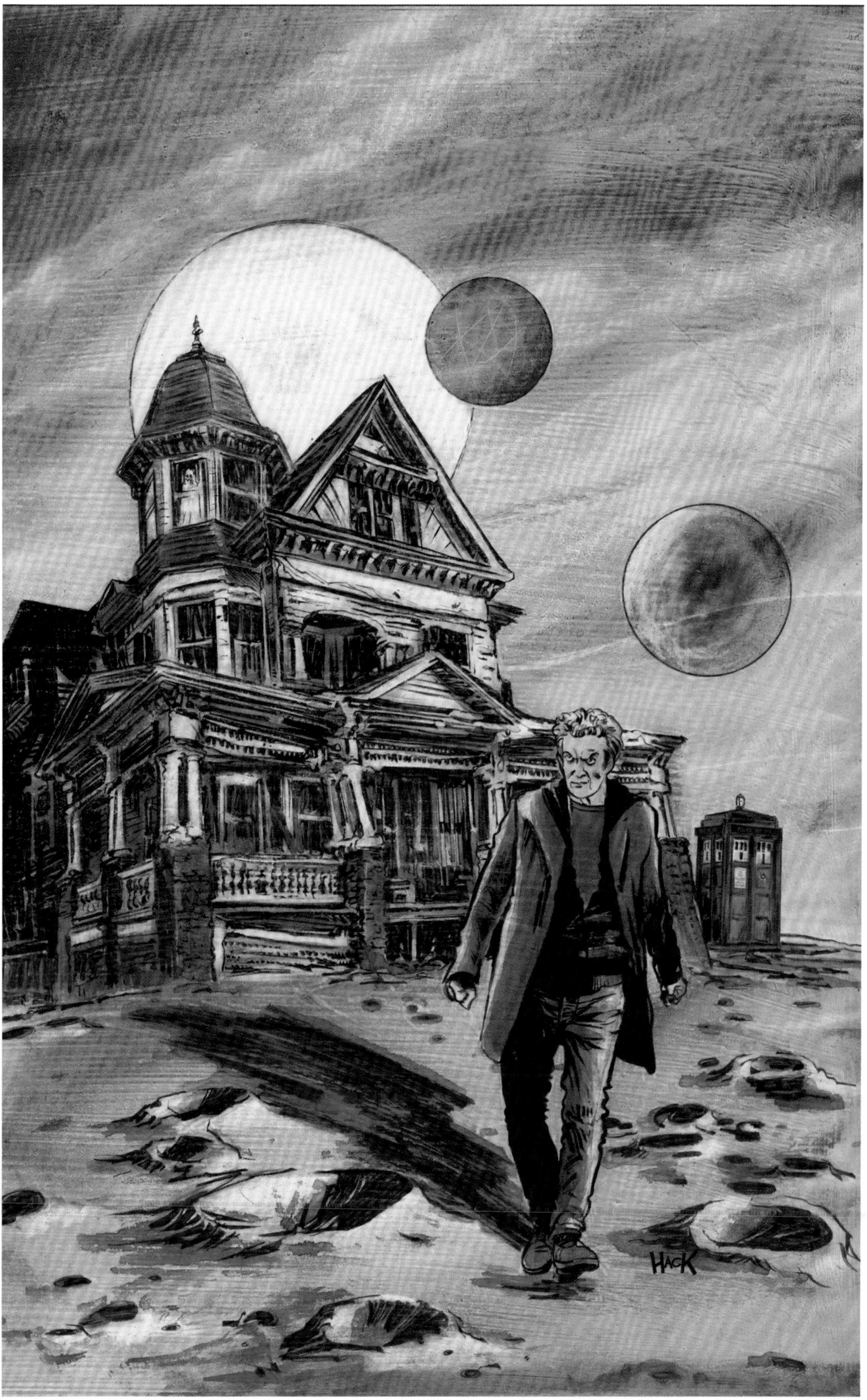
HACK

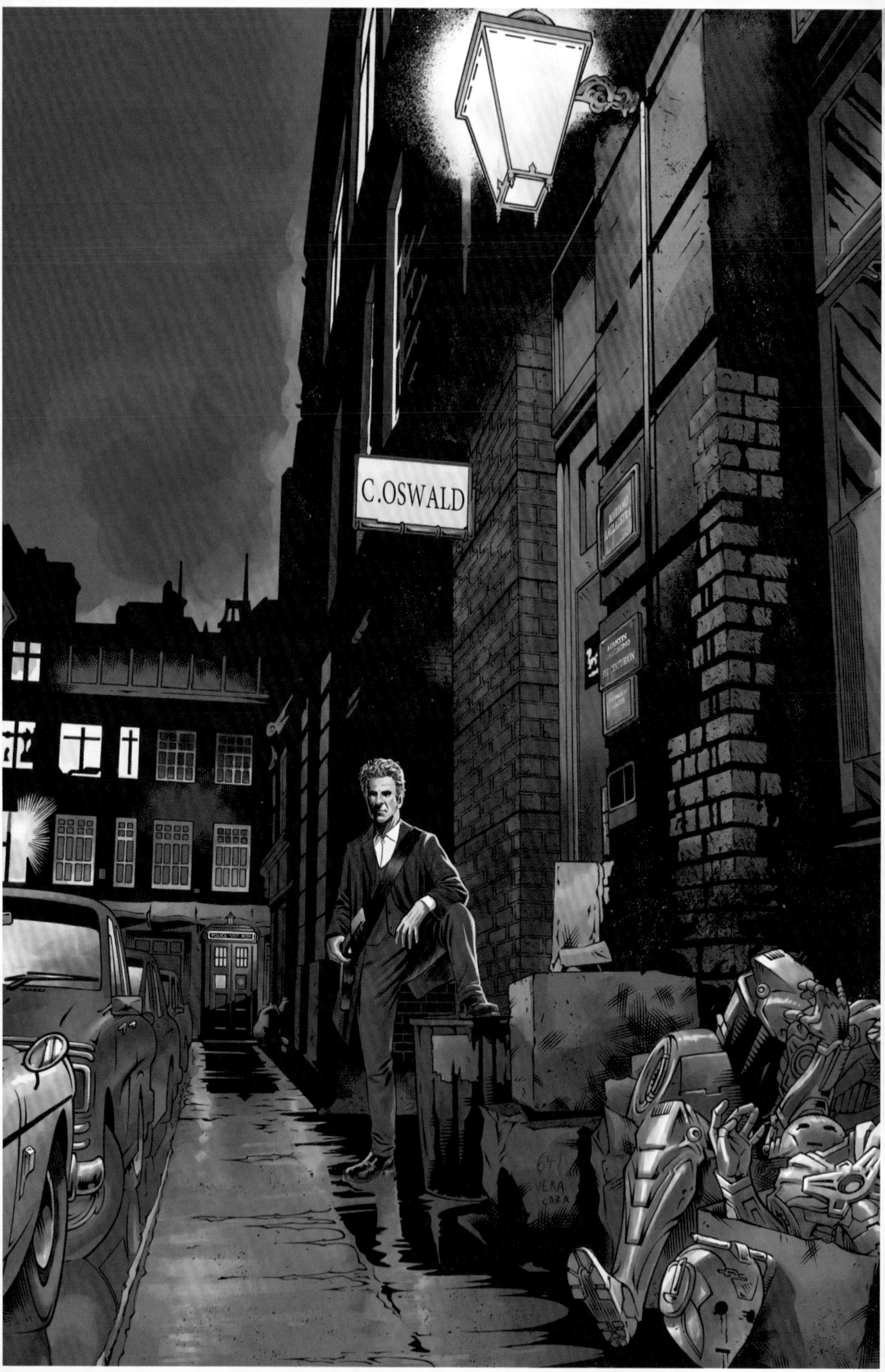
C.OSWALD
MARIANO LACLAUSTRA
AGUSTIN CALCAGNO
FER CENTURION
VERA CABA

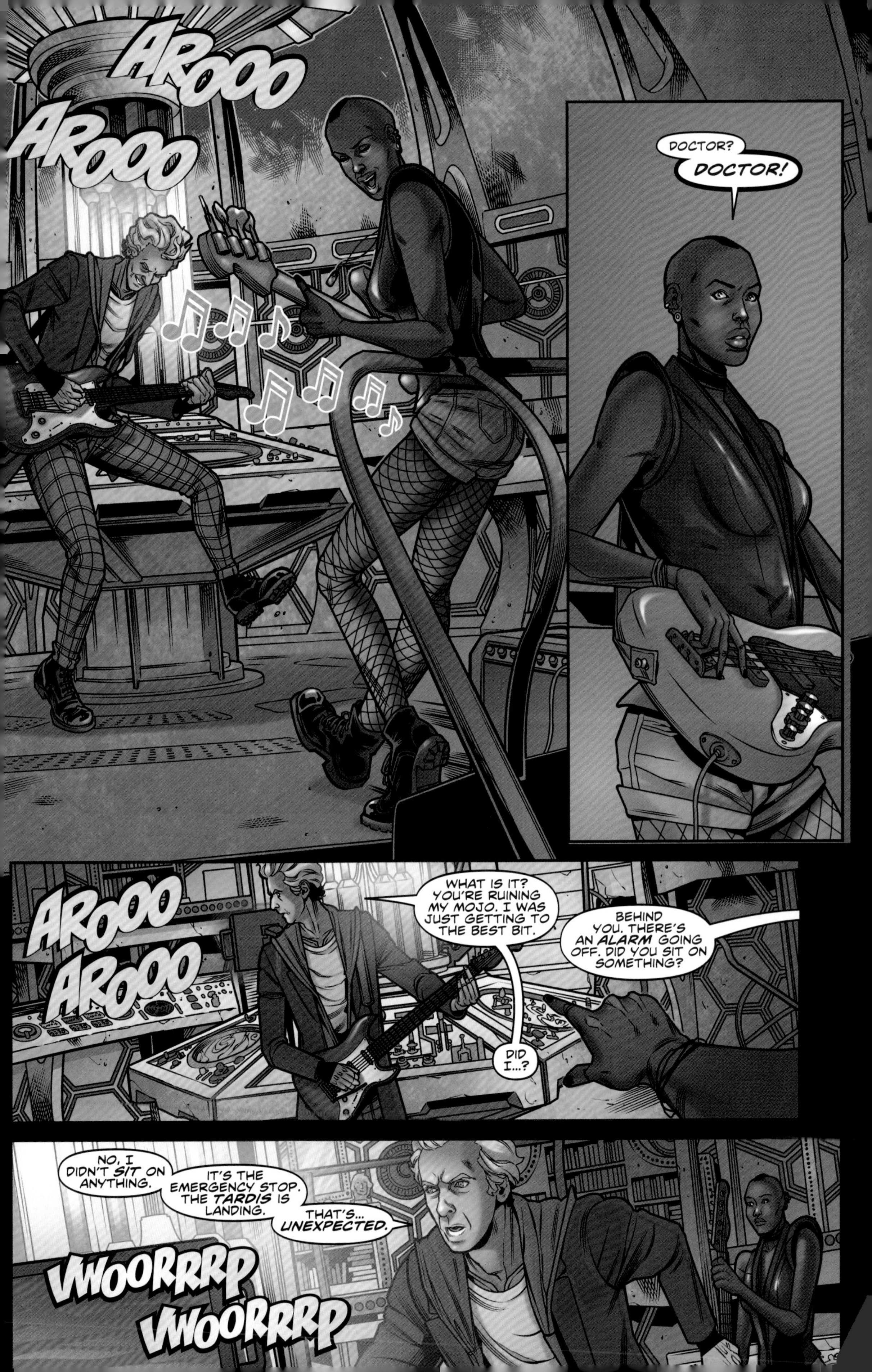
AROOO
AROOO
DOCTOR?
DOCTOR!
AROOO
AROOO
WHAT IS IT? YOU'RE RUINING MY MOJO. I WAS JUST GETTING TO THE BEST BIT.
BEHIND YOU. THERE'S AN ALARM GOING OFF. DID YOU SIT ON SOMETHING?
DID I...?
NO, I DIDN'T SIT ON ANYTHING.
IT'S THE EMERGENCY STOP. THE TARDIS IS LANDING.
THAT'S... UNEXPECTED.
VWOORRRP
VWOORRRP

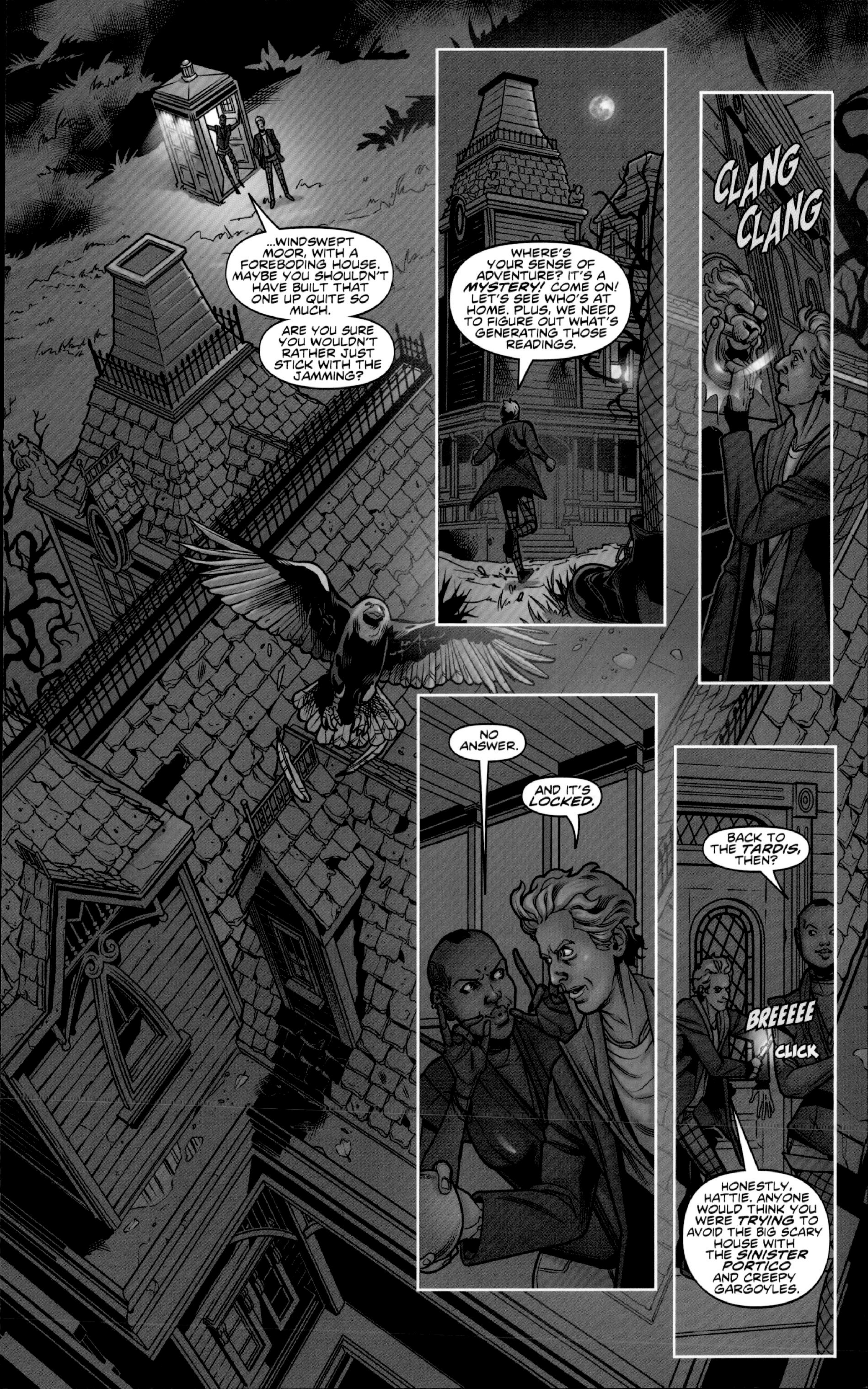
...WINDSWEPT MOOR, WITH A FOREBODING HOUSE. MAYBE YOU SHOULDN'T HAVE BUILT THAT ONE UP QUITE SO MUCH.
ARE YOU SURE YOU WOULDN'T RATHER JUST STICK WITH THE JAMMING?
WHERE'S YOUR SENSE OF ADVENTURE? IT'S A *MYSTERY!* COME ON! LET'S SEE WHO'S AT HOME. PLUS, WE NEED TO FIGURE OUT WHAT'S GENERATING THOSE READINGS.
CLANG CLANG
NO ANSWER.
AND IT'S *LOCKED.*
BACK TO THE *TARDIS,* THEN?
BREEEEE
CLICK
HONESTLY, HATTIE. ANYONE WOULD THINK YOU WERE *TRYING* TO AVOID THE BIG SCARY HOUSE WITH THE *SINISTER PORTICO* AND CREEPY GARGOYLES.

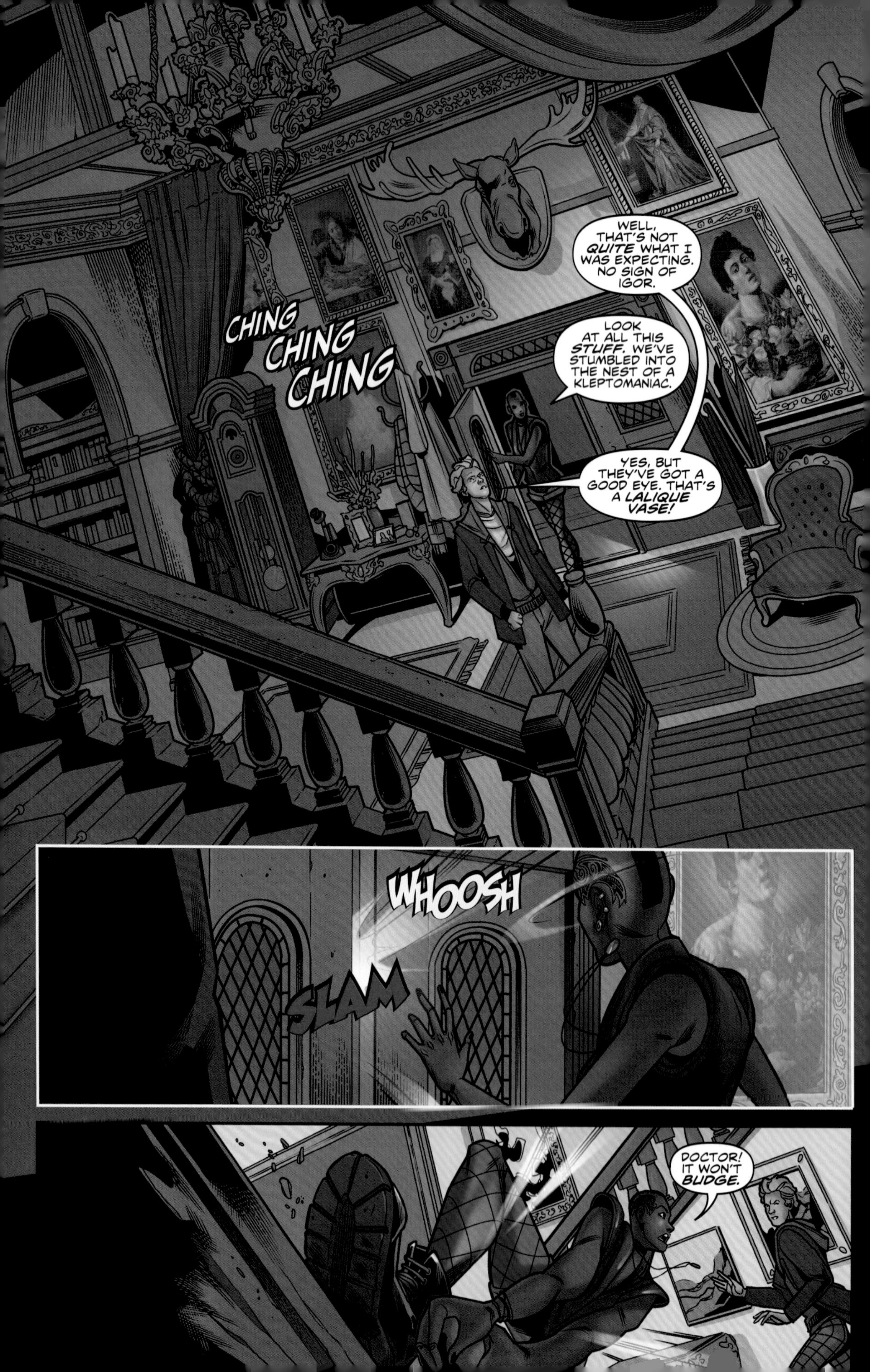
WELL, THAT'S NOT QUITE WHAT I WAS EXPECTING. NO SIGN OF IGOR.
LOOK AT ALL THIS STUFF. WE'VE STUMBLED INTO THE NEST OF A KLEPTOMANIAC.
CHING CHING CHING
YES, BUT THEY'VE GOT A GOOD EYE. THAT'S A LALIQUE VASE!
WHOOSH
SLAM
DOCTOR! IT WON'T BUDGE.

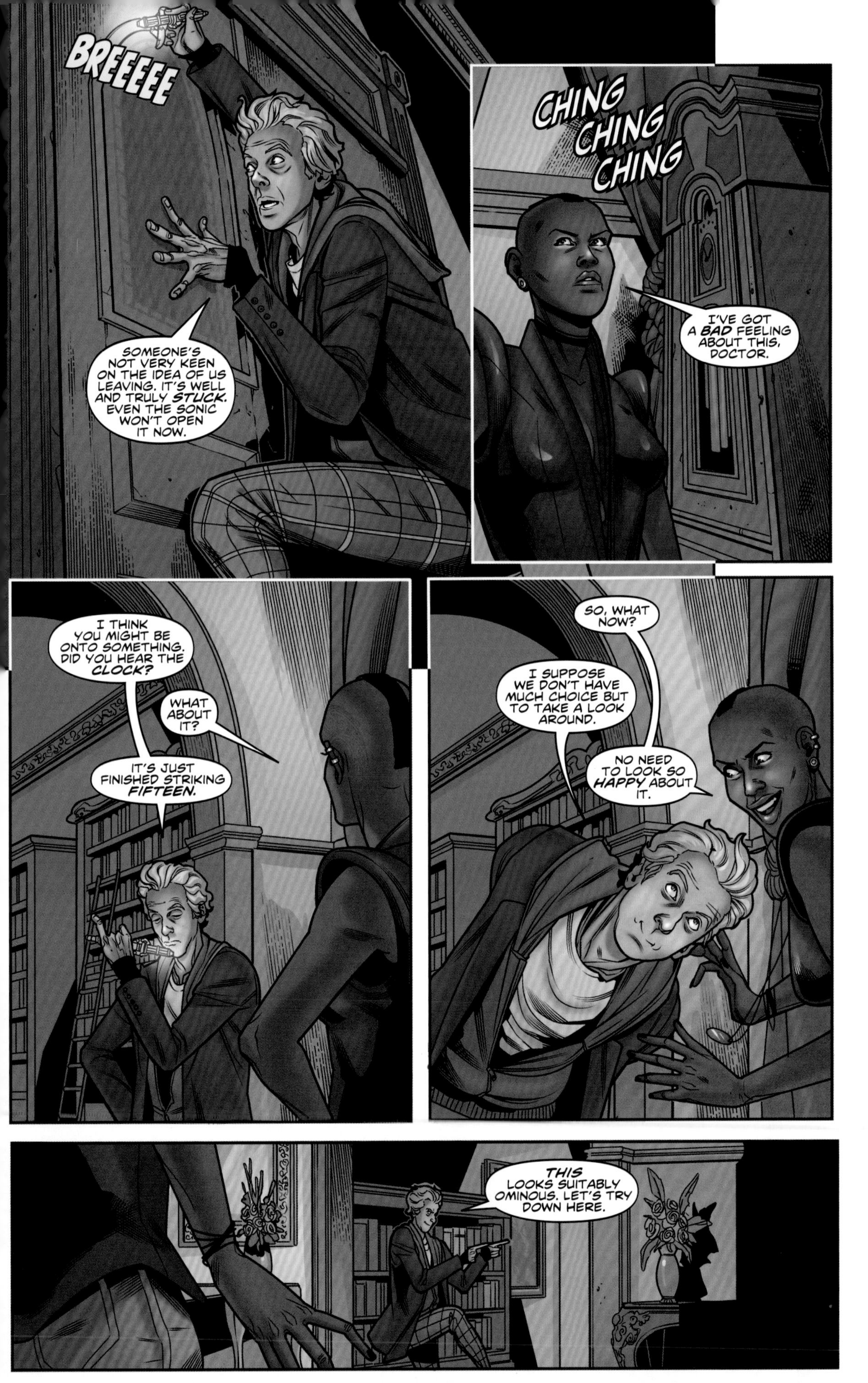
BREEEEE
SOMEONE'S NOT VERY KEEN ON THE IDEA OF US LEAVING. IT'S WELL AND TRULY STUCK. EVEN THE SONIC WON'T OPEN IT NOW.
CHING CHING CHING
I'VE GOT A BAD FEELING ABOUT THIS, DOCTOR.
I THINK YOU MIGHT BE ONTO SOMETHING. DID YOU HEAR THE CLOCK?
WHAT ABOUT IT?
IT'S JUST FINISHED STRIKING FIFTEEN.
SO, WHAT NOW?
I SUPPOSE WE DON'T HAVE MUCH CHOICE BUT TO TAKE A LOOK AROUND.
NO NEED TO LOOK SO HAPPY ABOUT IT.
THIS LOOKS SUITABLY OMINOUS. LET'S TRY DOWN HERE.

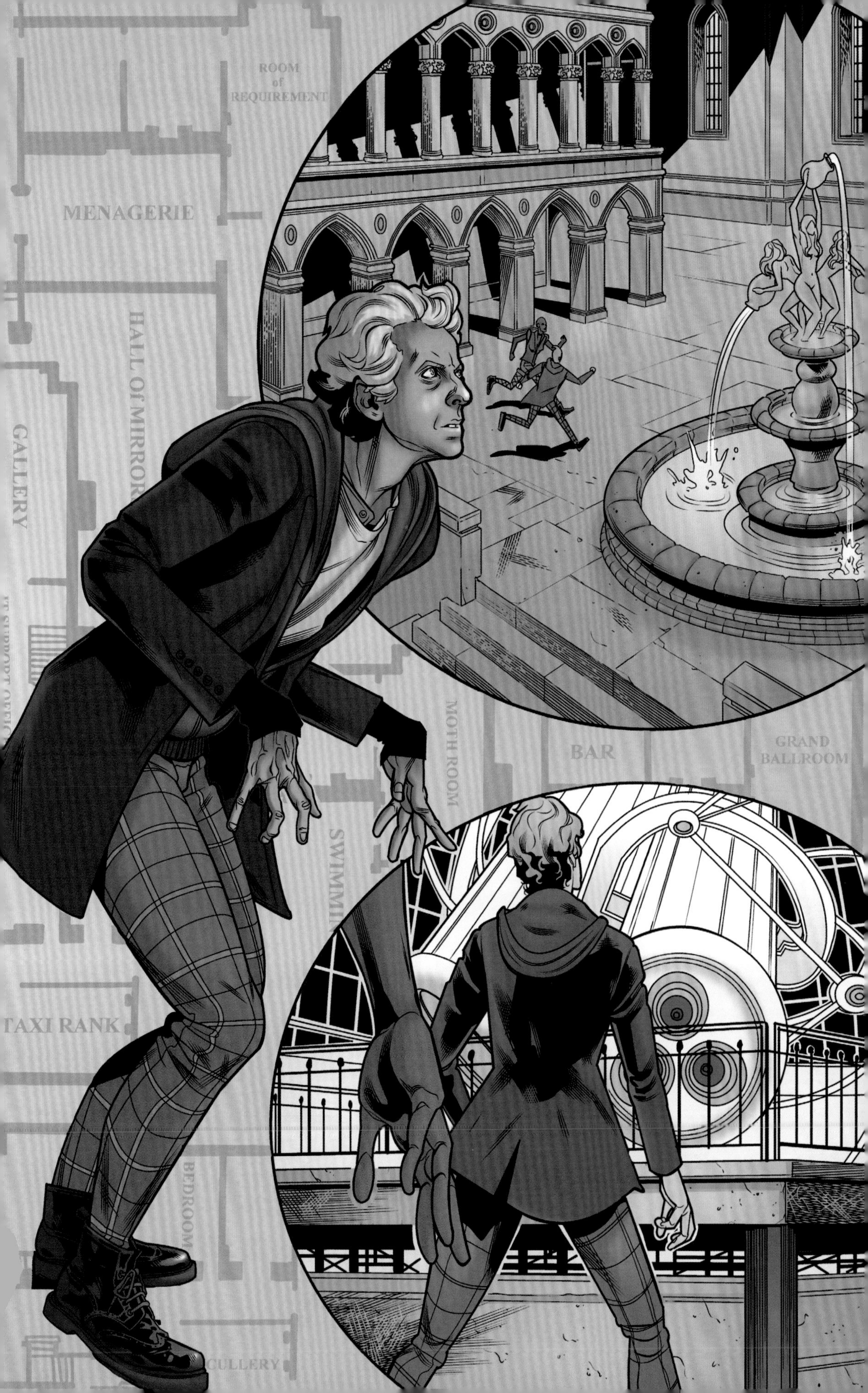
ROOM of REQUIREMENT
MENAGERIE
GALLERY
MOTH ROOM
BAR
GRAND BALLROOM
TAXI RANK
BEDROOM

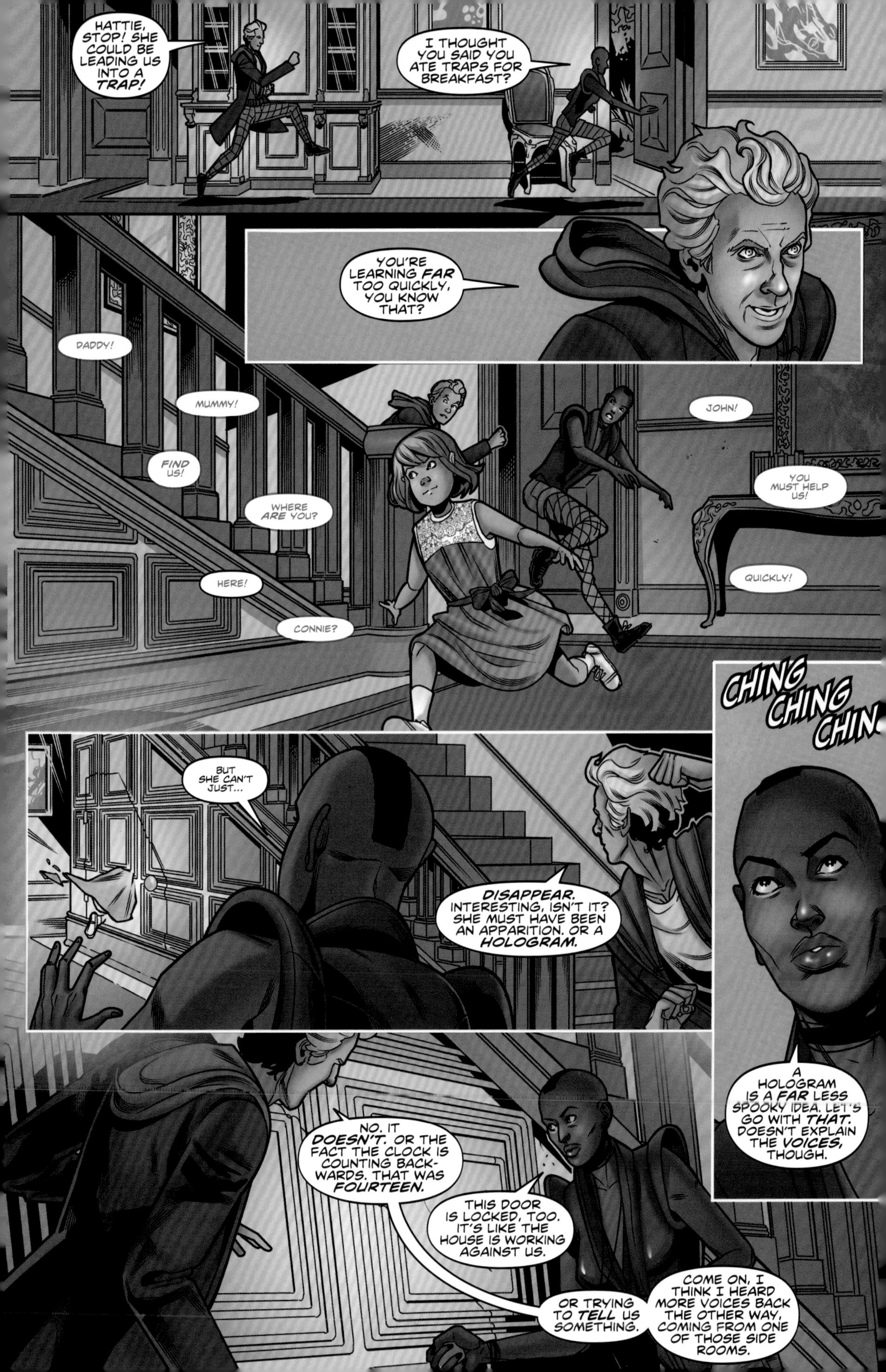

HATTIE, STOP! SHE COULD BE LEADING US INTO A *TRAP!*
I THOUGHT YOU SAID YOU ATE TRAPS FOR BREAKFAST?
YOU'RE LEARNING *FAR* TOO QUICKLY, YOU KNOW THAT?
DADDY!
MUMMY!
FIND US!
WHERE *ARE* YOU?
HERE!
CONNIE?
JOHN!
YOU MUST HELP US!
QUICKLY!
CHING CHING CHIN
BUT SHE CAN'T JUST...
DISAPPEAR. INTERESTING, ISN'T IT? SHE MUST HAVE BEEN AN APPARITION. OR A *HOLOGRAM.*
A HOLOGRAM IS A *FAR* LESS SPOOKY IDEA. LET'S GO WITH *THAT.* DOESN'T EXPLAIN THE *VOICES,* THOUGH.
NO. IT *DOESN'T.* OR THE FACT THE CLOCK IS COUNTING BACK-WARDS. THAT WAS *FOURTEEN.*
THIS DOOR IS LOCKED, TOO. IT'S LIKE THE HOUSE IS WORKING AGAINST US.
OR TRYING TO *TELL* US SOMETHING.
COME ON, I THINK I HEARD MORE VOICES BACK THE OTHER WAY, COMING FROM ONE OF THOSE SIDE ROOMS.

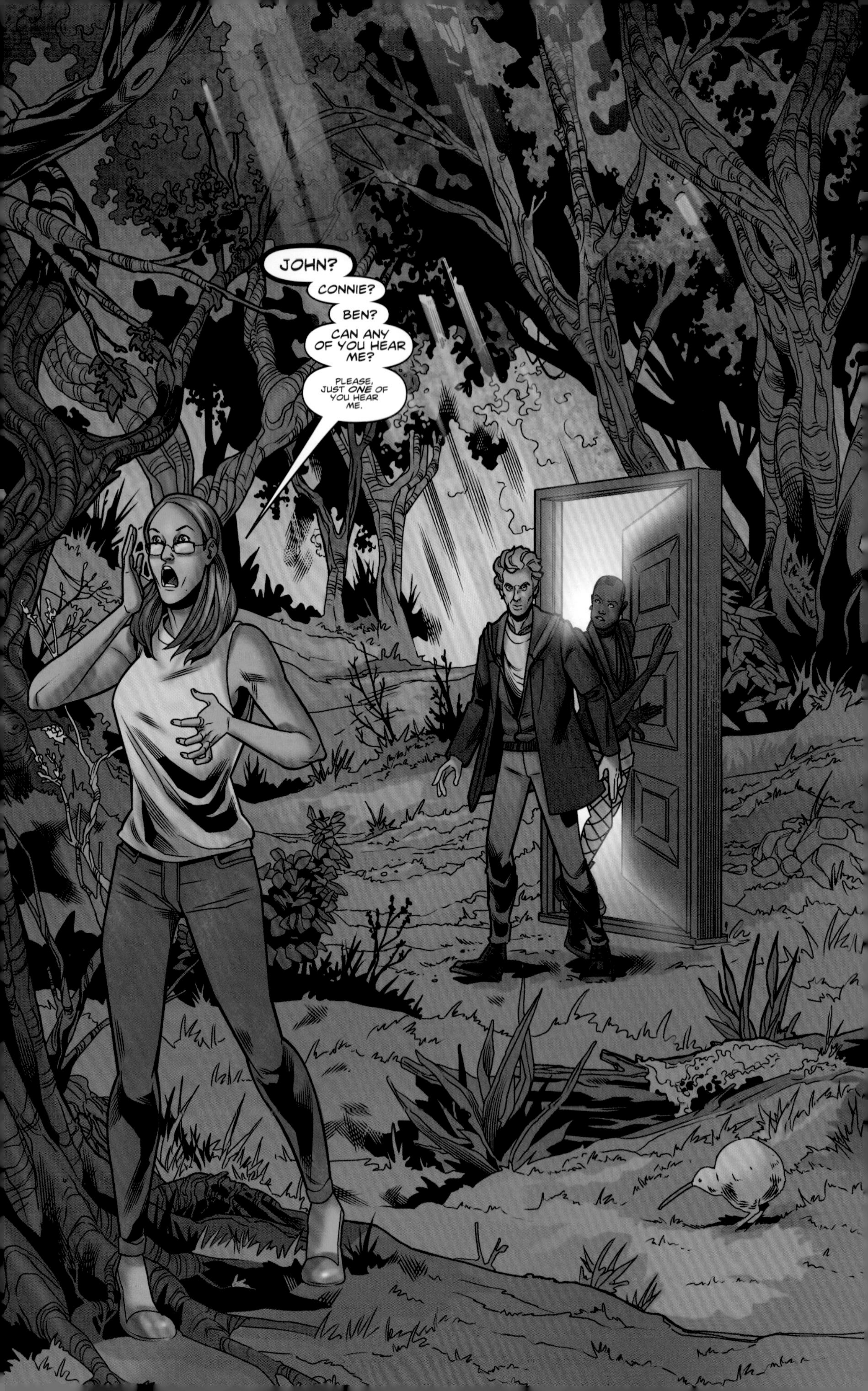
JOHN?
CONNIE?
BEN?
CAN ANY OF YOU HEAR ME?
PLEASE, JUST *ONE* OF YOU HEAR ME.

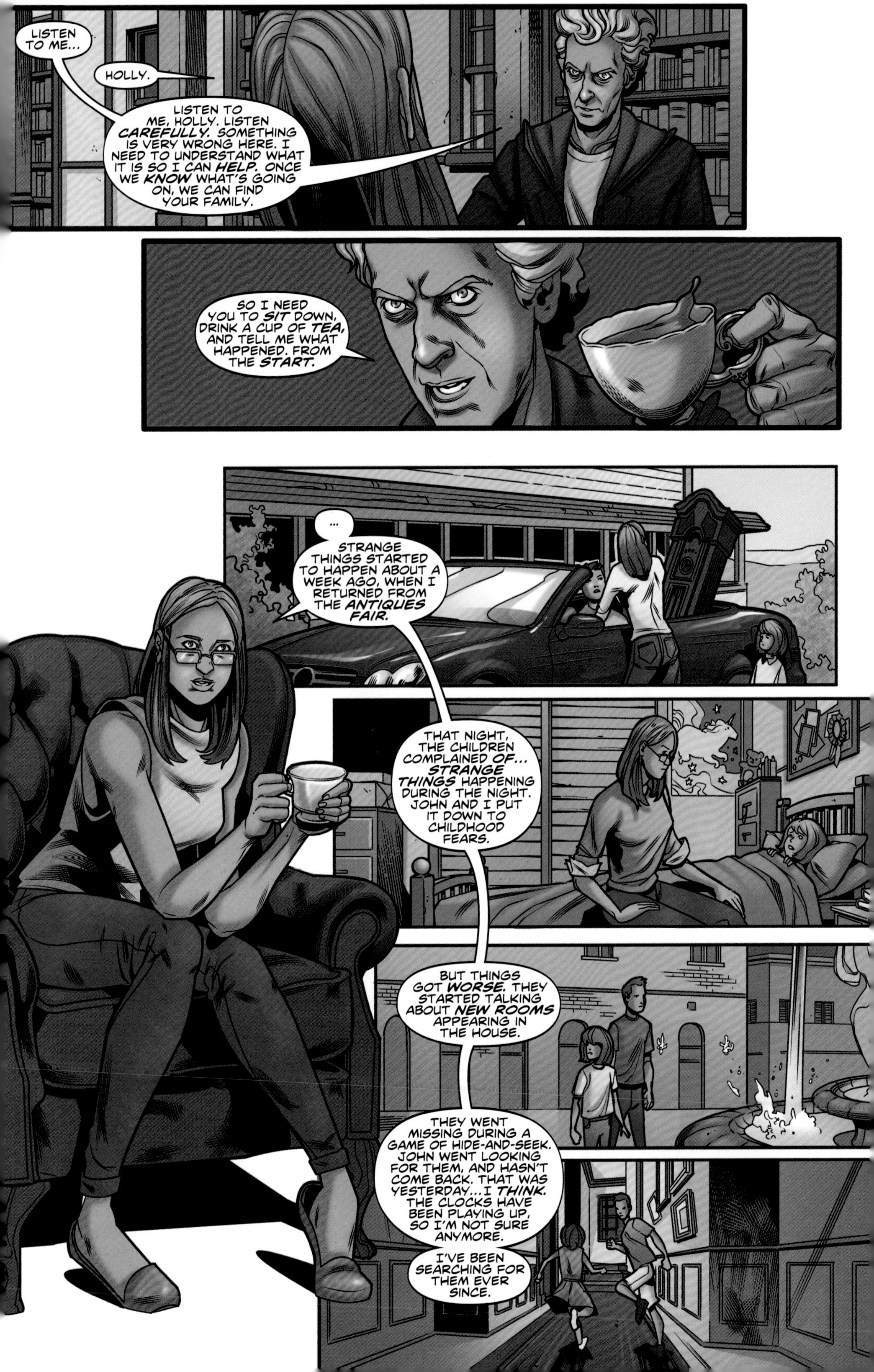
LISTEN TO ME...
HOLLY.
LISTEN TO ME, HOLLY. LISTEN CAREFULLY. SOMETHING IS VERY WRONG HERE. I NEED TO UNDERSTAND WHAT IT IS SO I CAN HELP. ONCE WE KNOW WHAT'S GOING ON, WE CAN FIND YOUR FAMILY.
SO I NEED YOU TO SIT DOWN, DRINK A CUP OF TEA, AND TELL ME WHAT HAPPENED. FROM THE START.
...
STRANGE THINGS STARTED TO HAPPEN ABOUT A WEEK AGO, WHEN I RETURNED FROM THE ANTIQUES FAIR.
THAT NIGHT, THE CHILDREN COMPLAINED OF... STRANGE THINGS HAPPENING DURING THE NIGHT. JOHN AND I PUT IT DOWN TO CHILDHOOD FEARS.
BUT THINGS GOT WORSE. THEY STARTED TALKING ABOUT NEW ROOMS APPEARING IN THE HOUSE.
THEY WENT MISSING DURING A GAME OF HIDE-AND-SEEK. JOHN WENT LOOKING FOR THEM, AND HASN'T COME BACK. THAT WAS YESTERDAY...I THINK. THE CLOCKS HAVE BEEN PLAYING UP, SO I'M NOT SURE ANYMORE.
I'VE BEEN SEARCHING FOR THEM EVER SINCE.

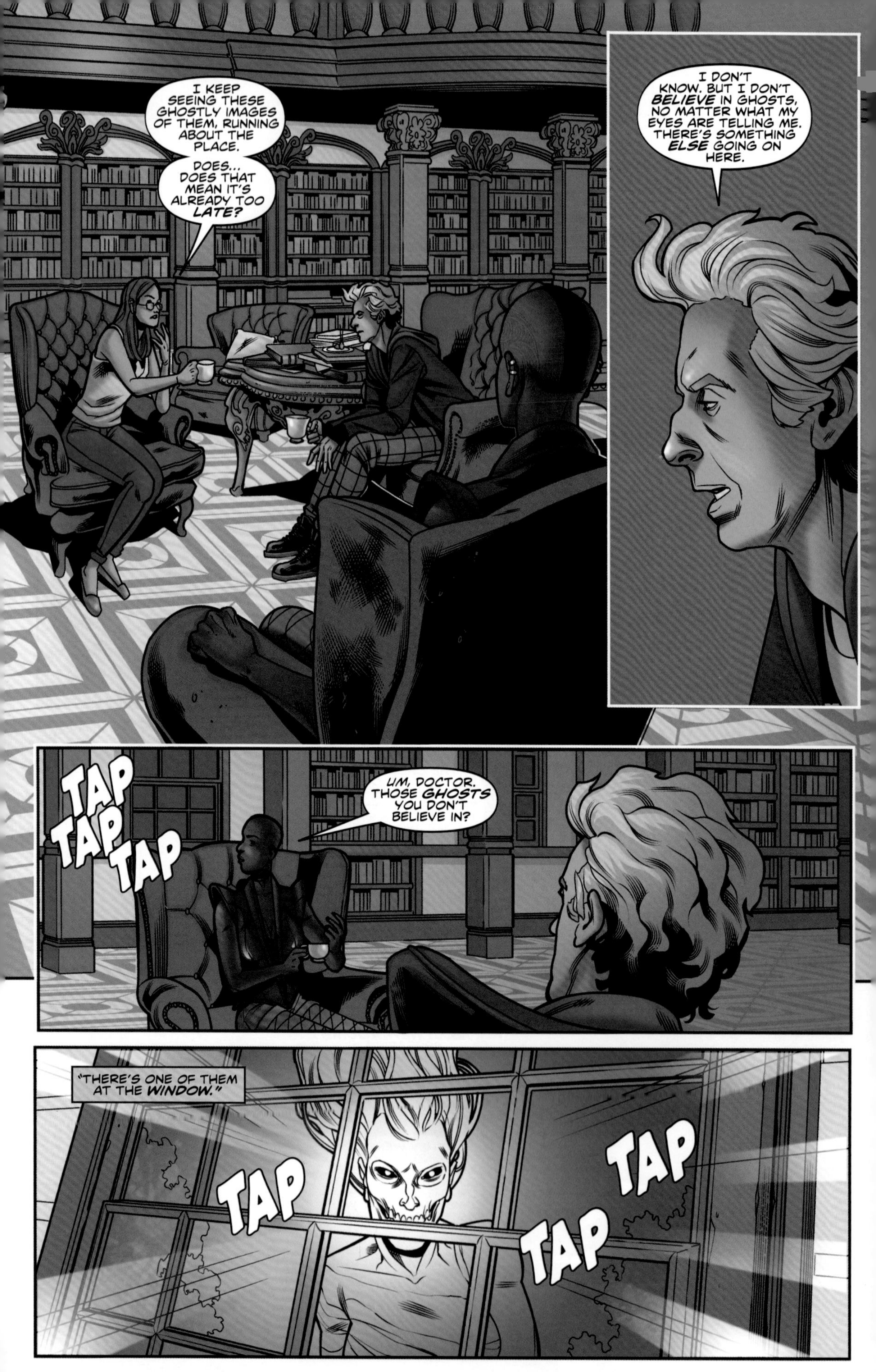
I KEEP SEEING THESE GHOSTLY IMAGES OF THEM, RUNNING ABOUT THE PLACE.
DOES... DOES THAT MEAN IT'S ALREADY TOO *LATE?*
I DON'T KNOW. BUT I DON'T *BELIEVE* IN GHOSTS, NO MATTER WHAT MY EYES ARE TELLING ME. THERE'S SOMETHING *ELSE* GOING ON HERE.
TAP TAP TAP
UM, DOCTOR. THOSE *GHOSTS* YOU DON'T BELIEVE IN?
"THERE'S ONE OF THEM AT THE *WINDOW.*"
TAP
TAP
TAP

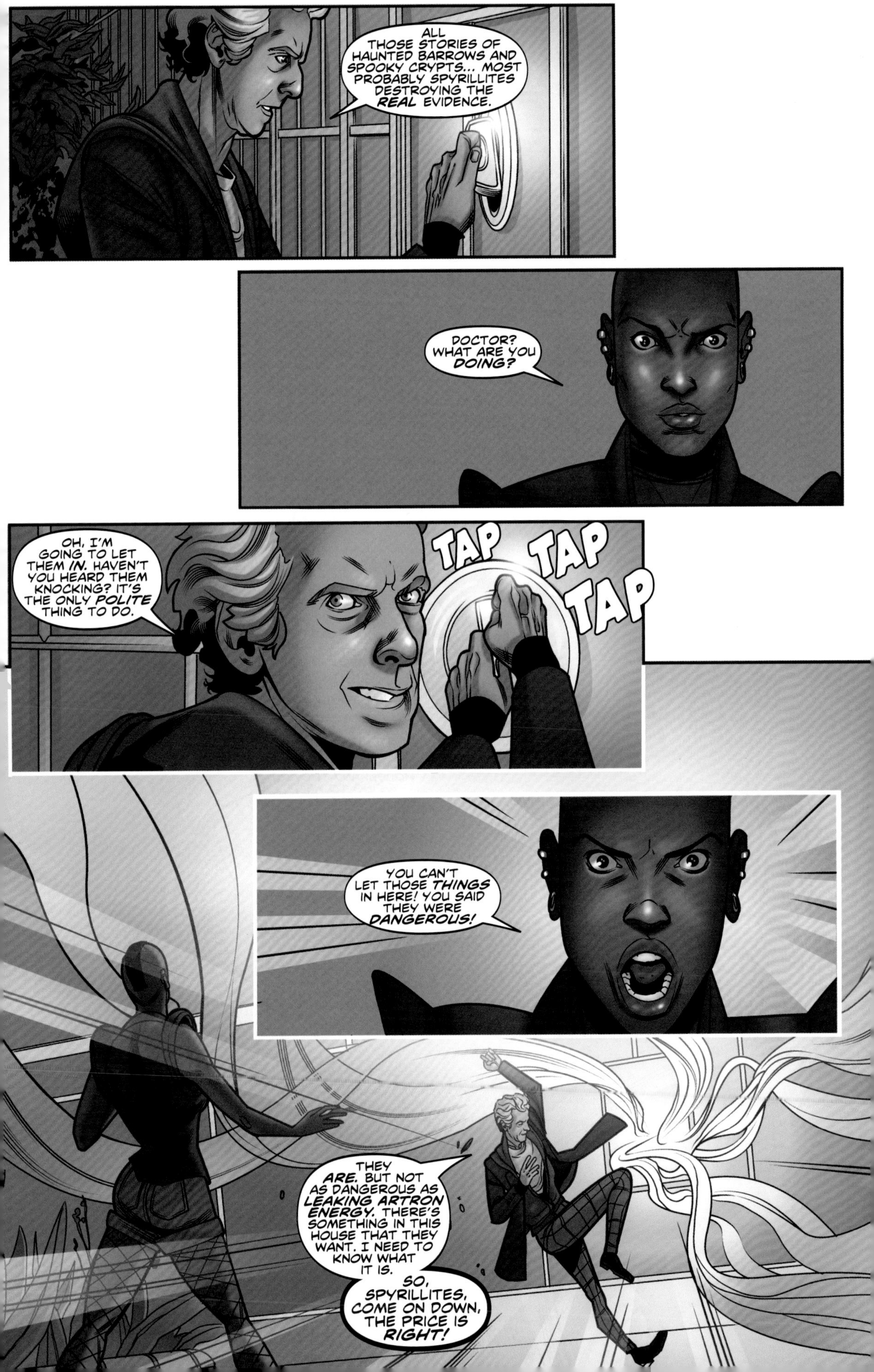
ALL THOSE STORIES OF HAUNTED BARROWS AND SPOOKY CRYPTS... MOST PROBABLY SPYRILLITES DESTROYING THE *REAL* EVIDENCE.
DOCTOR? WHAT ARE YOU *DOING?*
OH, I'M GOING TO LET THEM *IN.* HAVEN'T YOU HEARD THEM KNOCKING? IT'S THE ONLY *POLITE* THING TO DO.
TAP TAP TAP
YOU CAN'T LET THOSE *THINGS* IN HERE! YOU SAID THEY WERE *DANGEROUS!*
THEY *ARE.* BUT NOT AS DANGEROUS AS *LEAKING ARTRON ENERGY.* THERE'S SOMETHING IN THIS HOUSE THAT THEY WANT. I NEED TO KNOW WHAT IT IS.
SO, SPYRILLITES, COME ON DOWN, THE PRICE IS *RIGHT!*

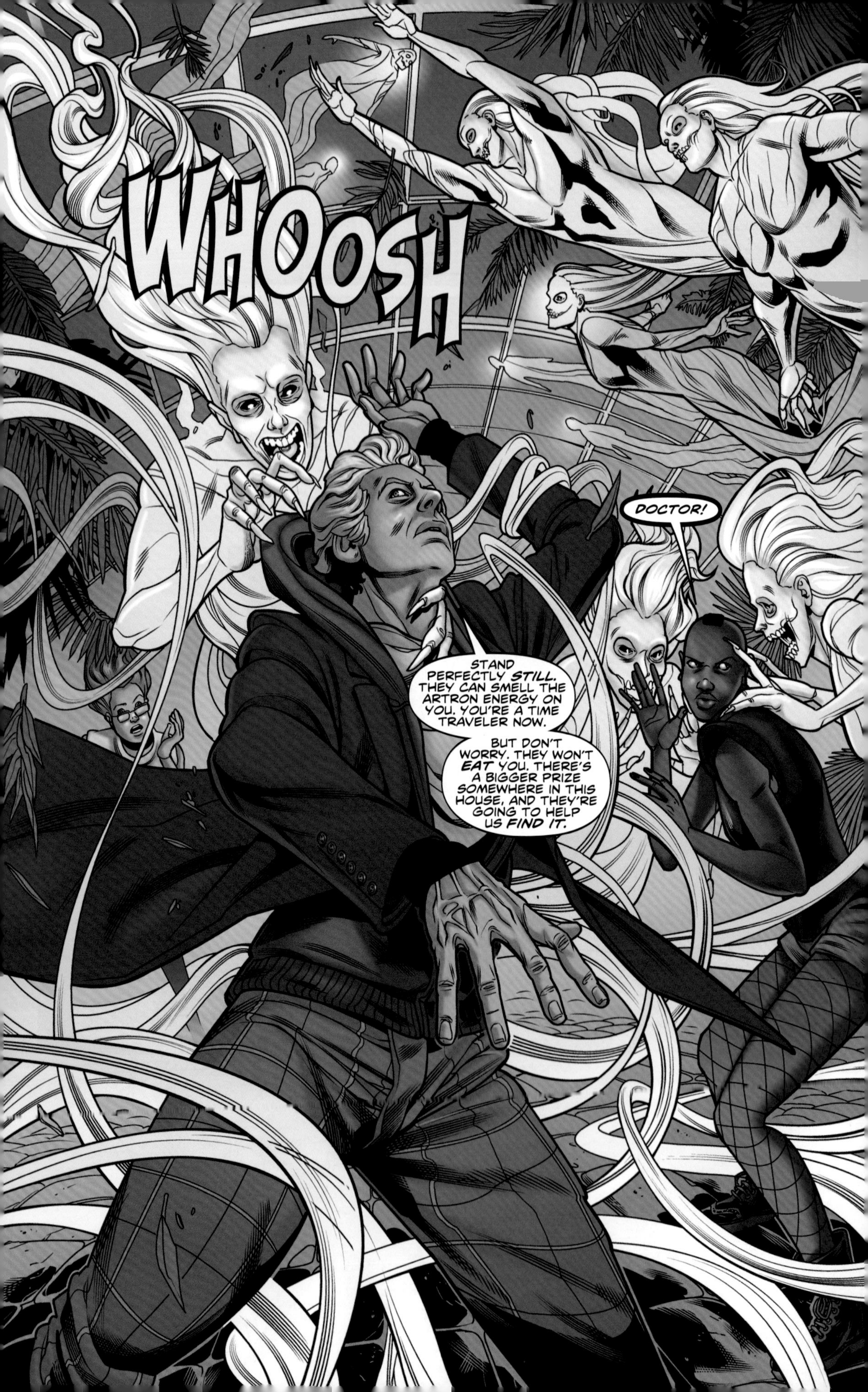
WHOOSH
DOCTOR!
STAND PERFECTLY STILL. THEY CAN SMELL THE ARTRON ENERGY ON YOU. YOU'RE A TIME TRAVELER NOW.
BUT DON'T WORRY. THEY WON'T EAT YOU. THERE'S A BIGGER PRIZE SOMEWHERE IN THIS HOUSE, AND THEY'RE GOING TO HELP US FIND IT.

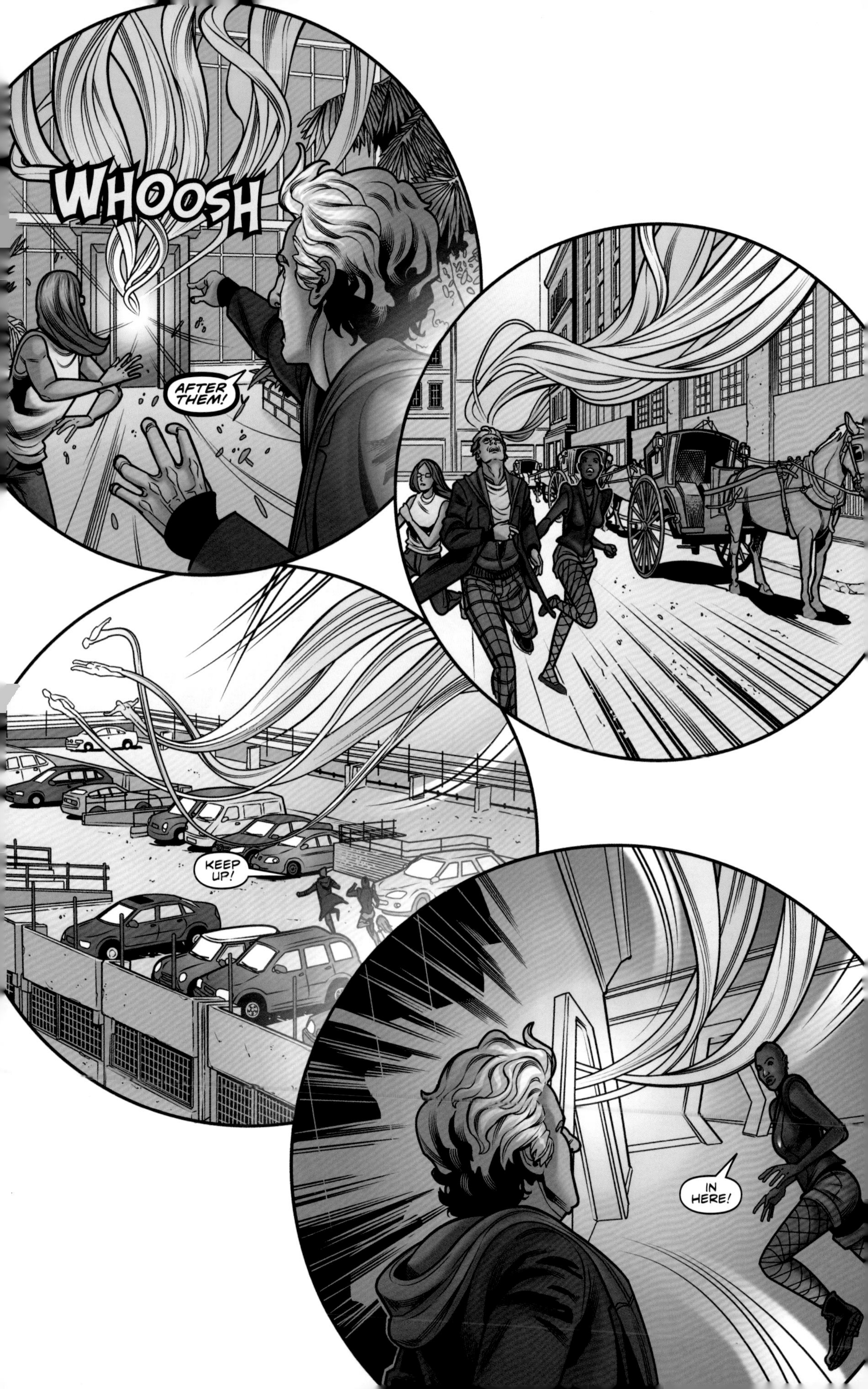
WHOOSH
AFTER THEM!
KEEP UP!
IN HERE!

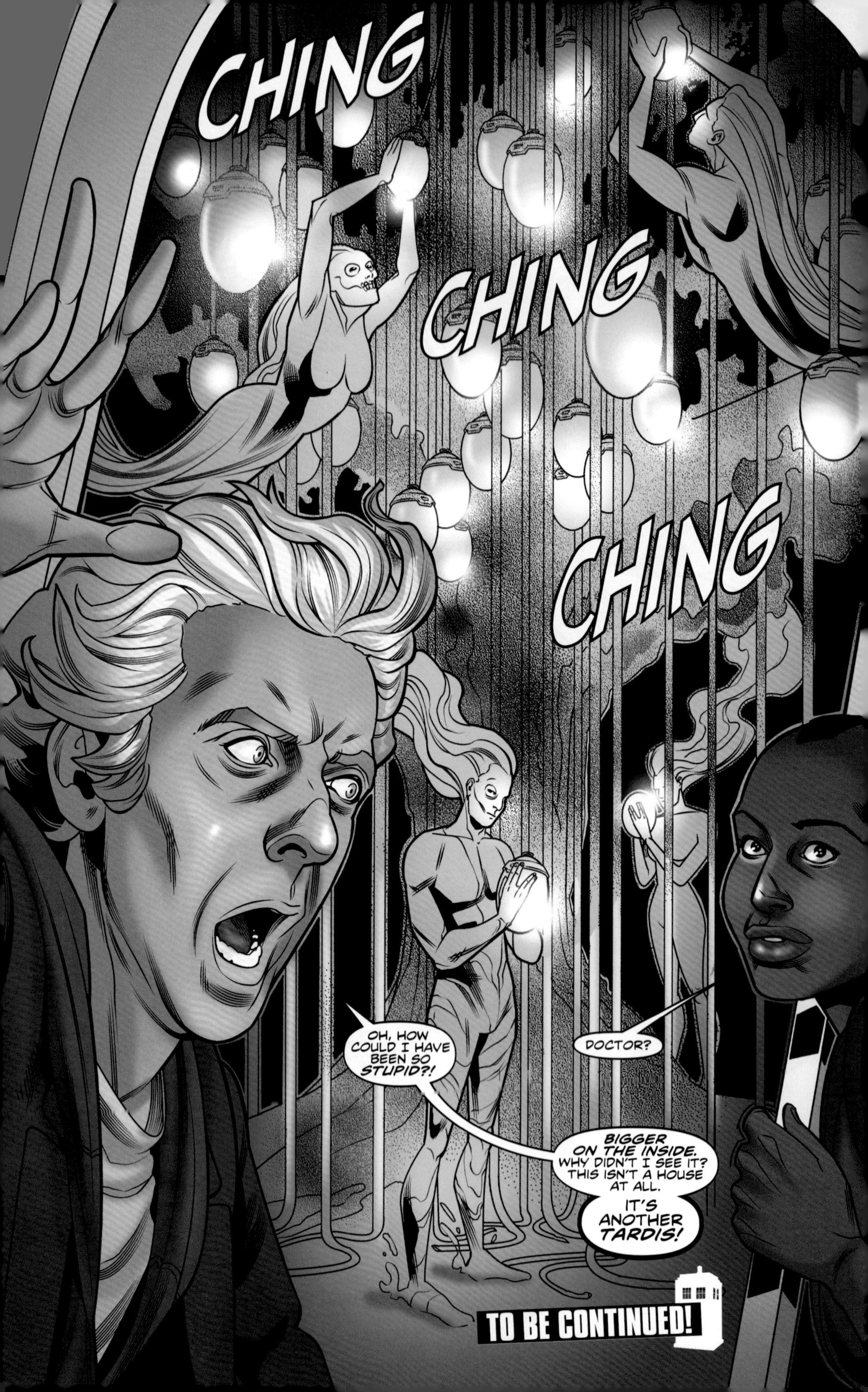
CHING
CHING
CHING
OH, HOW COULD I HAVE BEEN SO STUPID?!
DOCTOR?
BIGGER ON THE INSIDE. WHY DIDN'T I SEE IT? THIS ISN'T A HOUSE AT ALL.
IT'S ANOTHER TARDIS!
TO BE CONTINUED!

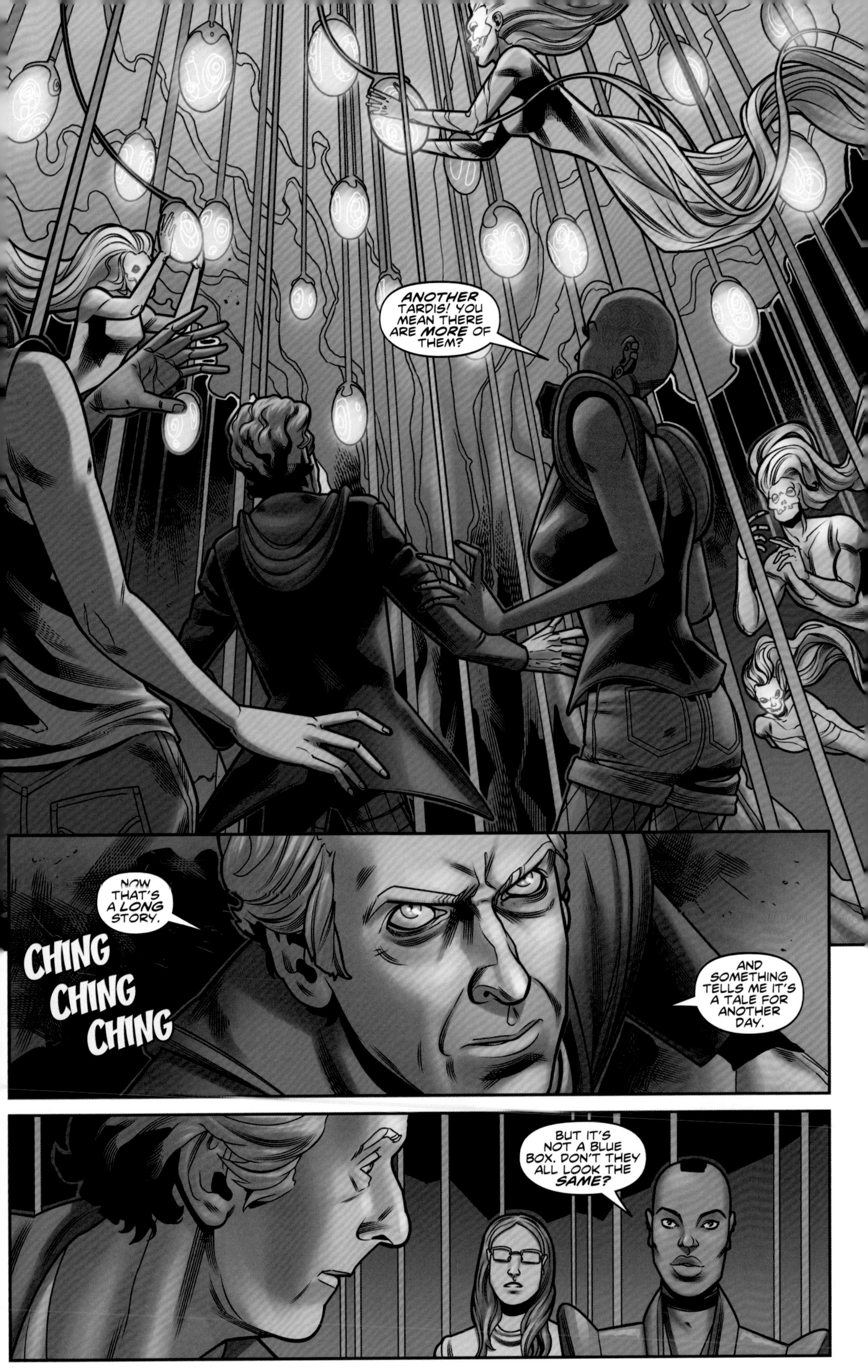
ANOTHER TARDIS! YOU MEAN THERE ARE MORE OF THEM?
NOW THAT'S A LONG STORY.
CHING CHING CHING
AND SOMETHING TELLS ME IT'S A TALE FOR ANOTHER DAY.
BUT IT'S NOT A BLUE BOX. DON'T THEY ALL LOOK THE SAME?

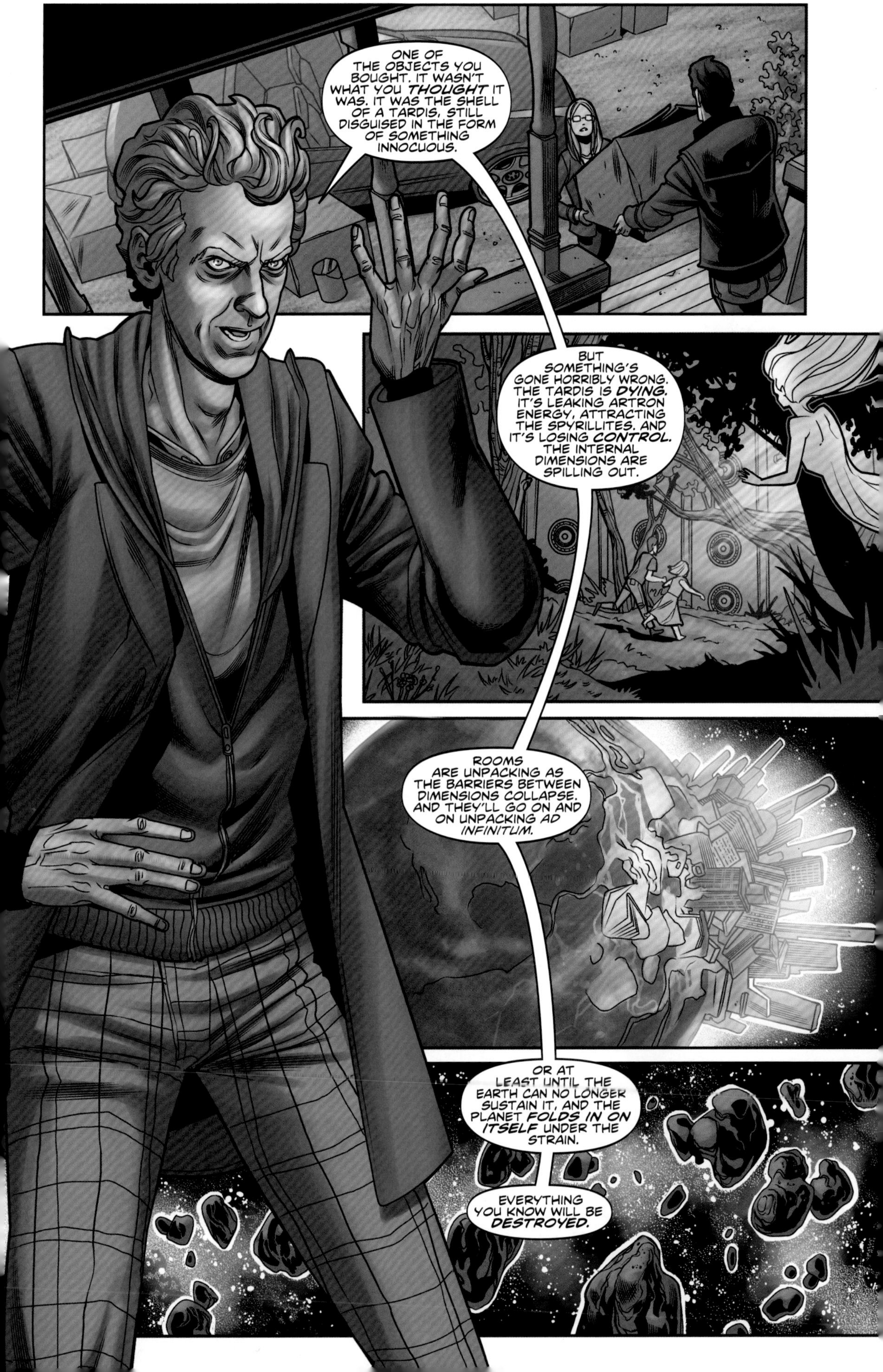
ONE OF THE OBJECTS YOU BOUGHT. IT WASN'T WHAT YOU *THOUGHT* IT WAS. IT WAS THE SHELL OF A TARDIS, STILL DISGUISED IN THE FORM OF SOMETHING INNOCUOUS.
BUT SOMETHING'S GONE HORRIBLY WRONG. THE TARDIS IS *DYING.* IT'S LEAKING ARTRON ENERGY, ATTRACTING THE SPYRILLITES. AND IT'S LOSING *CONTROL.* THE INTERNAL DIMENSIONS ARE SPILLING OUT.
ROOMS ARE UNPACKING AS THE BARRIERS BETWEEN DIMENSIONS COLLAPSE. AND THEY'LL GO ON AND ON UNPACKING AD *INFINITUM.*
OR AT LEAST UNTIL THE EARTH CAN NO LONGER SUSTAIN IT, AND THE PLANET *FOLDS IN ON ITSELF* UNDER THE STRAIN.
EVERYTHING YOU KNOW WILL BE *DESTROYED.*

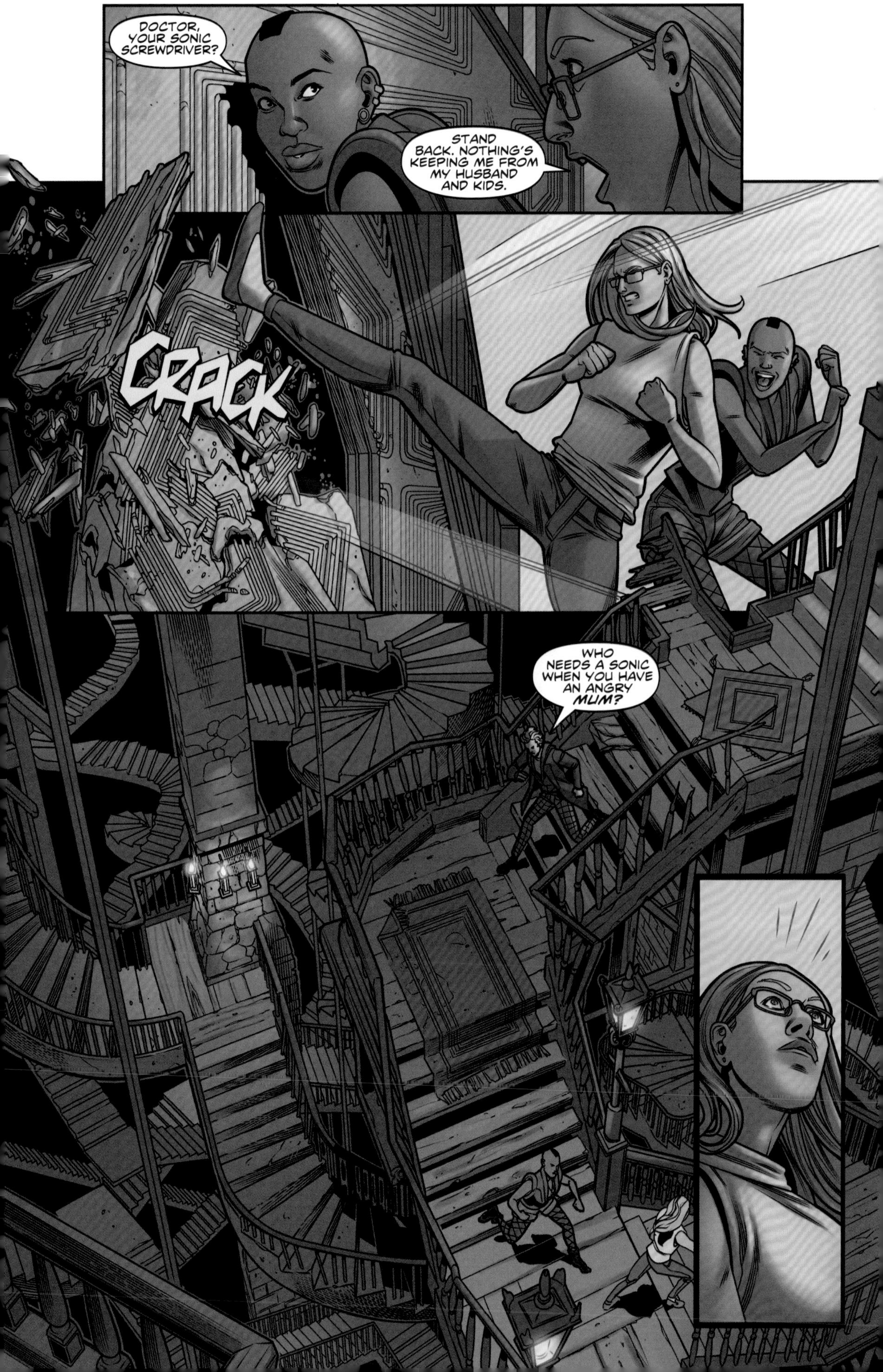
DOCTOR, YOUR SONIC SCREWDRIVER?
STAND BACK. NOTHING'S KEEPING ME FROM MY HUSBAND AND KIDS.
CRACK
WHO NEEDS A SONIC WHEN YOU HAVE AN ANGRY *MUM?*

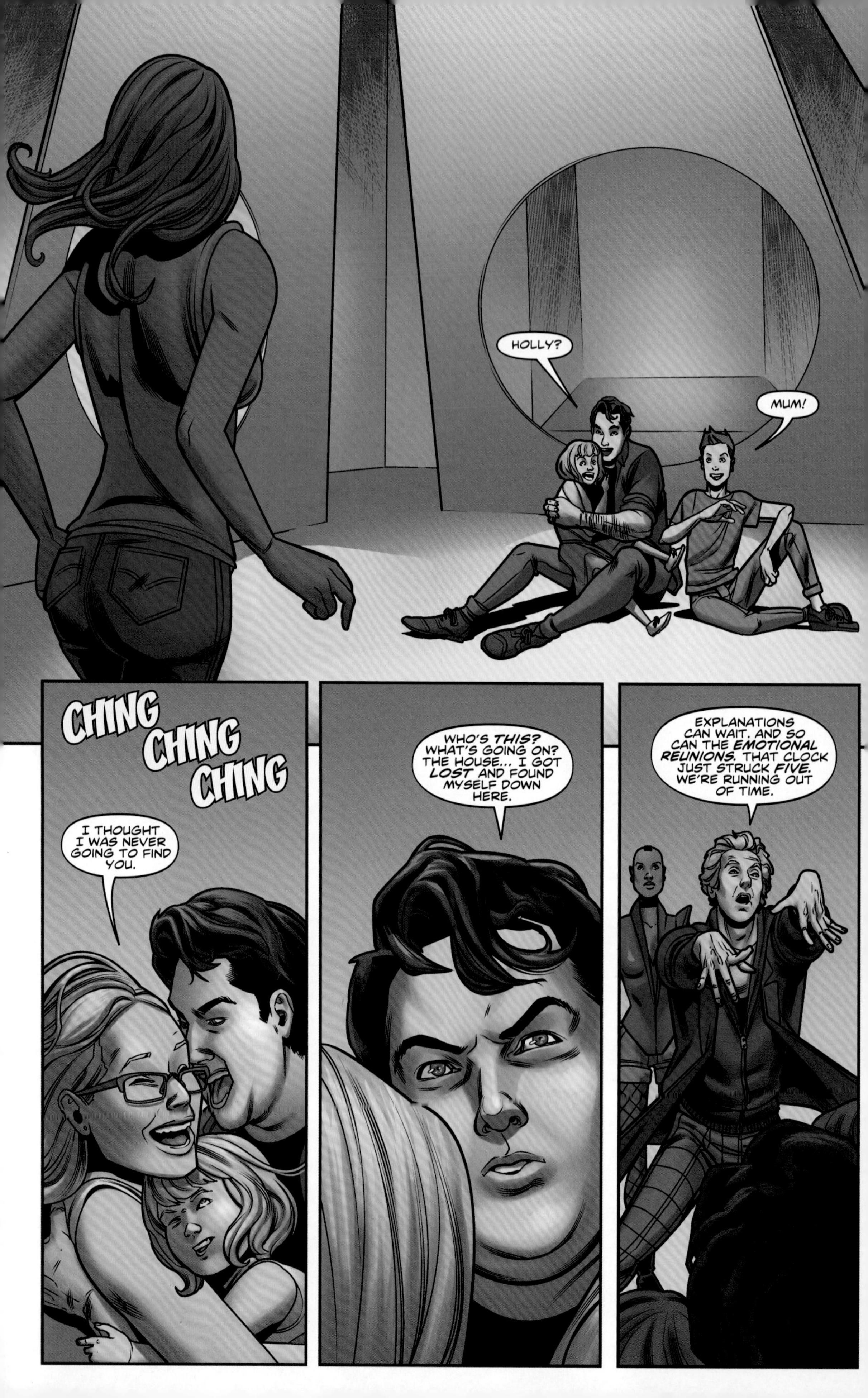
HOLLY?
MUM!
CHING CHING CHING
I THOUGHT I WAS NEVER GOING TO FIND YOU.
WHO'S THIS? WHAT'S GOING ON? THE HOUSE... I GOT LOST AND FOUND MYSELF DOWN HERE.
EXPLANATIONS CAN WAIT. AND SO CAN THE EMOTIONAL REUNIONS. THAT CLOCK JUST STRUCK FIVE. WE'RE RUNNING OUT OF TIME.

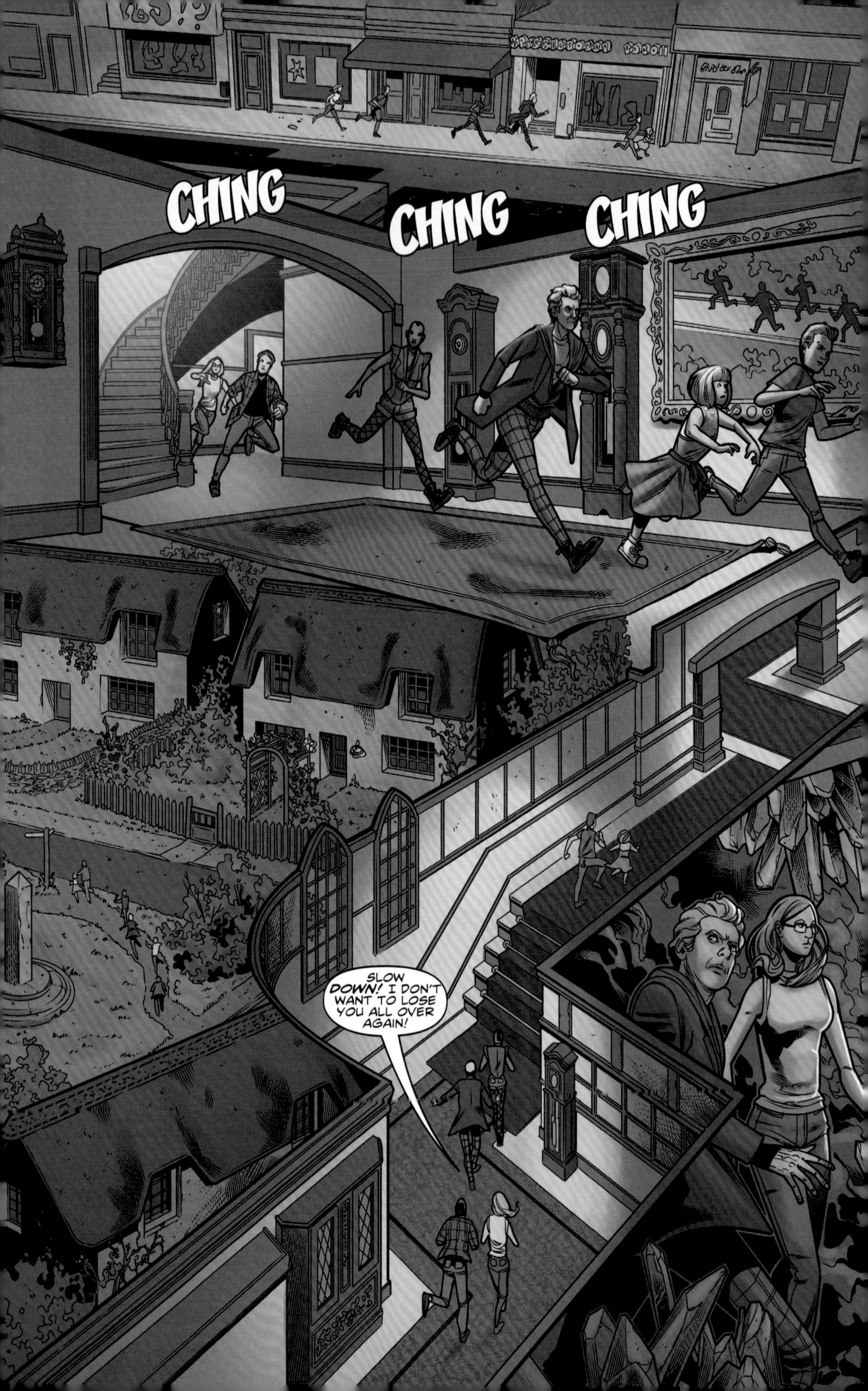
CHING
CHING
CHING
SLOW DOWN! I DON'T WANT TO LOSE YOU ALL OVER AGAIN!

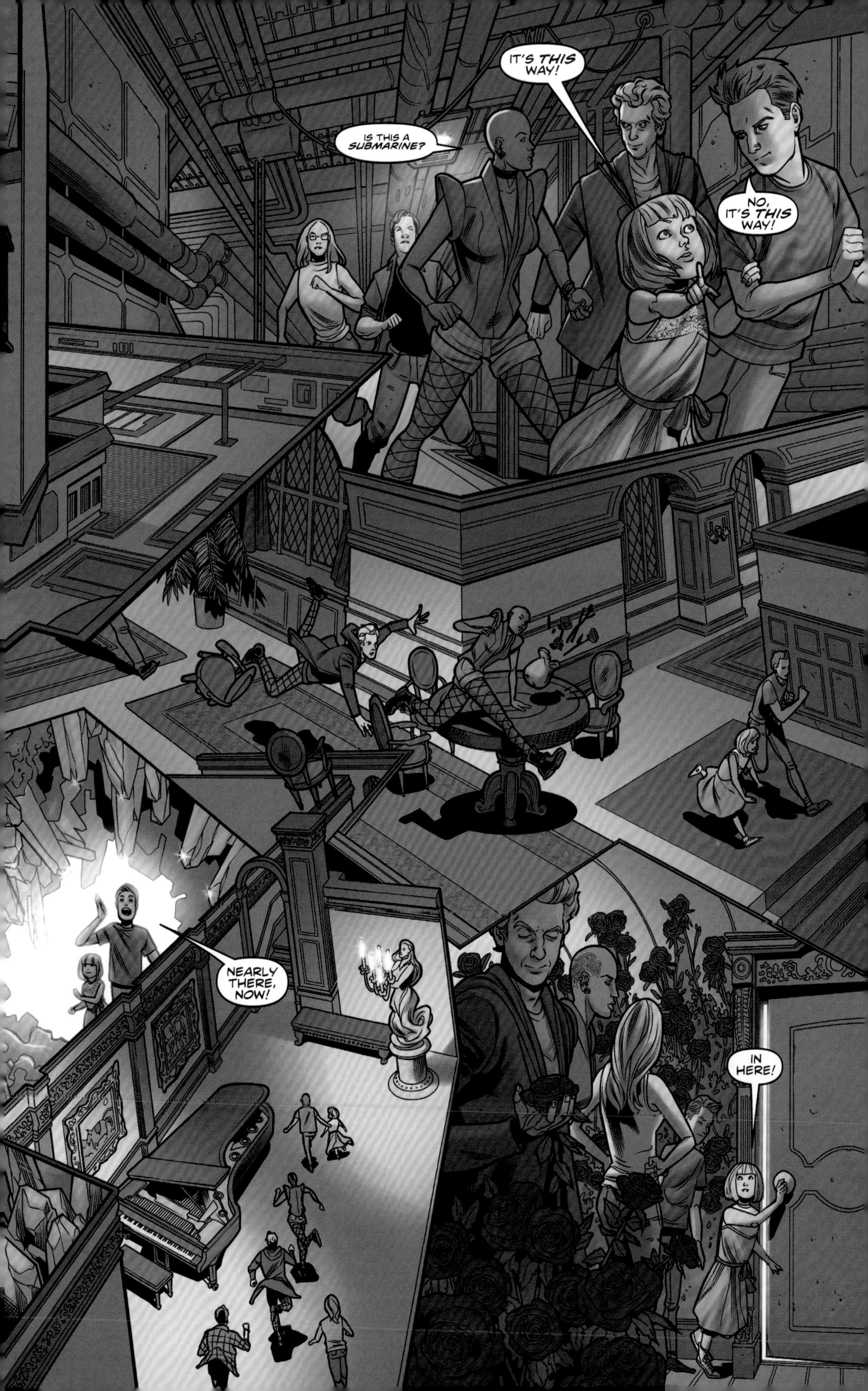
IS THIS A SUBMARINE?
IT'S THIS WAY!
NO, IT'S THIS WAY!
NEARLY THERE, NOW!
IN HERE!

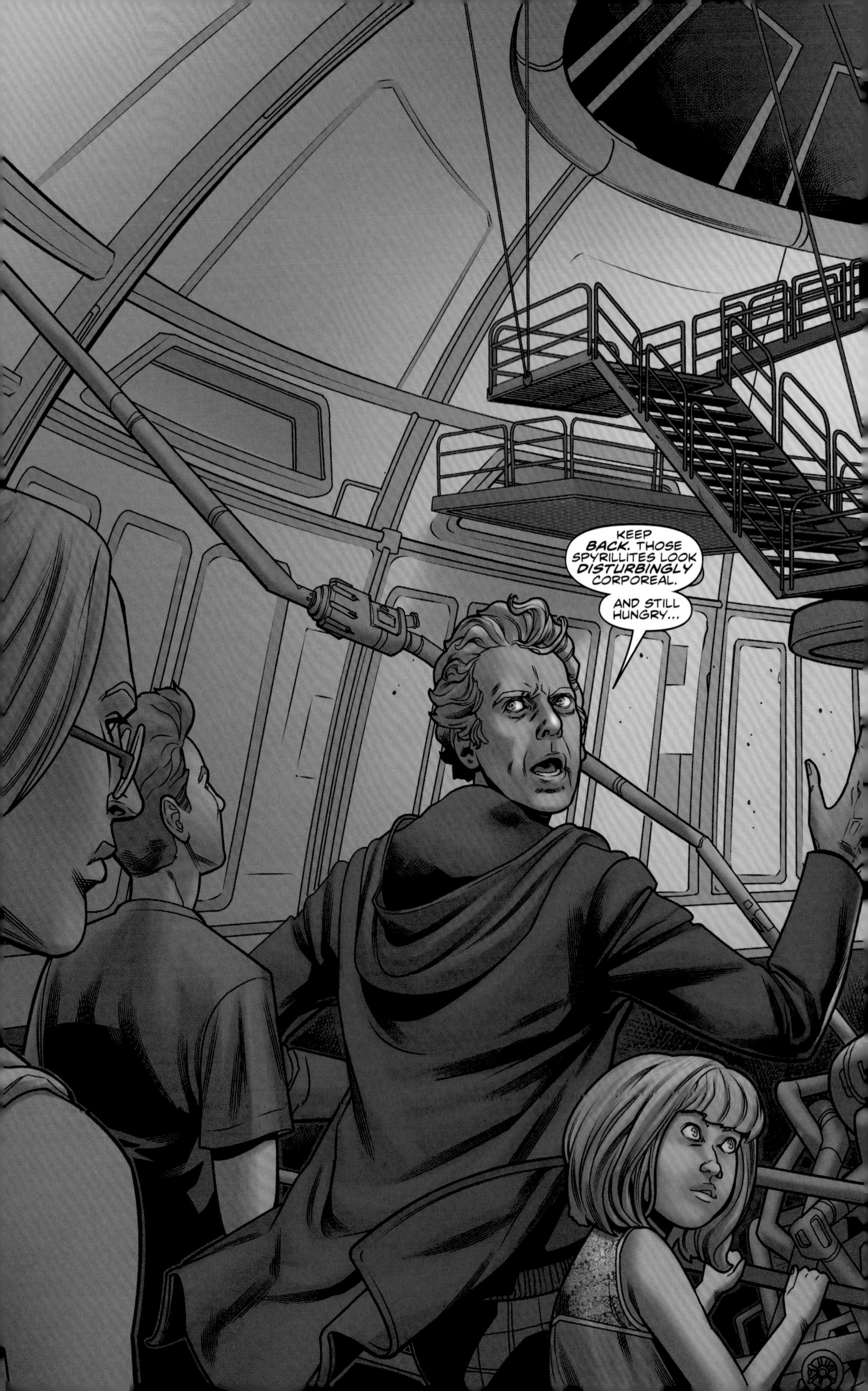
KEEP BACK. THOSE SPYRILLITES LOOK DISTURBINGLY CORPOREAL.
AND STILL HUNGRY...

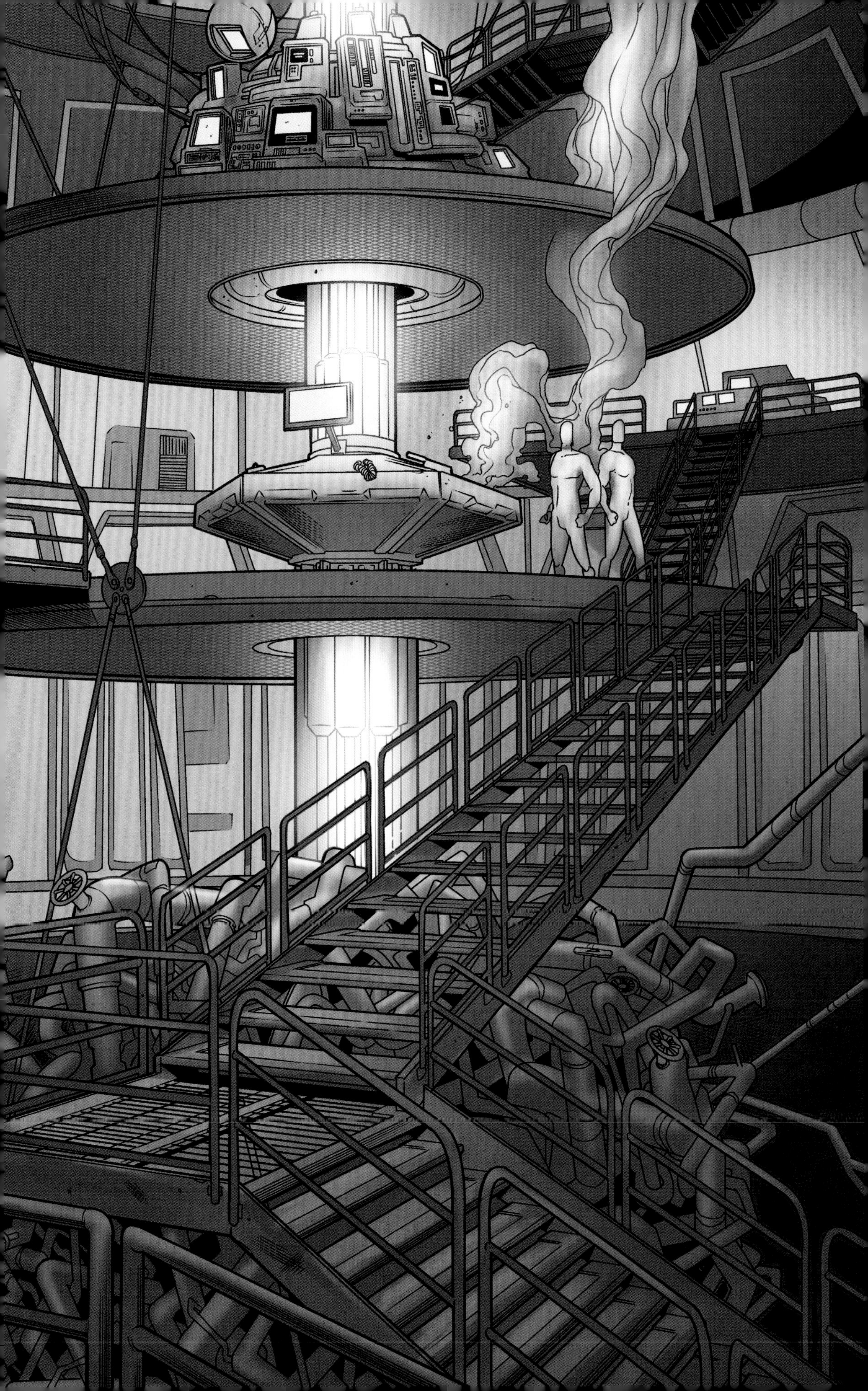

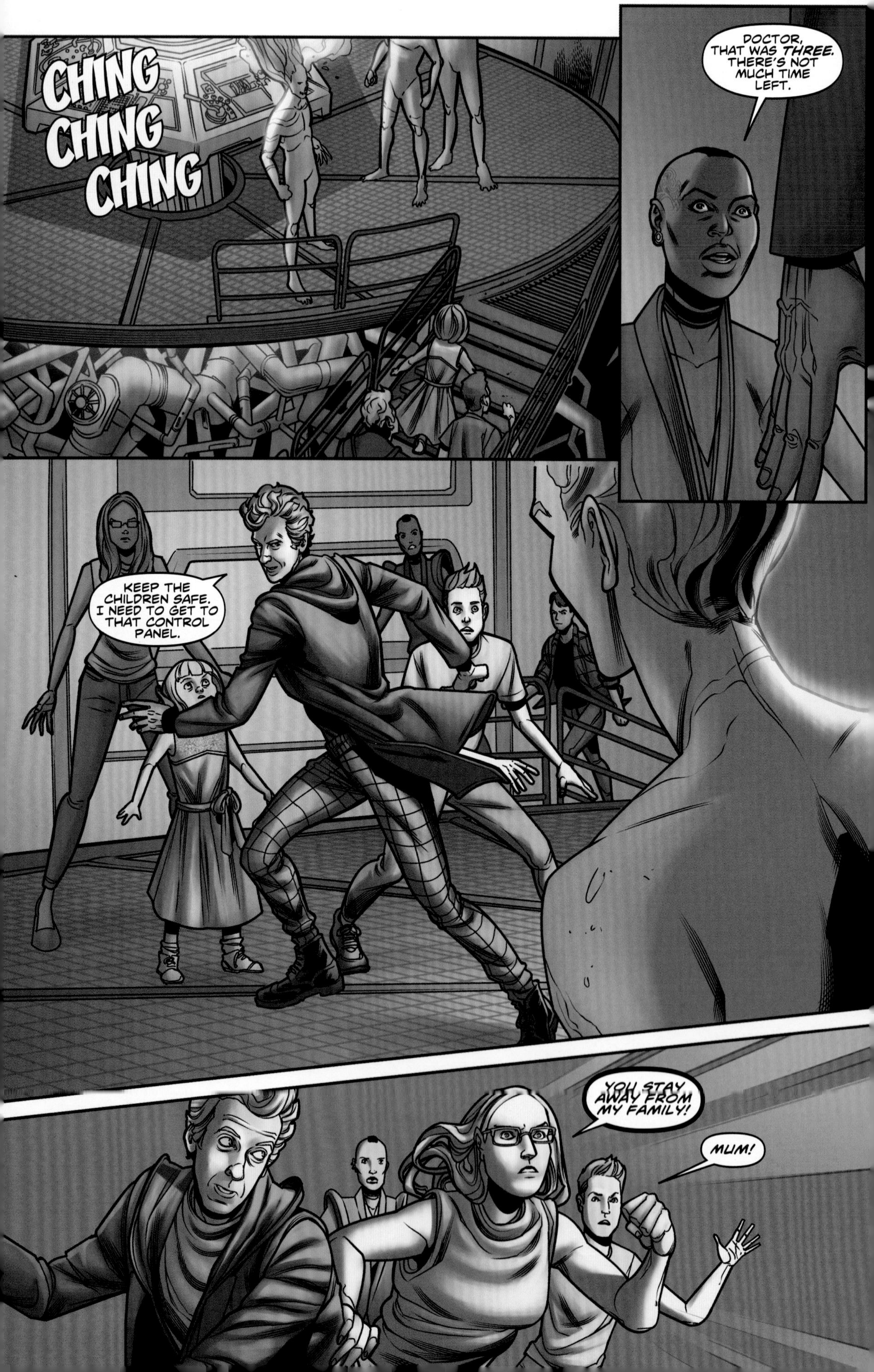
CHING CHING CHING
DOCTOR, THAT WAS THREE. THERE'S NOT MUCH TIME LEFT.
KEEP THE CHILDREN SAFE. I NEED TO GET TO THAT CONTROL PANEL.
YOU STAY AWAY FROM MY FAMILY!
MUM!

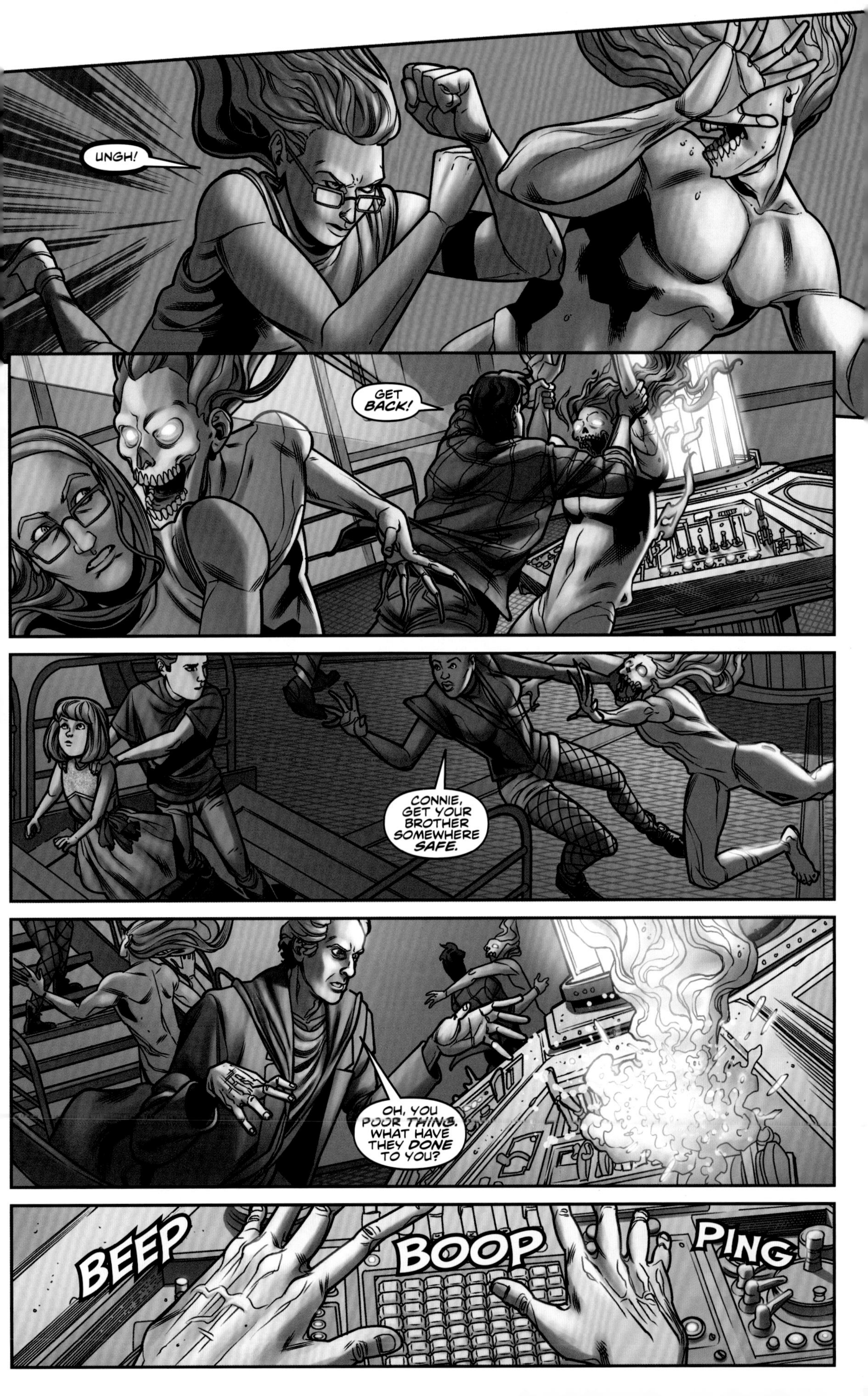
UNGH!
GET BACK!
CONNIE, GET YOUR BROTHER SOMEWHERE SAFE.
OH, YOU POOR THING. WHAT HAVE THEY DONE TO YOU?
BEEP
BOOP
PING

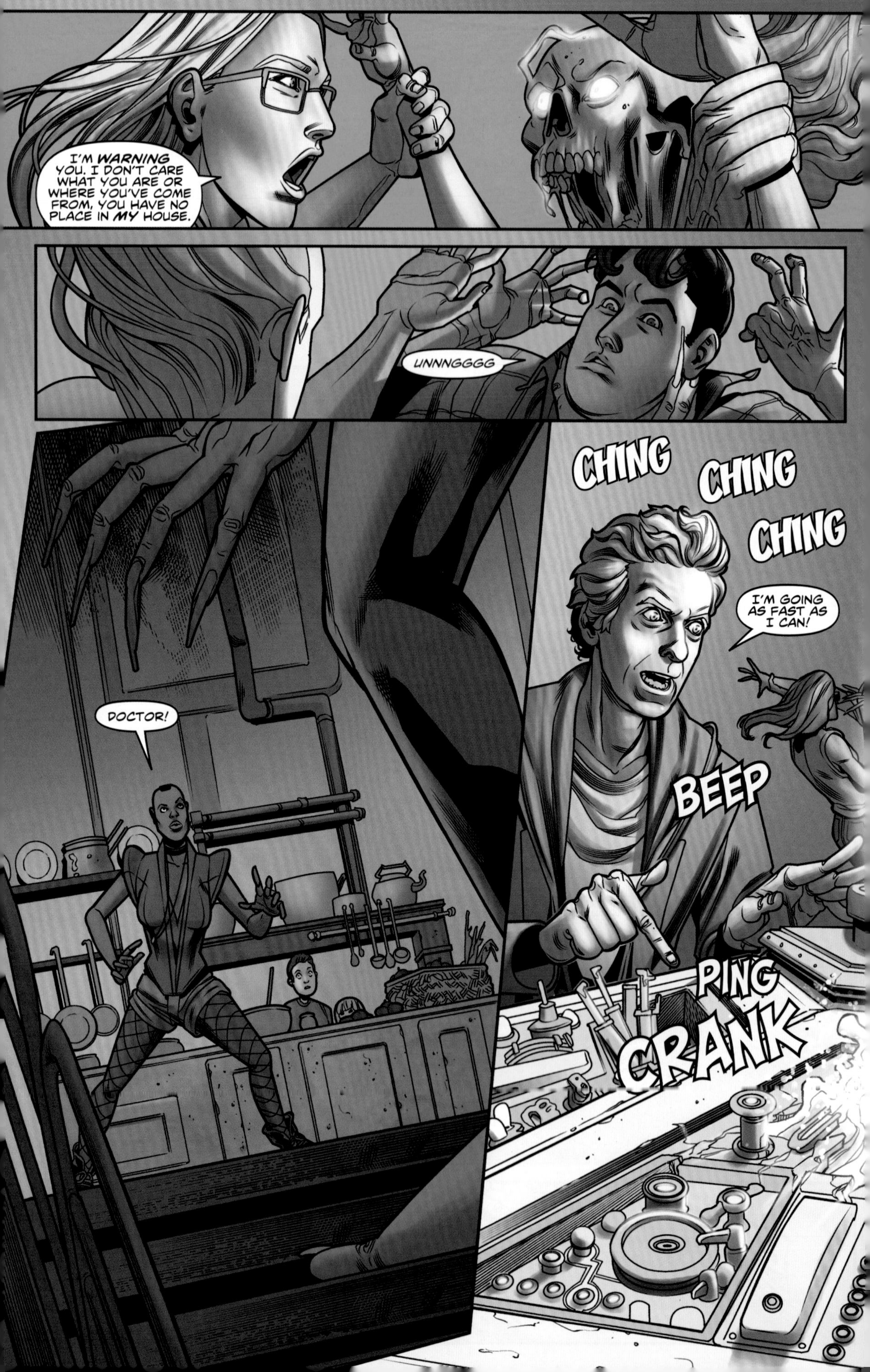
I'M WARNING YOU. I DON'T CARE WHAT YOU ARE OR WHERE YOU'VE COME FROM, YOU HAVE NO PLACE IN MY HOUSE.
UNNNGGGG
CHING
CHING
CHING
I'M GOING AS FAST AS I CAN!
DOCTOR!
BEEP
PING
CRANK

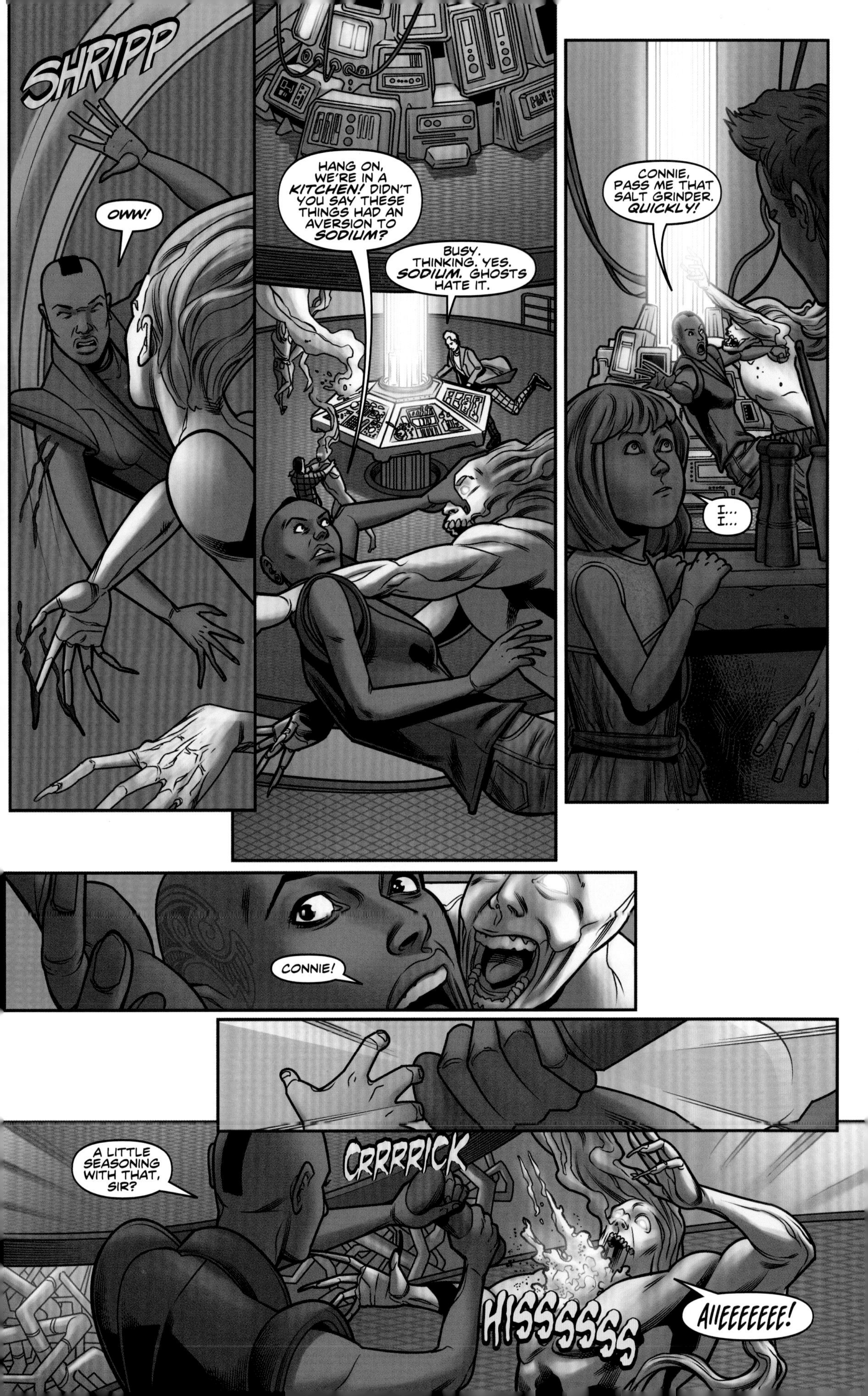

SHRIPP
OWW!
HANG ON, WE'RE IN A KITCHEN! DIDN'T YOU SAY THESE THINGS HAD AN AVERSION TO SODIUM?
BUSY. THINKING. YES. SODIUM. GHOSTS HATE IT.
CONNIE, PASS ME THAT SALT GRINDER. QUICKLY!
I... I...
CONNIE!
A LITTLE SEASONING WITH THAT, SIR?
CRRRRICK
HISSSSSS
AIIEEEEEEE!

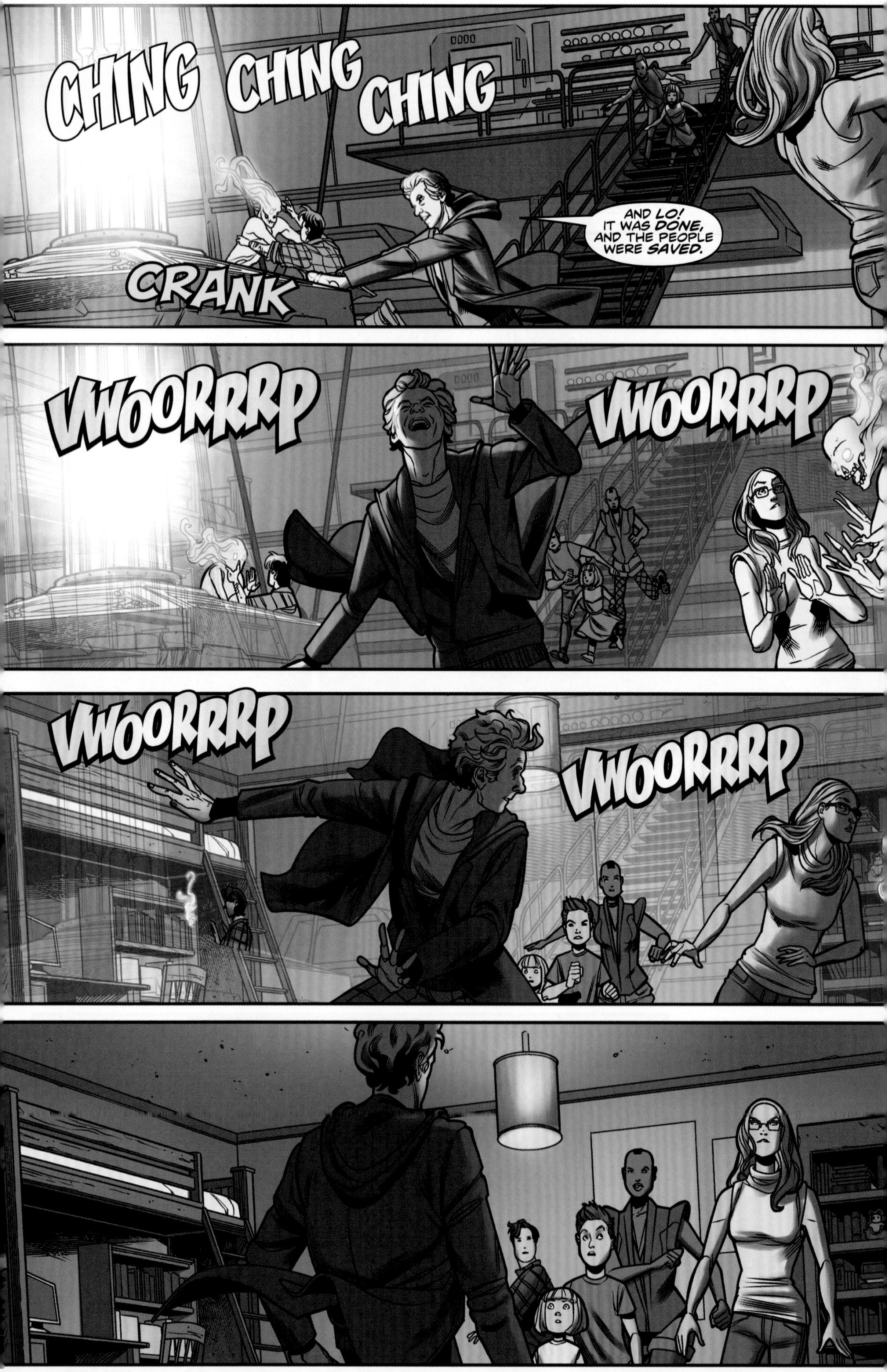
CHING CHING CHING
CRANK
AND LO! IT WAS DONE, AND THE PEOPLE WERE SAVED.
VWOORRRP
VWOORRRP
VWOORRRP
VWOORRRP

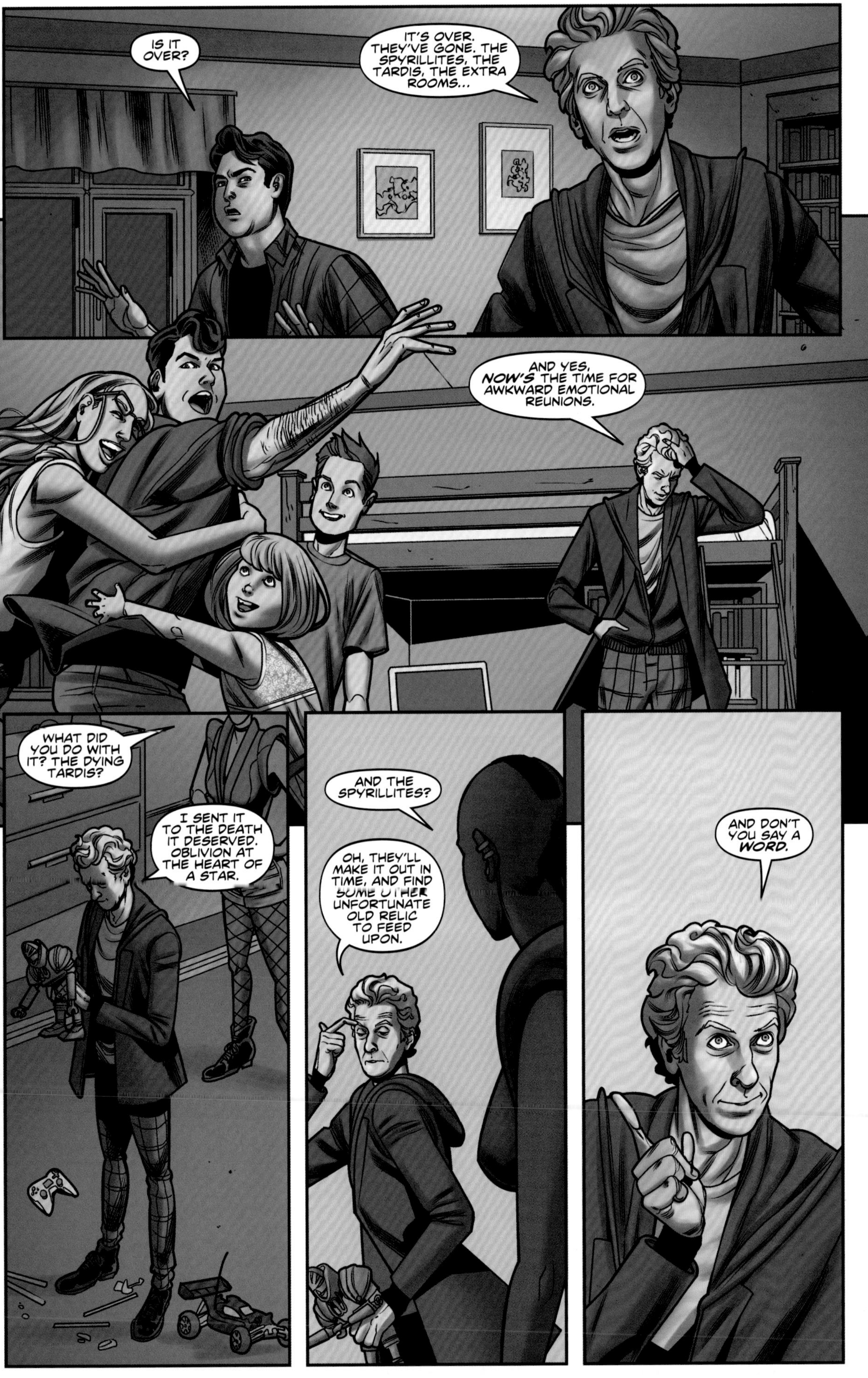
IS IT OVER?
IT'S OVER. THEY'VE GONE. THE SPYRILLITES, THE TARDIS, THE EXTRA ROOMS...
AND YES, NOW'S THE TIME FOR AWKWARD EMOTIONAL REUNIONS.
WHAT DID YOU DO WITH IT? THE DYING TARDIS?
I SENT IT TO THE DEATH IT DESERVED. OBLIVION AT THE HEART OF A STAR.
AND THE SPYRILLITES?
OH, THEY'LL MAKE IT OUT IN TIME, AND FIND SOME OTHER UNFORTUNATE OLD RELIC TO FEED UPON.
AND DON'T YOU SAY A WORD.

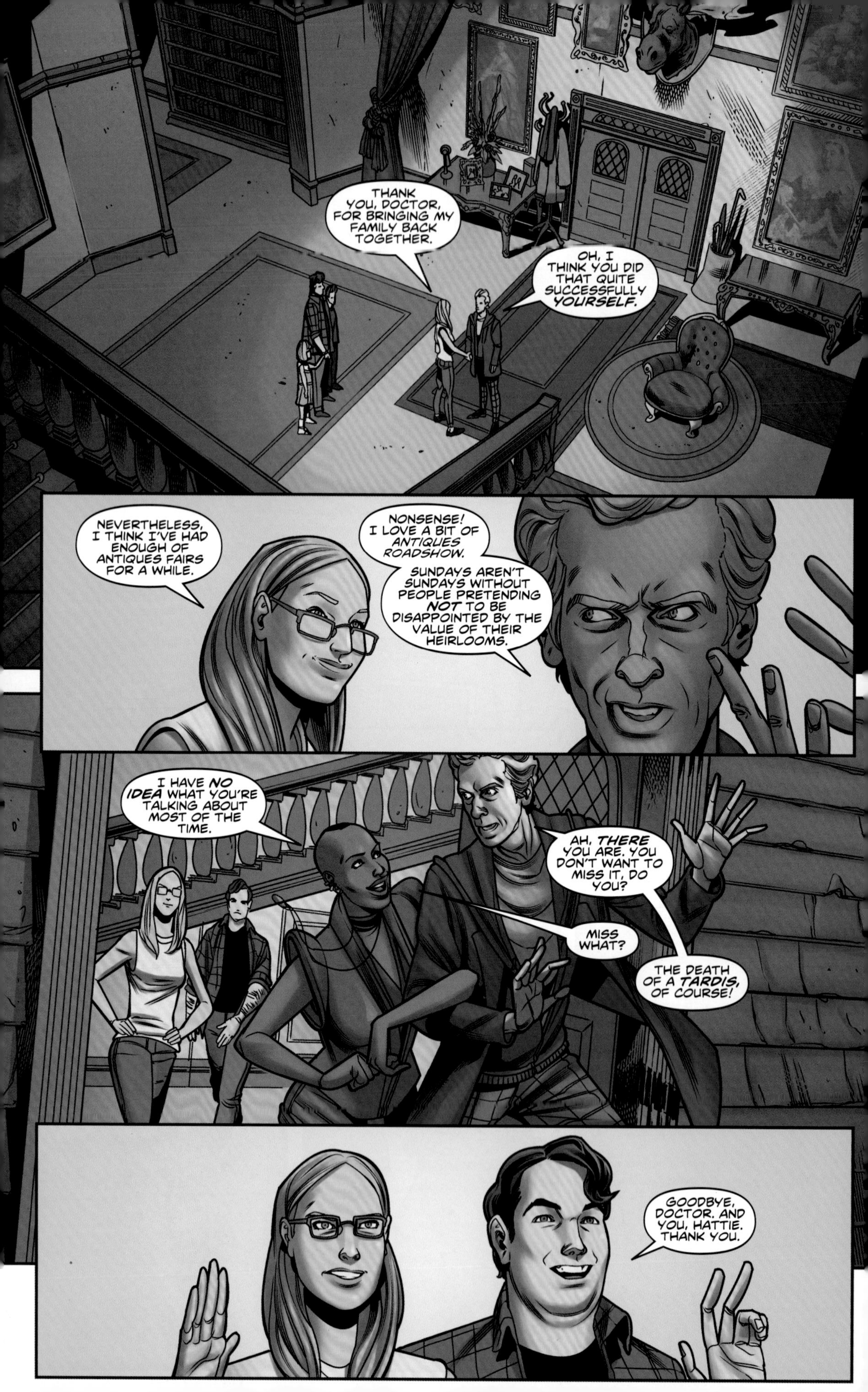
THANK YOU, DOCTOR, FOR BRINGING MY FAMILY BACK TOGETHER.
OH, I THINK YOU DID THAT QUITE SUCCESSFULLY YOURSELF.
NEVERTHELESS, I THINK I'VE HAD ENOUGH OF ANTIQUES FAIRS FOR A WHILE.
NONSENSE! I LOVE A BIT OF ANTIQUES ROADSHOW.
SUNDAYS AREN'T SUNDAYS WITHOUT PEOPLE PRETENDING NOT TO BE DISAPPOINTED BY THE VALUE OF THEIR HEIRLOOMS.
I HAVE NO IDEA WHAT YOU'RE TALKING ABOUT MOST OF THE TIME.
AH, THERE YOU ARE. YOU DON'T WANT TO MISS IT, DO YOU?
MISS WHAT?
THE DEATH OF A TARDIS, OF COURSE!
GOODBYE, DOCTOR. AND YOU, HATTIE. THANK YOU.

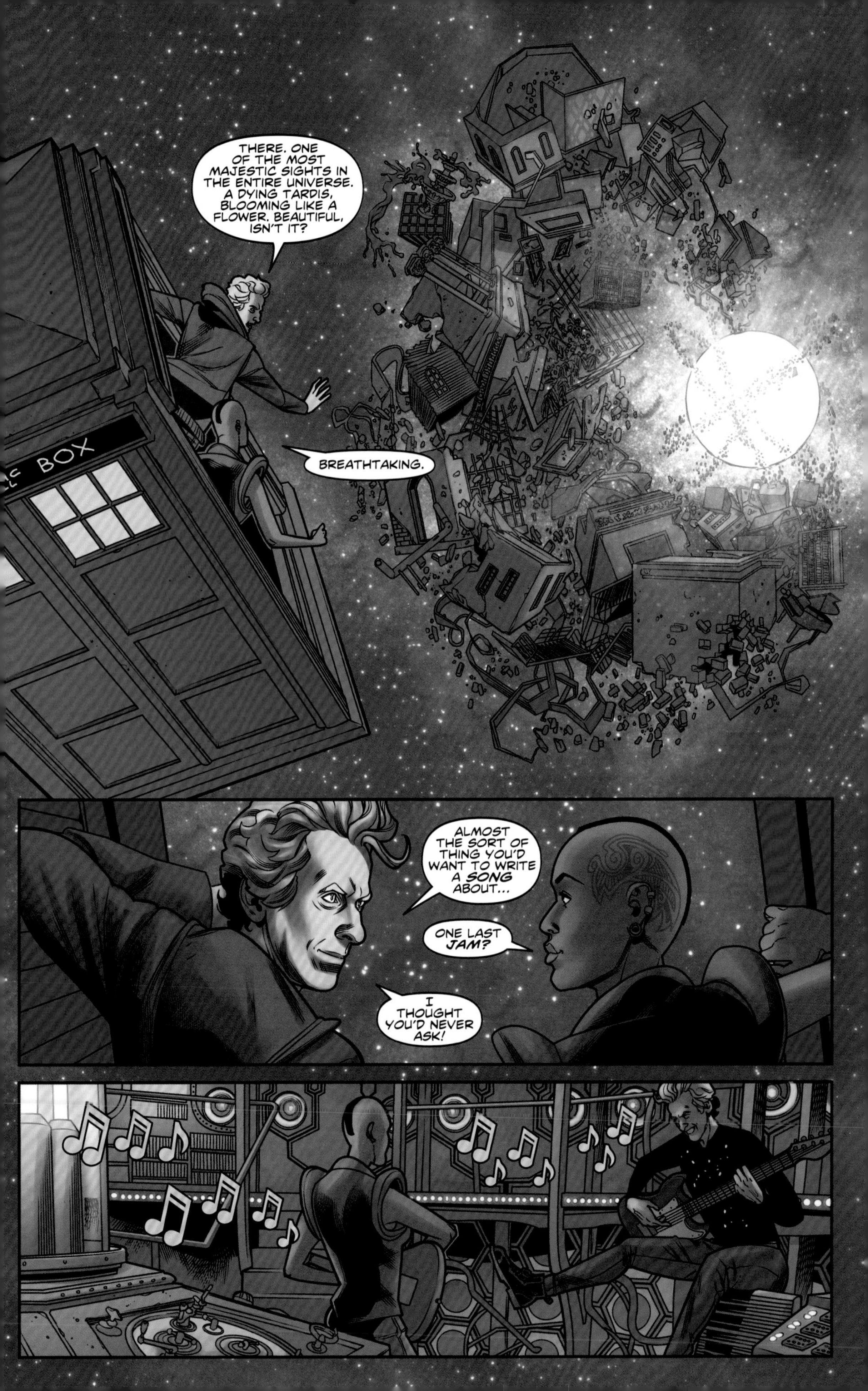
THERE. ONE OF THE MOST MAJESTIC SIGHTS IN THE ENTIRE UNIVERSE. A DYING TARDIS, BLOOMING LIKE A FLOWER. BEAUTIFUL, ISN'T IT?
BREATHTAKING.
ALMOST THE SORT OF THING YOU'D WANT TO WRITE A SONG ABOUT...
ONE LAST JAM?
I THOUGHT YOU'D NEVER ASK!

COVER GALLERY

A

BBC THE TWELFTH DOCTOR ADVENTURES YEAR TWO
DOCTOR WHO
DOCTOR WHO
GEORGE MANN
MARIANO LACLAUSTRA
CARLOS CABRERA
06 | JUN'16 $3.99
COVER A STEVE PUGH

BBC THE TWELFTH DOCTOR ADVENTURES YEAR TWO
DOCTOR WHO
DOCTOR WHO
FREE
PUBLIC
PULL TO OPEN

B

C

BBC THE TWELFTH DOCTOR ADVENTURES YEAR TWO
DOCTOR WHO
DOCTOR WHO
GEORGE MANN
MARIANO LACLAUSTRA
CARLOS CABRERA

D

BBC THE TWELFTH DOCTOR ADVENTURES YEAR TWO
DOCTOR WHO
DOCTOR WHO
GEORGE MANN
MARIANO LACLAUSTRA
CARLOS CABRERA
HACK

E

BBC THE TWELFTH DOCTOR ADVENTURES YEAR TWO
DOCTOR WHO
DOCTOR WHO
GEORGE MANN
MARIANO LACLAUSTRA
CARLOS CABRERA

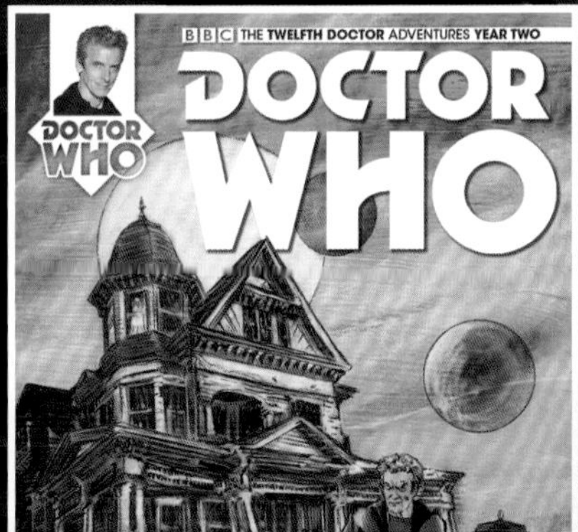

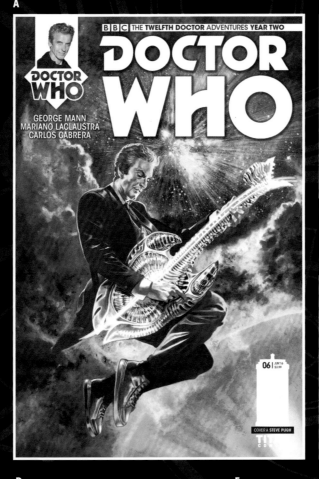

ISSUE #6

A. STEVE PUGH
B. PHOTO – WILL BROOKS
C. TODD NAUCK
D. ROBERT HACK
E. SIMON MYERS

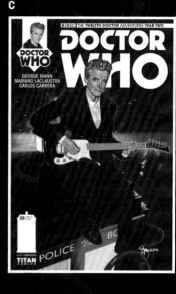

ISSUE #8

A. MARK WHEATLEY
B. PHOTO – WILL BROOKS
C. SIMON MYERS

ISSUE #9

A. MARIANO LACLAUSTRA
B. PHOTO – WILL BROOKS
C. WARREN PLEECE

DOCTOR WHO
THE NINTH DOCTOR

COVER GALLERY

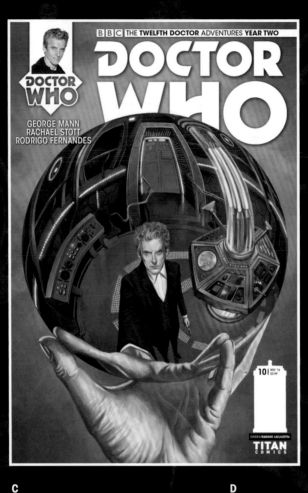

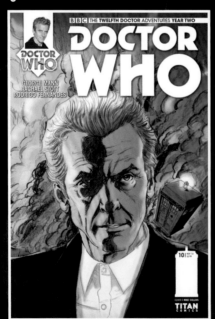

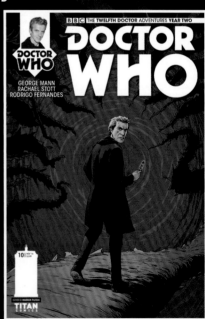

ISSUE #10

A. MARIANO LACLAUSTRA
B. PHOTO – WILL BROOKS
C. MIKE COLLINS
D. WARREN PLEECE

DOCTOR WHO

RACHAEL STOTT

TAKE A LOOK BEHIND THE SCENES AT SOME OF ARTIST
RACHAEL STOTT'S MOST INCREDIBLE INKED PAGES
FROM ISSUES #2.9 AND #2.10!

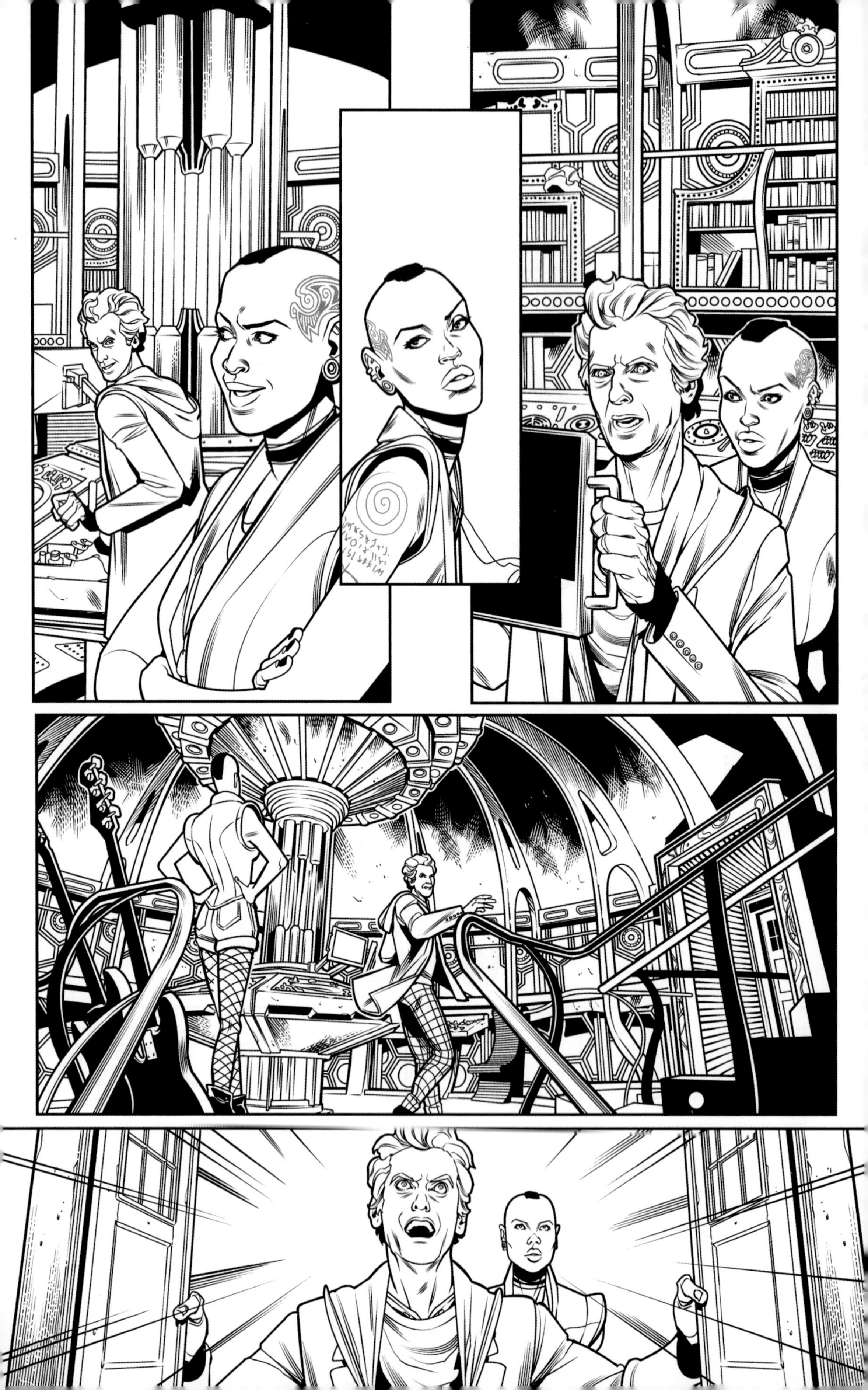

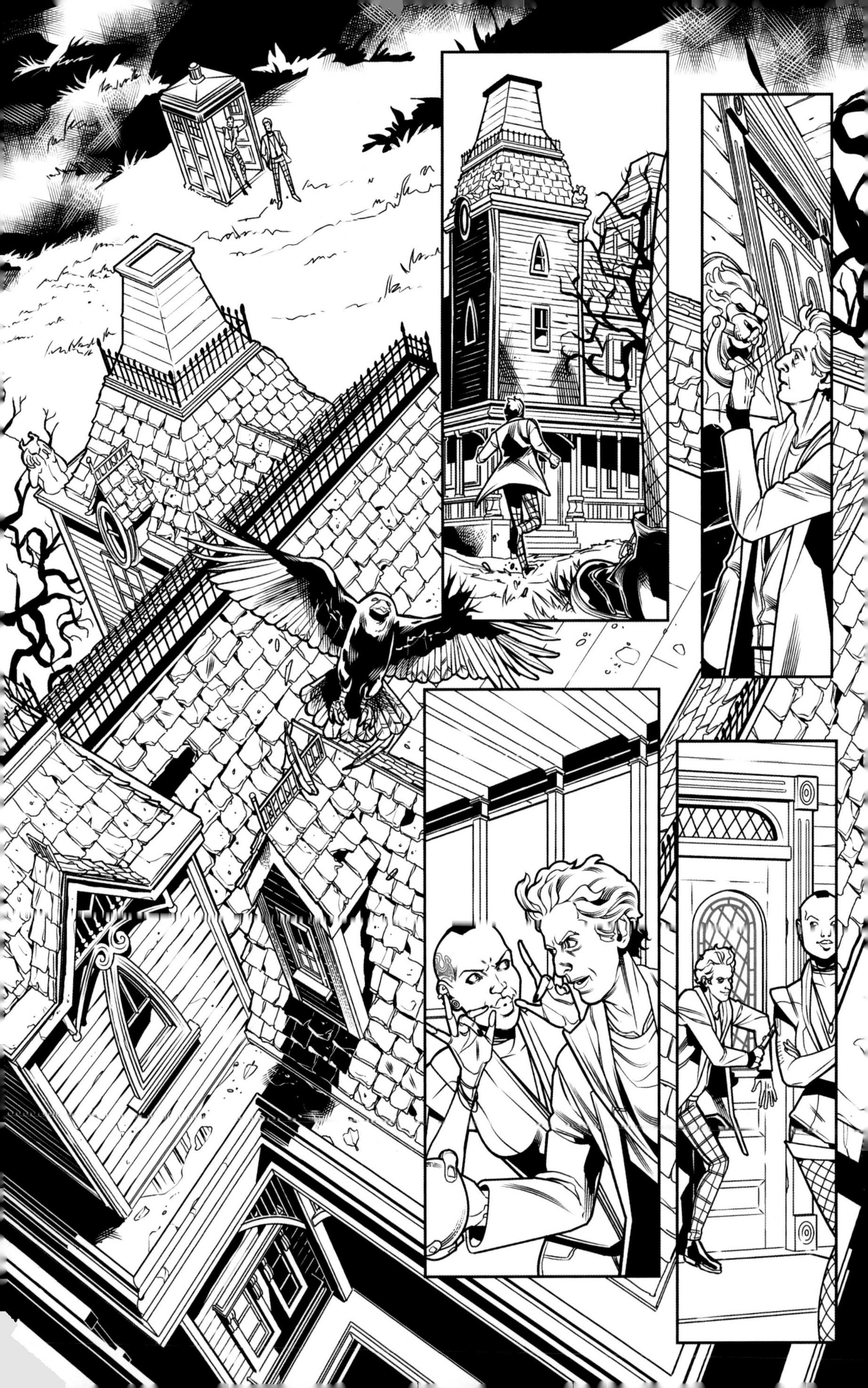

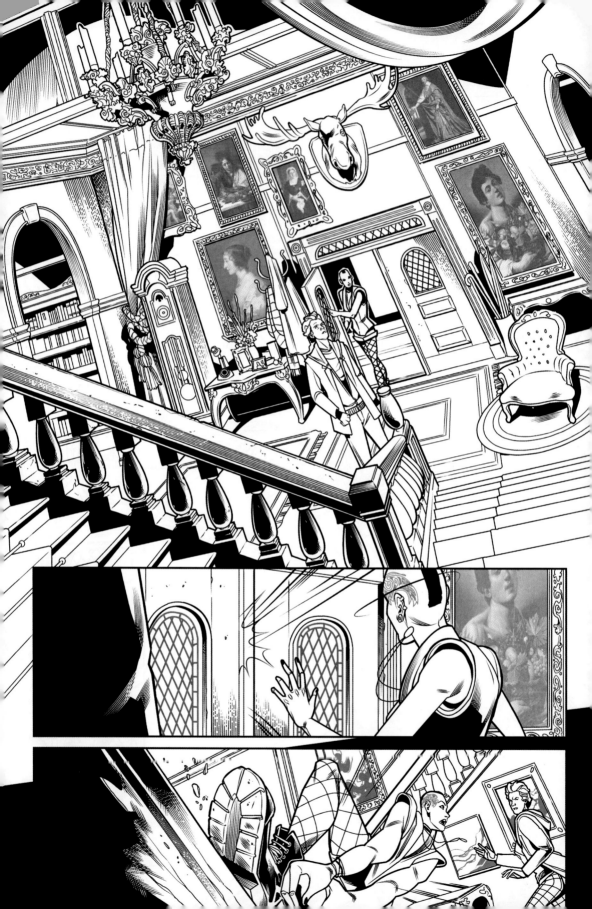

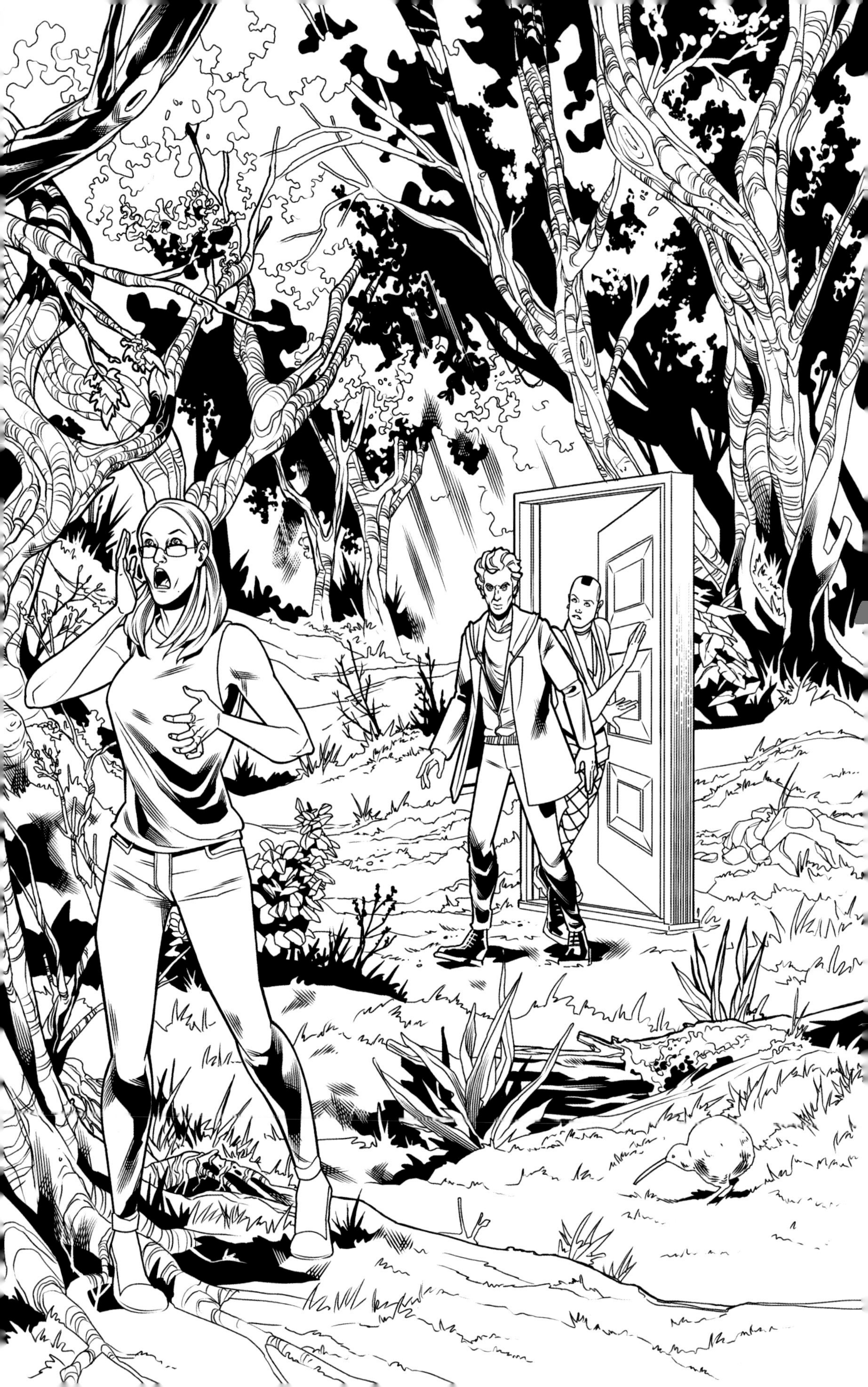

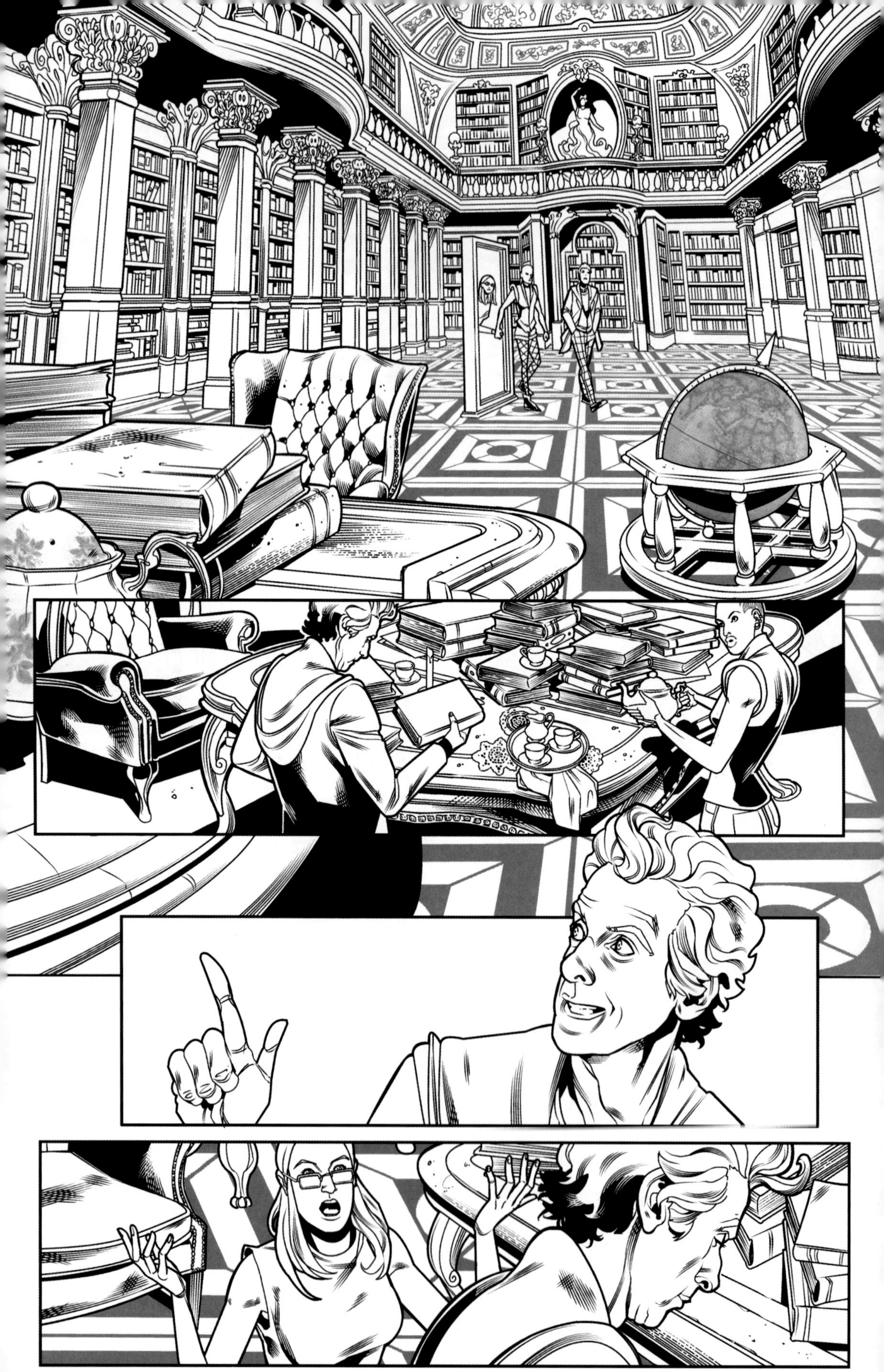

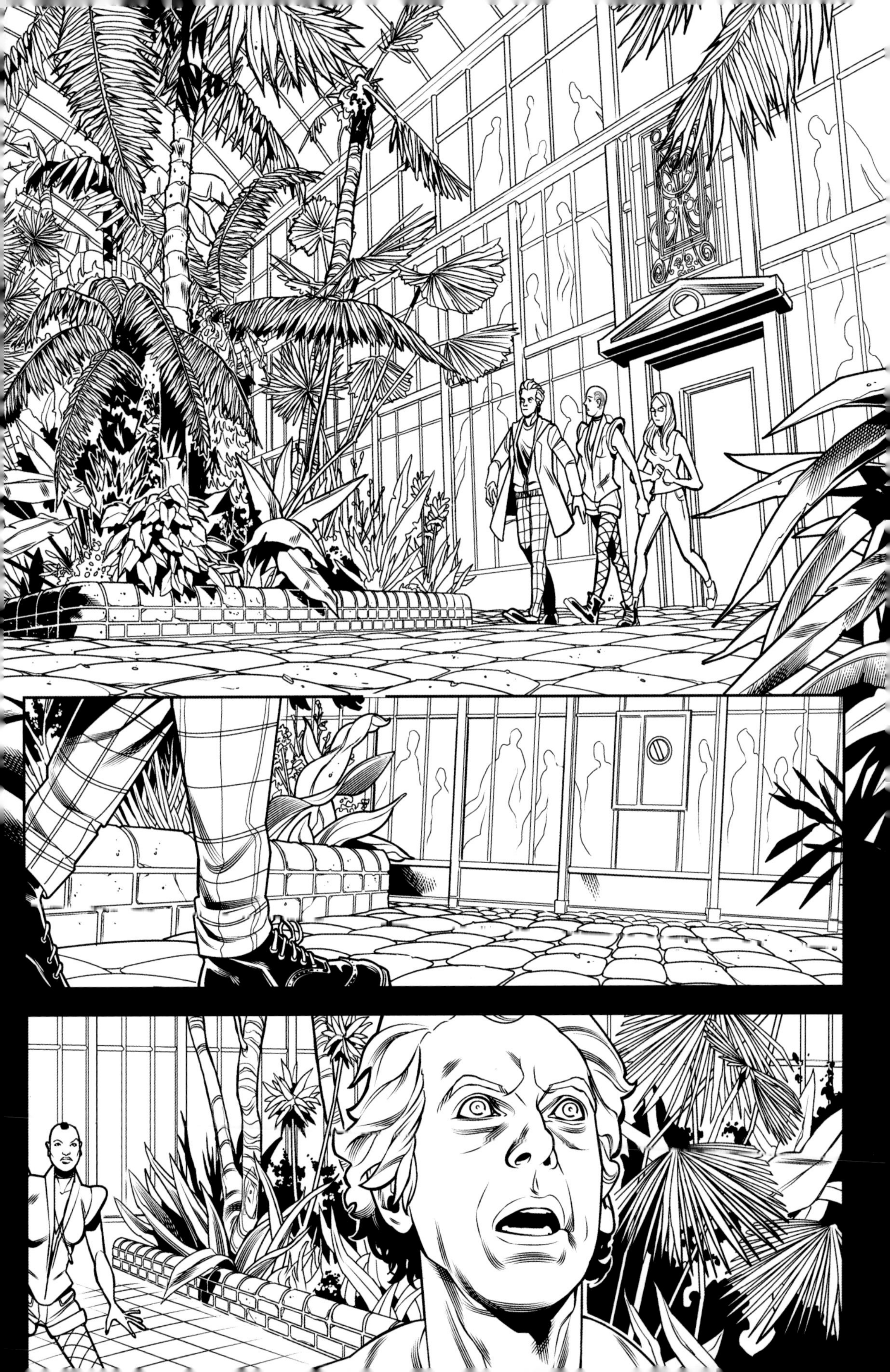

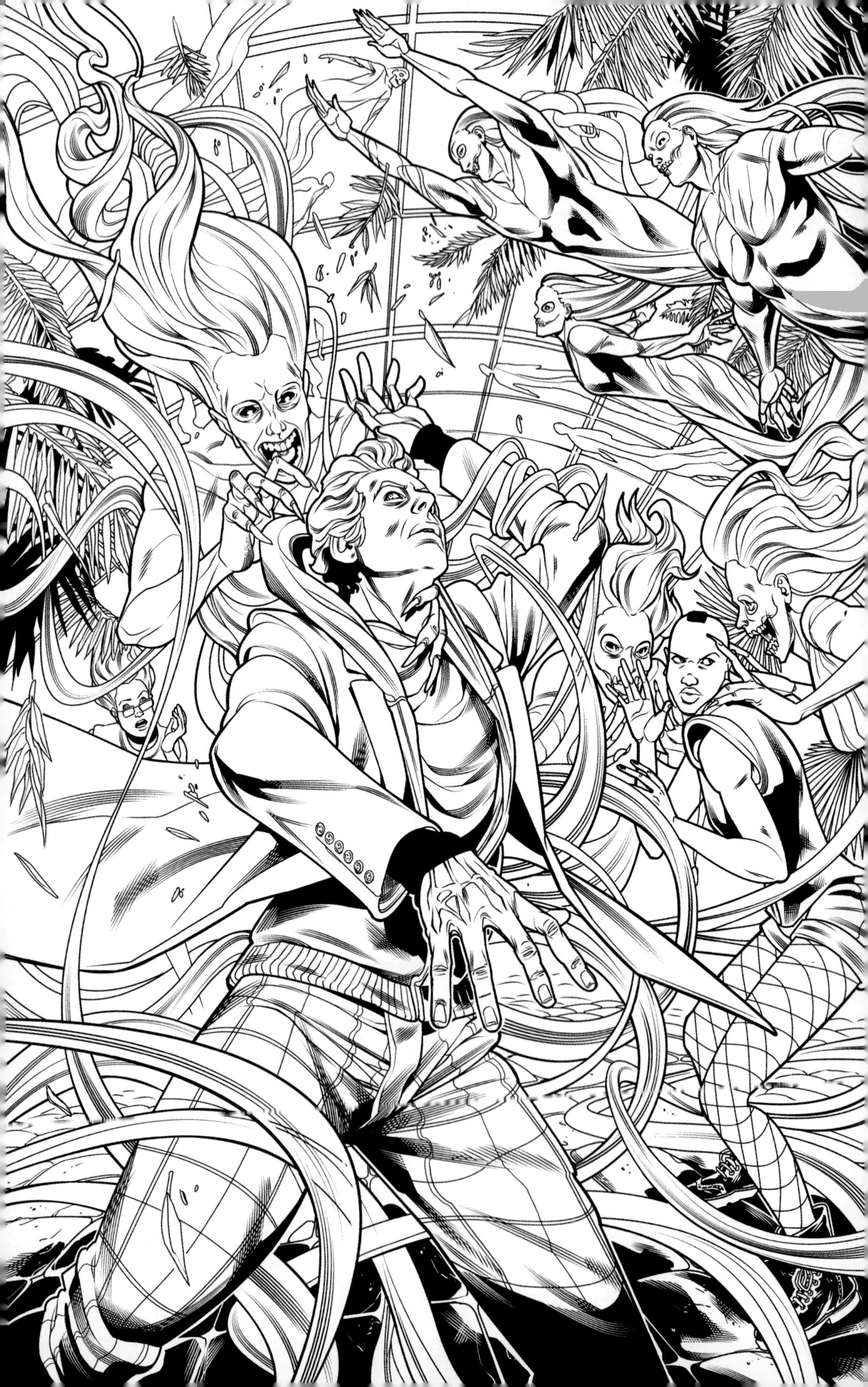

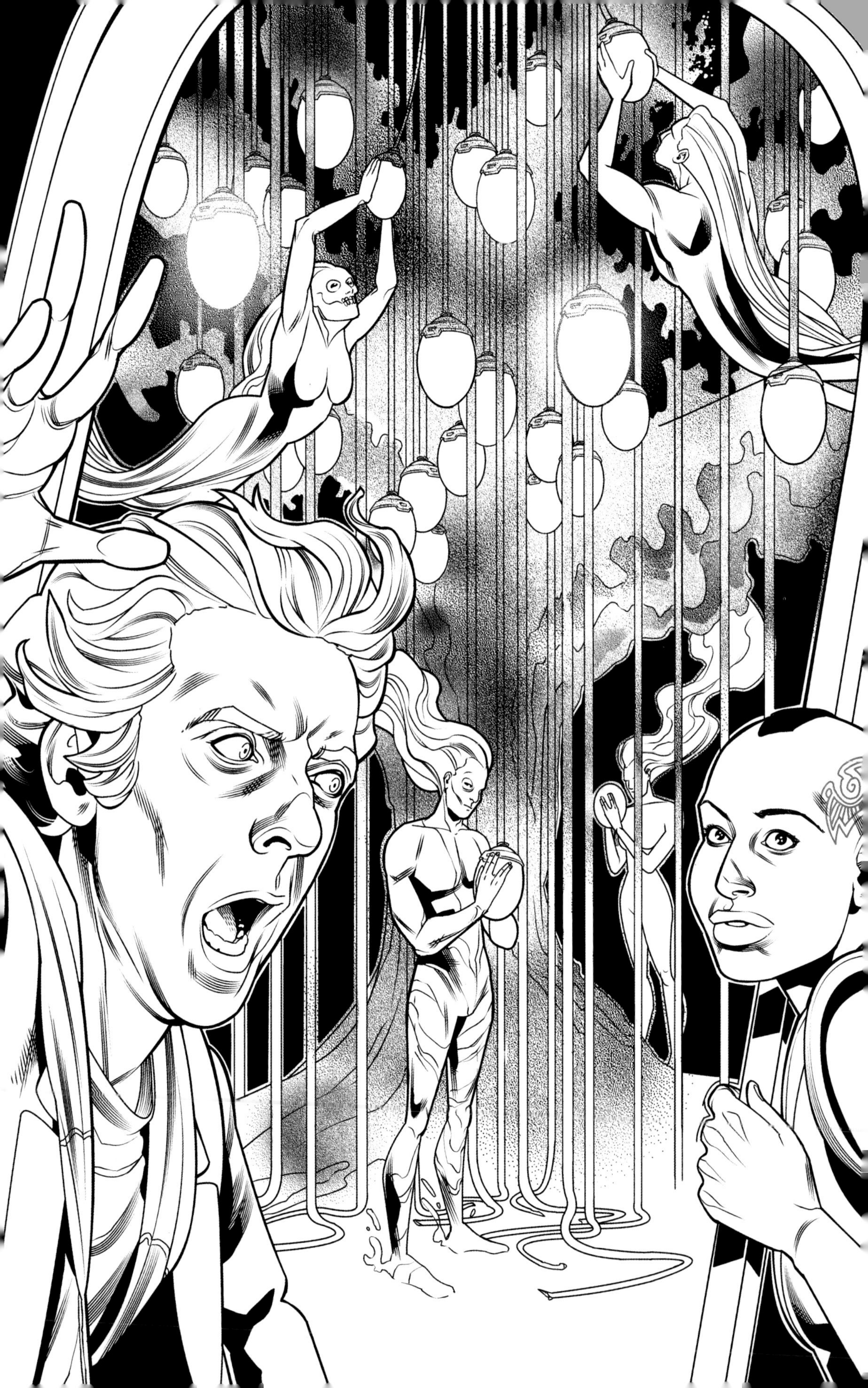

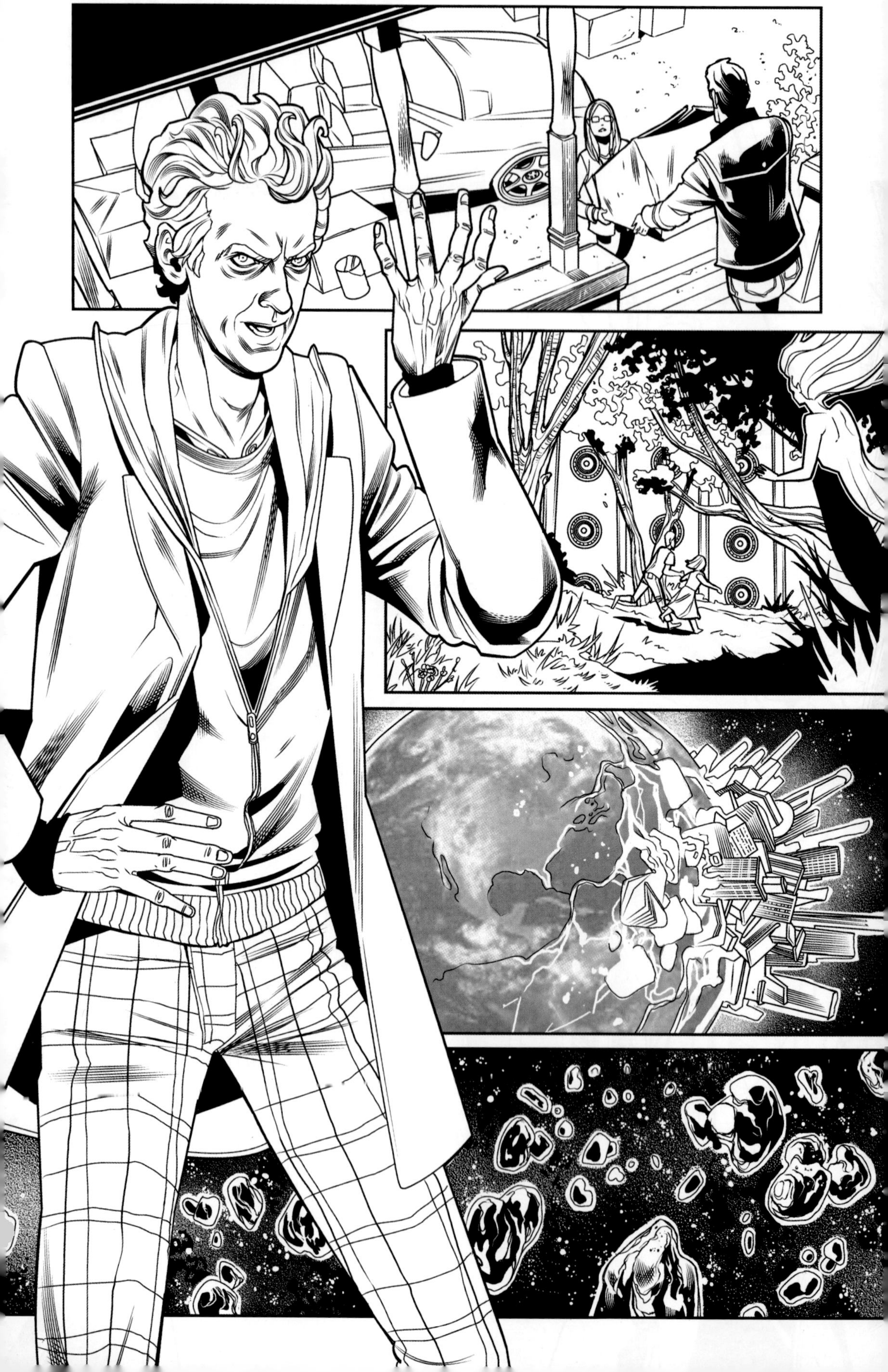

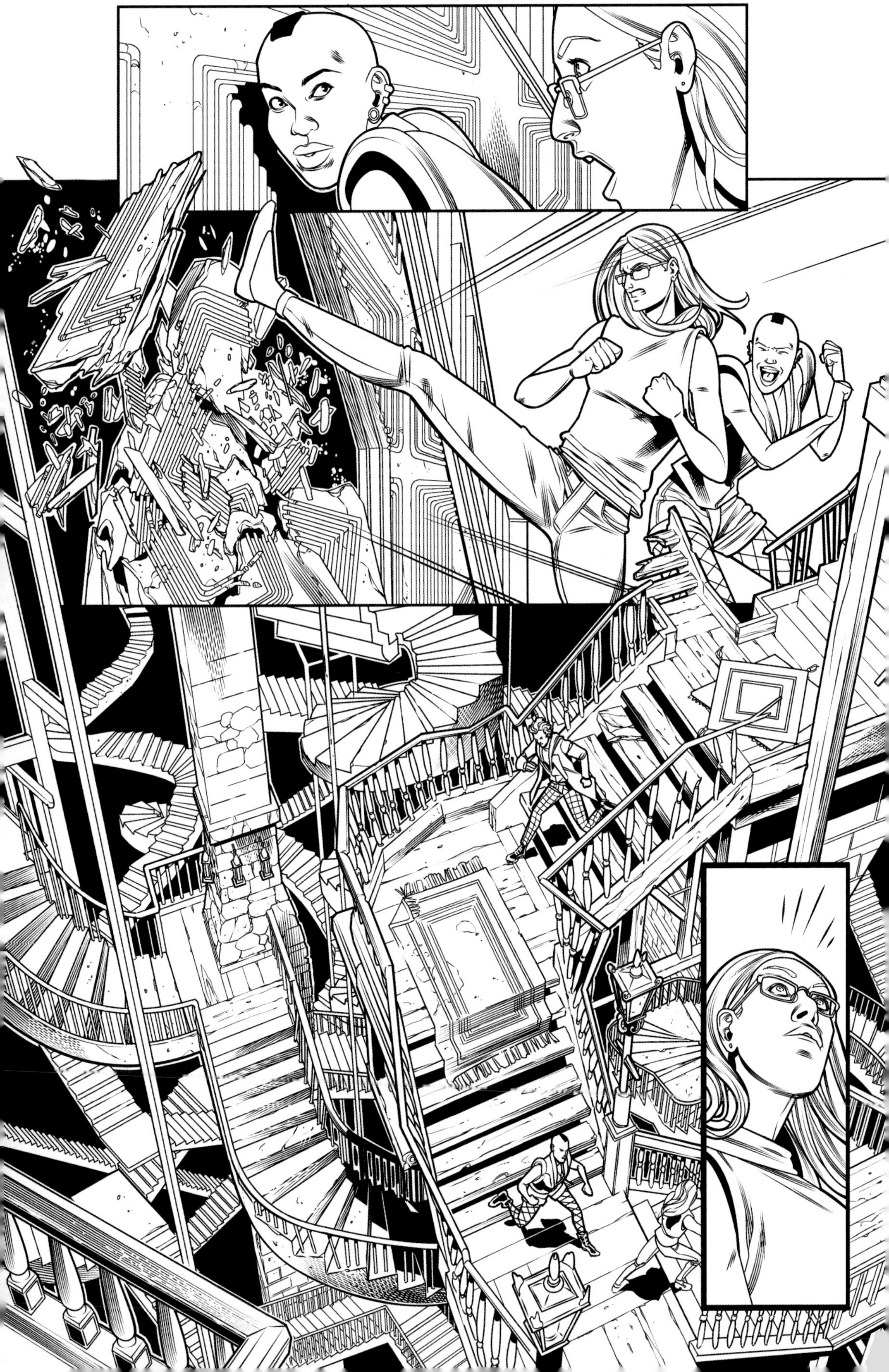

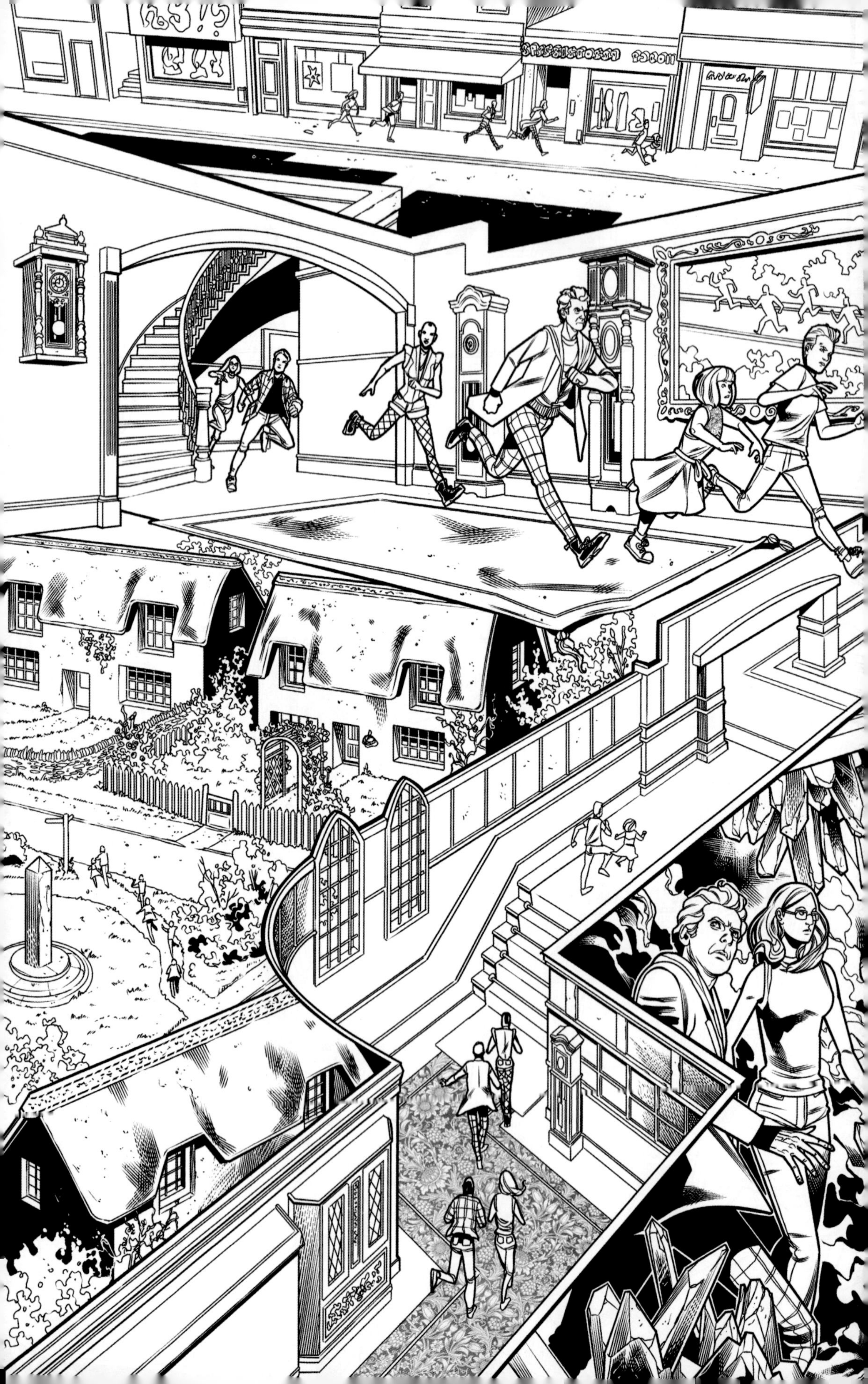

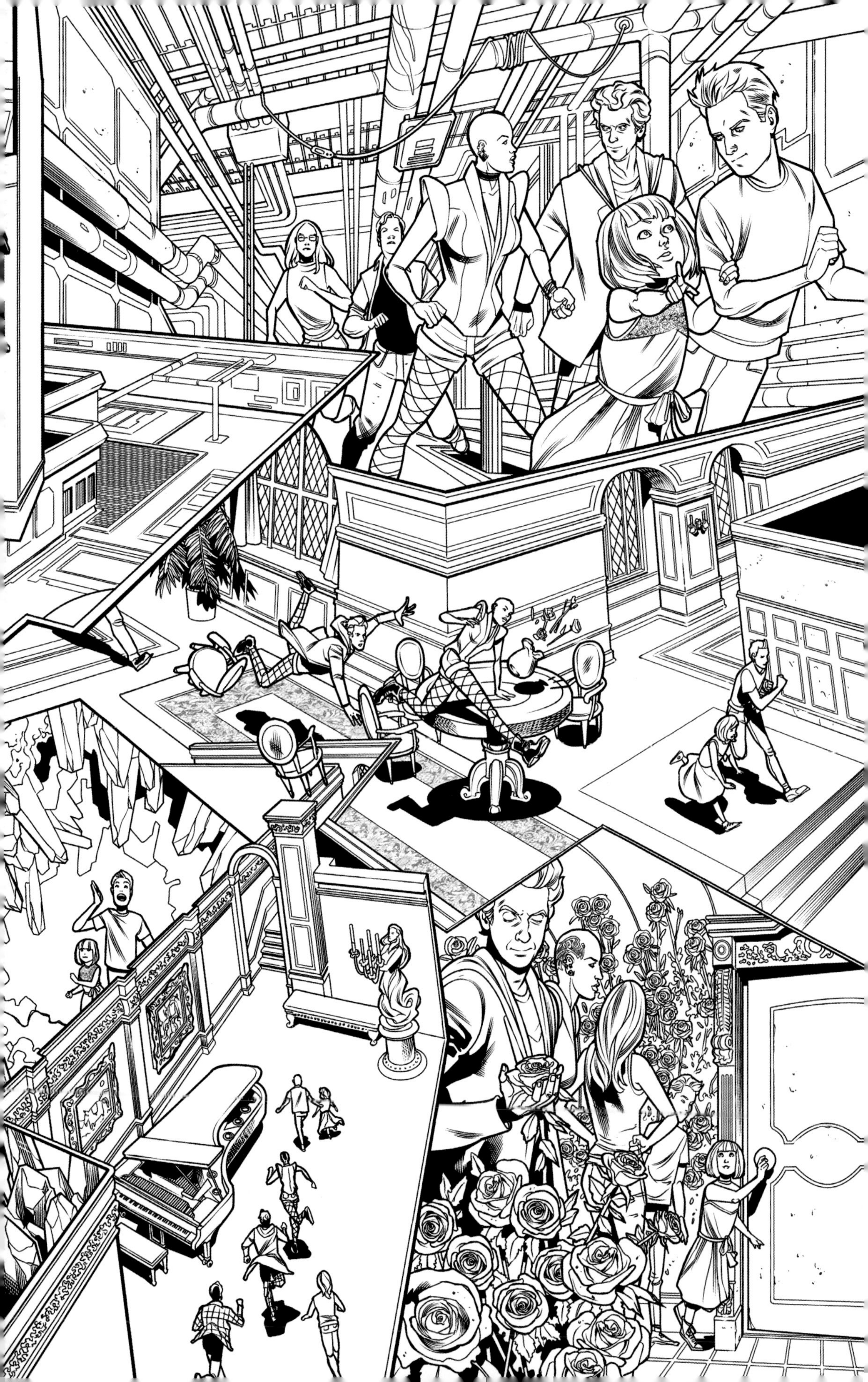

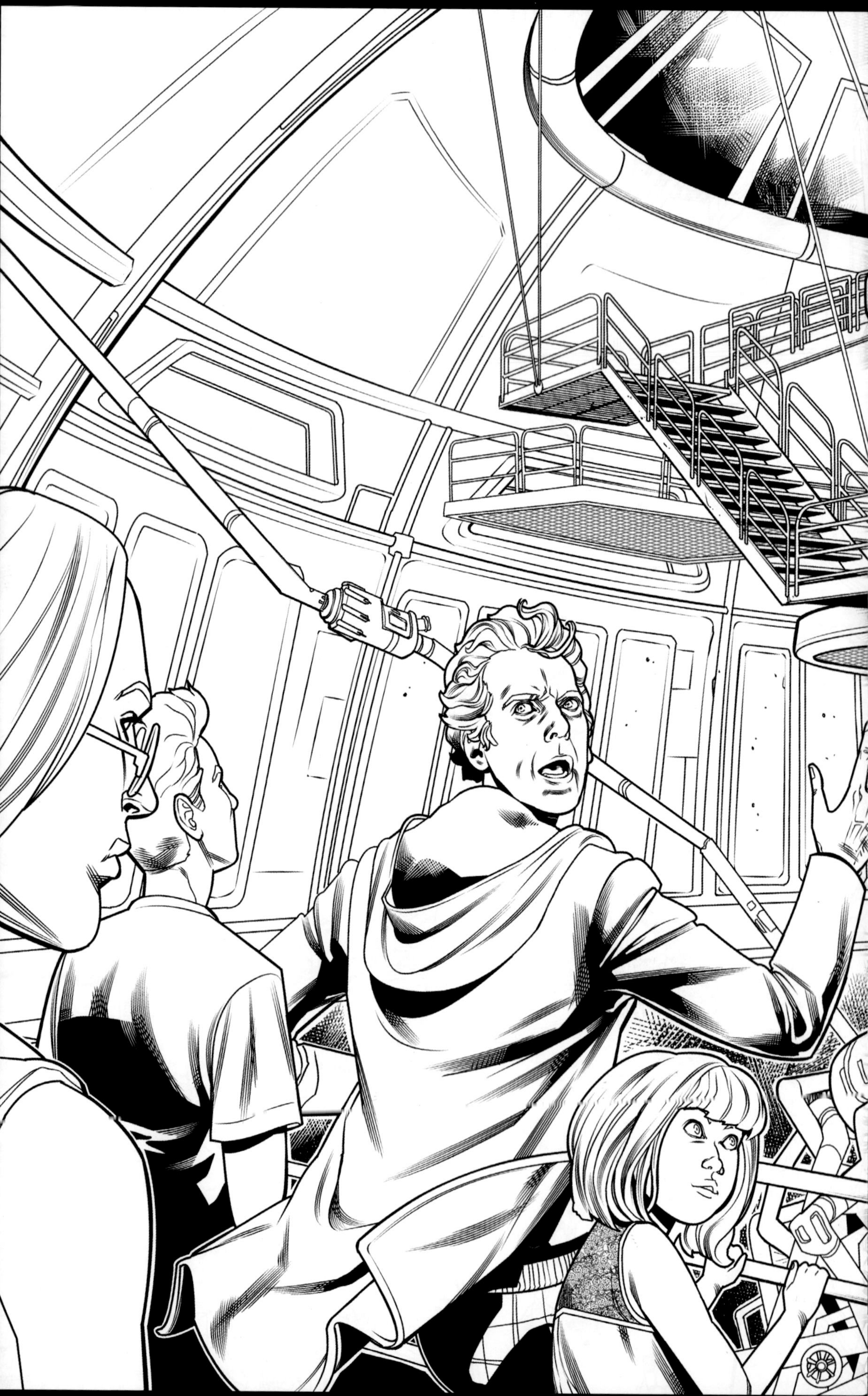

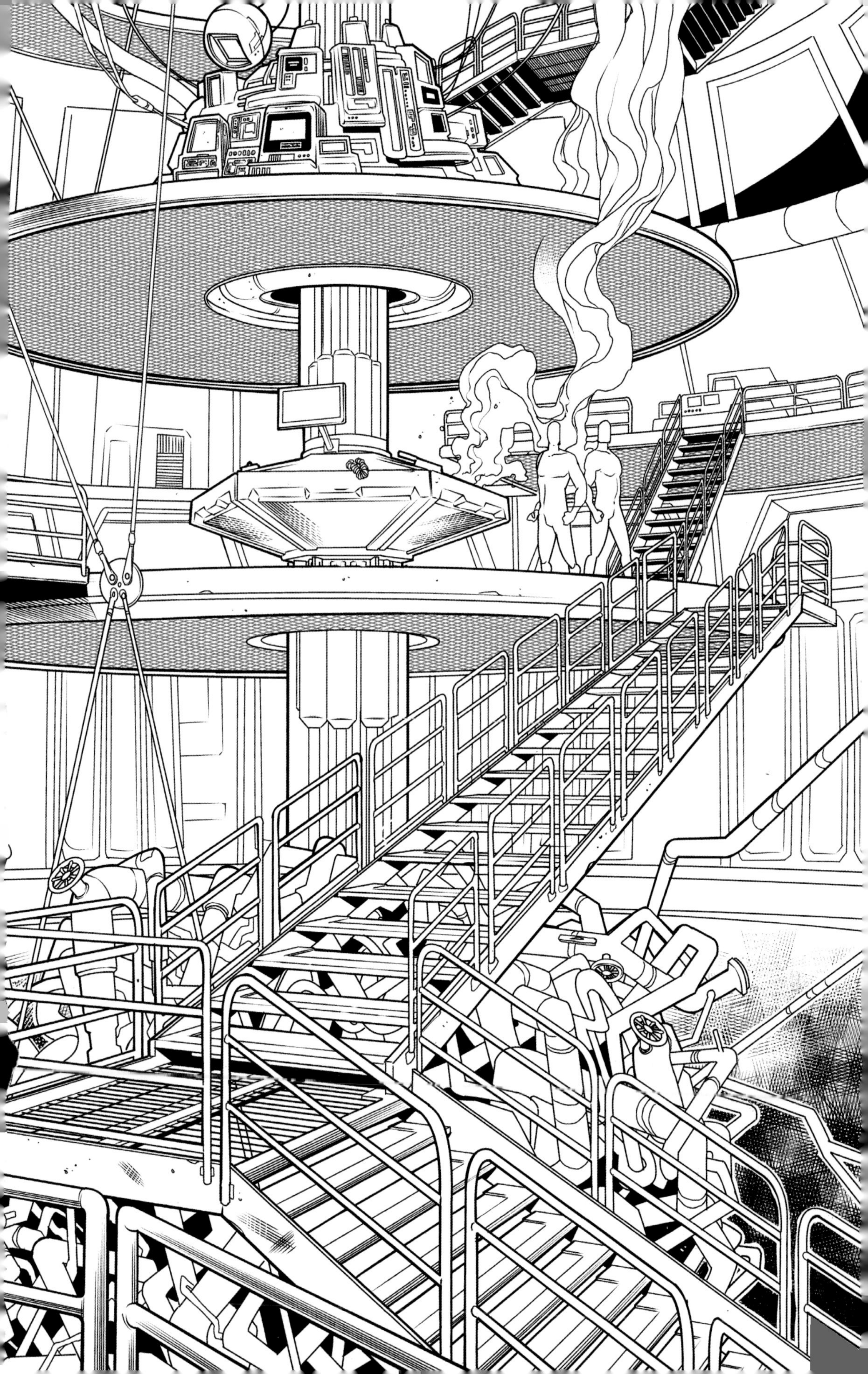

FOLLOW YOUR FAVORITE INCARNATIONS ACROSS THESE FANTASTIC COLLECTIONS!

DOCTOR WHO: THE TWELFTH DOCTOR VOL. 1: TERRORFORMER

ISBN: 9781782761778
ON SALE NOW - $19.99 /
$22.95 CAN / £10.99
(UK EDITION ISBN: 9781782763864)

DOCTOR WHO: THE TWELFTH DOCTOR VOL. 2: FRACTURES

ISBN: 9781782763017
ON SALE NOW - $19.99 /
$25.99 CAN / £10.99
(UK EDITION ISBN: 9781782766599)

DOCTOR WHO: THE TWELFTH DOCTOR VOL. 3: HYPERION

ISBN: 9781782767473
ON SALE NOW- $19.99 /
$25.99 CAN / £10.99
(UK EDITION ISBN: 9781782767444)

DOCTOR WHO: THE TWELFTH DOCTOR VOL. 4: THE SCHOOL OF DEATH

ISBN: 9781785851087
COMING SOON - $19.99 /
$25.99 CAN / £10.99
(UK EDITION ISBN: 9781785851070)

DOCTOR WHO: THE ELEVENTH DOCTOR VOL. 1: AFTER LIFE

ISBN: 9781782761747
ON SALE NOW - $19.99 /
$22.95 CAN / £10.99
(UK EDITION ISBN: 9781782763857)

DOCTOR WHO: THE ELEVENTH DOCTOR VOL. 2: SERVE YOU

ISBN: 9781782761754
ON SALE NOW - $19.99 /
$25.99 CAN / £10.99
(UK EDITION ISBN: 9781782766582)

DOCTOR WHO: THE ELEVENTH DOCTOR VOL. 3: CONVERSION

ISBN: 9781782763024
ON SALE NOW - $19.99 /
$25.99 CAN / £10.99
(UK EDITION ISBN: 9781782767435)

DOCTOR WHO: THE ELEVENTH DOCTOR VOL. 4: THE THEN AND THE NOW

ISBN: 9781782767466
ON SALE NOW - $19.99 /
$25.99 CAN / £10.99
(UK EDITION ISBN: 9781722767428)

For information on how to subscribe to our great Doctor Who titles,
or to purchase them digitally for your favorite device, visit:

WWW.TITAN-COMICS.COM

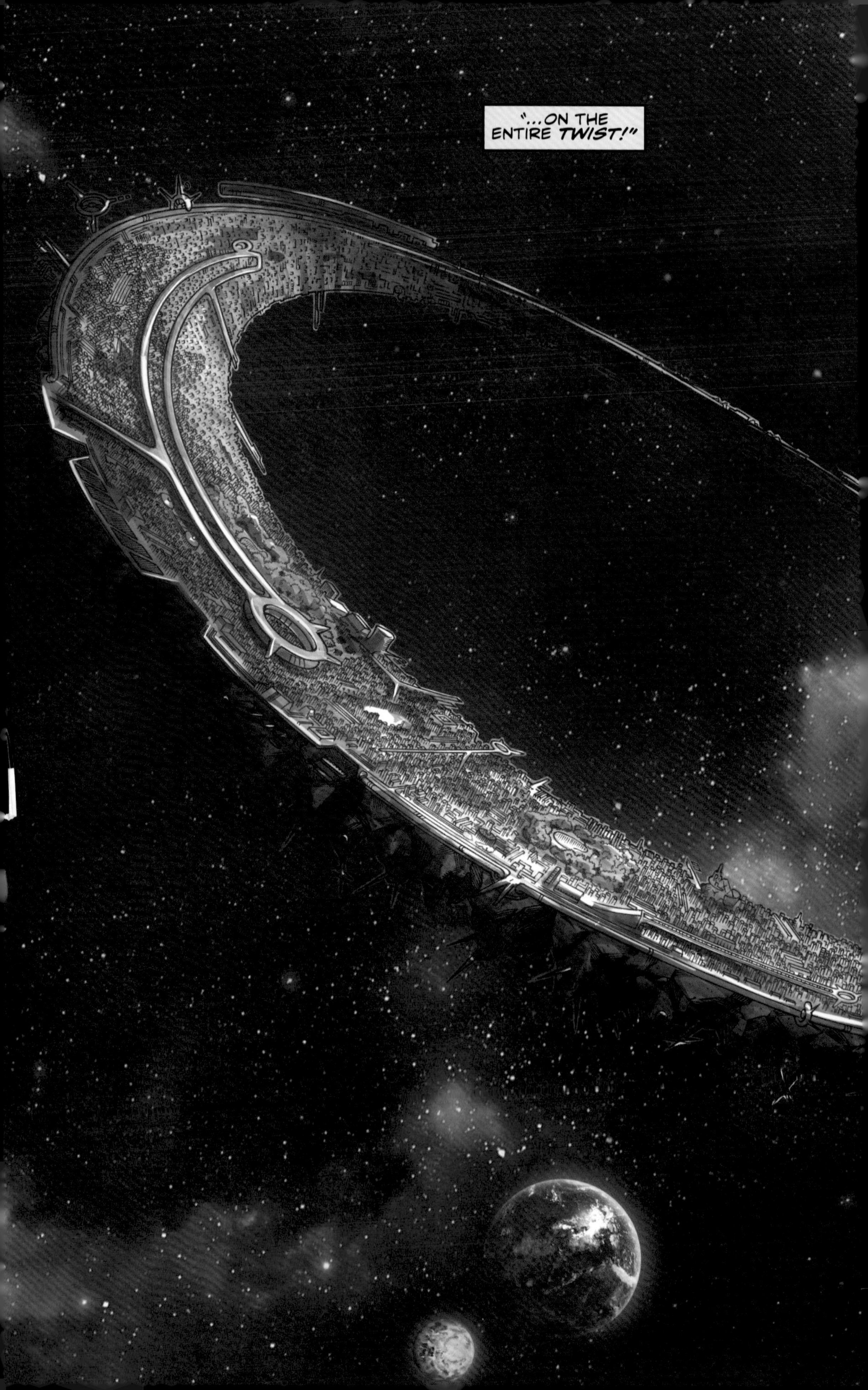
"...ON THE ENTIRE TWIST!"

COMPLETE YOUR COLLECTION!

DOCTOR WHO: THE TENTH DOCTOR VOL. 1: REVOLUTIONS OF TERROR

ISBN: 9781782761747
ON SALE NOW - $19.99 / $22.95 CAN / £10.99
(UK EDITION ISBN: 9781782763840)

DOCTOR WHO: THE TENTH DOCTOR VOL. 2: THE WEEPING ANGELS OF MONS

ISBN: 9781782761754
ON SALE NOW - $19.99 / $25.99 CAN / £10.99
(UK EDITION ISBN: 9781782766575)

DOCTOR WHO: THE TENTH DOCTOR VOL. 3: THE FOUNTAINS OF FOREVER

ISBN: 9781782763024
ON SALE NOW - $19.99 / $25.99 CAN / £10.99
(UK EDITION ISBN: 9781782767435)

DOCTOR WHO: THE TENTH DOCTOR VOL. 4: THE ENDLESS SONG

ISBN: 9781785854286
ON SALE NOW - $19.99 / $25.99 CAN / £10.99
(SC ISBN: 9781785853227)

DOCTOR WHO: THE NINTH DOCTOR VOL. 1: WEAPONS OF PAST DESTRUCTION

ISBN: 9781782763369
ON SALE NOW - $19.99 / $25.99 CAN / £10.99
(UK EDITION ISBN: 9781782761056)

DOCTOR WHO EVENT 2015 FOUR DOCTORS

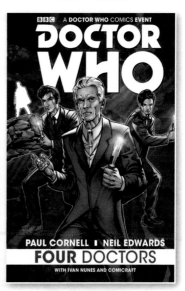

ISBN: 9781782765967
ON SALE NOW - $19.99 / $25.99 CAN / £10.99
(UK EDITION ISBN: 9781785851063)

AVAILABLE IN ALL GOOD COMIC STORES, BOOK STORES, AND DIGITAL PROVIDERS!

BIOGRAPHIES

George Mann is the author of *Dark Souls, The Affinity Bridge, The Osiris Ritual* and *Ghosts of Manhattan*, as well as numerous short stories, novellas and an original *Doctor Who* audiobook. He has edited a number of anthologies, including a retrospective collection of *Sexton Blake* stories, *Sexton Blake, Detective*. He lives near Grantham, UK, with his wife and children.

Mariano Laclaustra is a creator with a background in the Fine Arts. A freelance artist based in Argentina, he has worked with publishers across Europe and the United States, including for *Dark Horse Presents*. In between drawing and coloring comics, he teaches oil painting.

Rachael Stott is a talented illustrator and winner of the Best Newcomer Artist at the British Comic Awards 2015. She has worked on *Planet of the Apes, Star Trek, Doctor Who,* and *Ghostbusters International*.

Carlos Cabrera is an up and coming colorist with many diverse projects to his name, such as *Invincible Iron Man, Agents of Atlas* and *Doctor Who*.

Alexandre Siqueira is a fresh coloring talent who has worked on *Doctor Who*.

Rodrigo Fernandes is a colorist whose beautiful work can be seen on titles such as *Vikings, Independence Day* and *Doctor Who*.

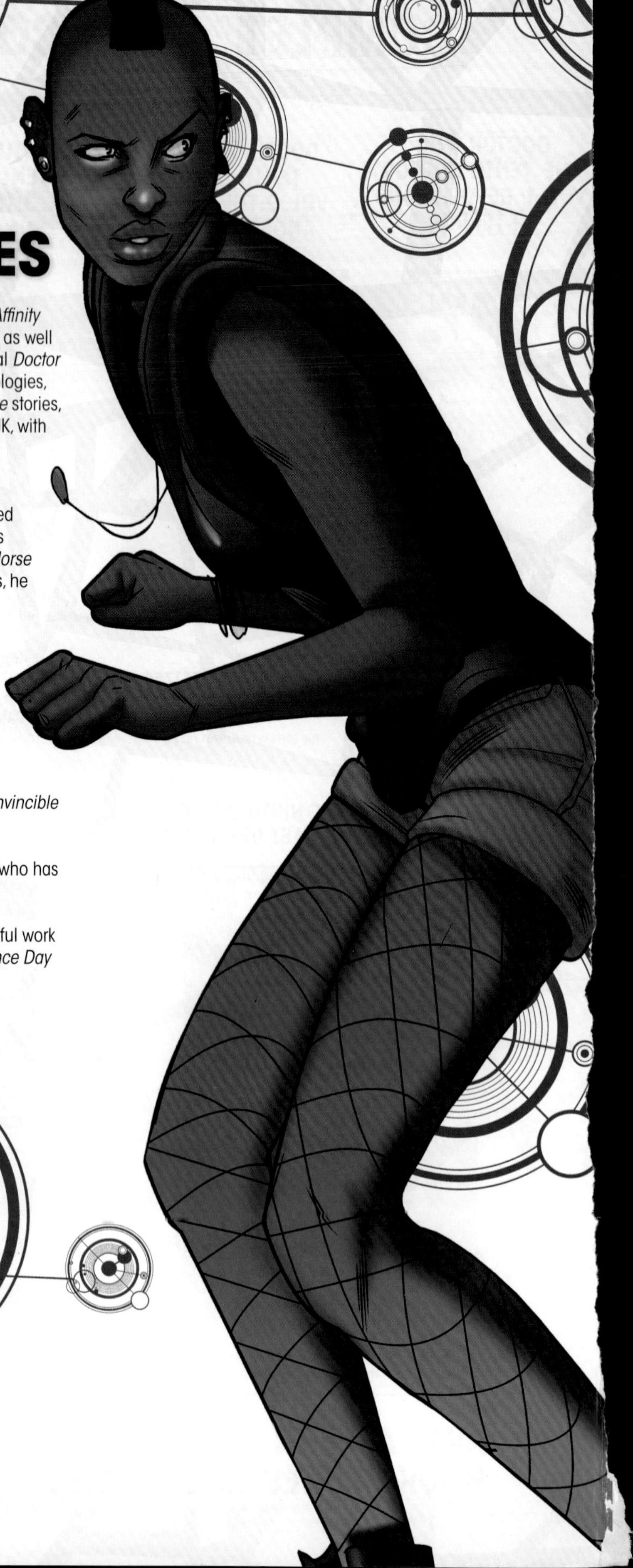